THE QUEST FOR KING ARTHUR

BY JAMES FROST

Order this book online at www.trafford.com
or email orders@trafford.com

Most Trafford titles are also available at major online book retailers.

Print information available on the last page.

ISBN: 978-1-4269-0352-6 (sc)
ISBN: 978-1-4269-0354-0 (e)

Trafford rev. 06/01/2015

 www.trafford.com

North America & international
toll-free: 1 888 232 4444 (USA & Canada)
fax: 812 355 4082

To my mother, Cecelia Frost who gave me a love of history

To my aunt Mary Connelly who taught me how to study it

To my brother Anthony Frost who convinced me to get published

Foreword

THIS BOOK is an experiment. It was written to present a philosophy of history, using the Arthurian debate as the test. All of the other researchers who have attempted to find the answer to this debate have openly stated that they stick to the documentation. They make a hierarchy of sources with documentation being considered more important than other sources and contemporary documentation being considered the most important of all. The idea followed here is that information is information. The only advantage documentation has over other sources is that it tends to provide more information. But that is quantity not quality. Qualitatively speaking all information is equal. Conclusions must be based upon facts. Documents are a collection of statements. Statements prove nothing. Only facts prove things. It is the nature of the study of history that researchers must accept certain things on faith but before that can be done it must be verified that the author of the primary source is trustworthy.

In order to find the answer to any problem all information must be cross referenced with anything else that might have a bearing on the topic, this includes the archeological record, linguistics and the ways that things are done. This last idea consists of two parts. The first is that each culture does certain things in specific ways. That is one of the most important ways in which cultures differ from one another. The second is that certain things are constant and can only happen one way, regardless of the specific time and place. Other examples of the same thing can shed light on contentious issues. The approach is concerned with verifying and explaining what the information reveals

Contents

Chapter I

ARTHUR AS MYTH

KING ARTHUR-THE name itself is enough to conjure up images of romance and tragedy, of a glittering Golden Age of peace and prosperity that was destroyed by betrayal. For centuries people have wondered if it was real or just an entertaining story. Did Arthur the Briton really live or was he simply a figure of legend? Although the question is simple enough the answer is very complex. Up until this point the approach to the debate has always emphasized the documentation. The approach taken here is to shift the emphasis on to the facts. Researchers always state that they interpret the information in an unbiased manner. In fact we interpret the information in terms that we are used to. For example everyone who studies Arthur emphasizes the fact that his name does not appear in reliable documentation. Someone who has a different experience, say by studying the Maya would not be impressed by such an argument.

The Maya were divided into over 120 kingdoms. For many centuries the two most powerful of these states were Tikal and Calakmul. Mayanists refer to them as the two superpowers. We are missing approximately one dozen names for the kings of Tikal and there is no king list for Calakmul at all. There are only a handful of names on stone inscriptions. Mayan scholars do not say that the kings did not exist because we do not have the names; they say the kings were real but the names are missing. To use another example, the important thing about William the Conqueror is not that he was named William, but that he conquered. To apply this to Arthur, the name is irrelevant, the important thing is to determine whether or not there is any evidence of a powerful king in the so-called Arthurian period or if there is any case of an Arthur–type character in the mythology. The approach is to keep the emphasis on the information, not the name. In other words this work will not go through the documentation it will go around it.

The present work is an attempt to make a systematic study of the topic. It is true that there is missing information from both the mythology and the history. But it is also true that there are certain things that are known for certain. In order to find the truth it is necessary to stick to the facts. To paraphrase Thomas Aquinas: in debate it is necessary to use arguments that your opponent will find persuasive, not arguments that you find persuasive, you are not trying to convince yourself. Interpretations of documentation are opinions and opinions do not convince the opposition. The problem with interpretation is that an idea may seem right and still be wrong.

This book presents a series of theories about King Arthur, the stories told about him and other characters in those stories. The reader is invited to examine, accept or reject any or all of these theories in part or in whole. The purpose is to engage the reader's interest and suggest new avenues of thought rather than to demand acceptance of the writer's claims. This is a history and not "the" history of King Arthur. This does not mean that no position is taken in the debate. It does mean that arguments for and against an idea are examined, detailed reasons for accepting or rejecting an argument are given and even the occasional weakness in the supported theory is admitted to.

The first step is to decide whether or not Arthur truly existed. A great many people believe that he was simply a character from mythology; either a god or a pagan hero whose tales continued to be told long after the Britons converted to Christianity. There are no accurate histories that mention him furthermore he could not possibly have lived in or even visited all of the places associated with him. These locations were probably centres dedicated to his worship.

In popular imagination Arthur is viewed as a figure of English literature. This impression is reinforced by the fact that he is connected with places like Glastonbury and Tintagel. But in the fifth and sixth centuries there were no such people as the English. Until relatively recently the ancient Britons were believed to have been a Celtic people with the English being descended from invaders called Anglo-Saxons. This traditional view has been challenged and a new view of the origins of the cultures of the island has emerged. Britain was culturally divided into two, the west and Highlands of the far north were inhabited by people who had been mistaken for Celts but were actually a distinct group whose various branches lived not only in Britain, but also in Ireland Brittany and Galacia in northwestern Spain. Irish legend indicates that they originated in Spain and sailed to the British Isles in prehistoric times. The dominant group in Ireland called themselves the Gaels. These people will be called the Britano-Gaels to represent their two main surviving groups: British (Welsh and Cornish) and Breton in one group, Irish (Gaels), Manx and Scots (both originally from Ireland), and Galacians in the other. Whether the Britano-Gaels were Celts or a separate people is not a question for this investigation. The term is used here only for purposes of convenience.

A people referred to as the Anglo-Saxons invaded Britain in the fifth century and conquered much of it over the course of the next two hundred years. Previously it was believed that the English language and culture were imported to the island through them. It now appears that in reality this language and culture were already there and the invaders gained political ascendancy and spread into areas where it had not been before, but did not introduce it. This native culture will be referred to as Germano-British.

At the time of the Roman invasion of Britain in the first century a large number of tribes inhabited the island. In the far north lived the Atecotti, a mysterious people for whom there is virtually no information. In fact it is not even clear if the Atecotti really were a distinct people, they may have been a group of the Picts. The Picts and Scots occupied most of the Highlands. The Scots originated in Ireland (Scotti is one of the Latin names for the Irish), but there is a disagreement about the Picts. Some argue that they were Britons that were never conquered by the Romans and developed independently. However both Welsh and Pictish sources indicate that they too originated in Ireland.

The Britons inhabited all of what is now southern Scotland, all of England and Wales. They were culturally divided between Britano-Gaels and Germano-British, with the second group being the minority. Many people in Ancient Europe were nomadic, or at least semi-nomadic. In *The Conquest of Gaul*, Caesar gave details of the tribes that occupied Belgium, (modern Belgium is smaller than the region in Caesar day but it is still roughly the same place). He listed 15 tribes, of which four were Germanic.[1] If Germanic tribes could settle in Belgium then they could easily have crossed the Channel and settled in Britain, especially since the Belgea themselves had invaded Britain and Caesar identified their king Diviciacus as ruler of Britain too. This nomadism would explain a Germanic presence in Britain before the arrival of the Anglo-Saxons.

Aside from a few references in Roman sources and what can be learned from archaeology everything that has been preserved about Britano-Gaelic mythology comes either from Ireland or Wales. The Irish material is older and there is more of it. The Arthurian stories are Welsh in origin, although many tales passed through Breton oral sources before being written down. A comparison with Irish tales is helpful in identifying common themes and characters. The Britano-Gaels did turn their gods into heroes-a process called euhemerisation. A favorite was the sun god Vin who appears in Irish traditions as Finn Mac Cool (also called Fion Mac Cumhaill). It should be pointed out that there is a school of thought that argues that Finn was real, but this is unlikely. He is supposed to have lived in a time period in which Ireland was still pagan. Finn was a sacred name, the name of a popular god who was widely worshipped. They never used divine names for real people. They sometimes associated a real person with a divine being, but that is not the same thing. For example one name was Cunobelin. This means "Hound of Belinus." Belinus or Benli was another sun god. But Cunobelin was not Benli; he was only the hound of Benli. Furthermore if Finn was real then one of the most popular gods in the mythology had no myths; which does not really make sense.

In the legends Finn was the leader of an elite group of fighters called the Fianna (Warriors). They almost certainly really existed. It is known that Ancient Europeans had warrior fraternities and the way that the Fianna are described fits with what is known of such groups. The similarities of the names is what led to the real organization being drawn into the mythology. It is these very same myths that led some people to conclude that Arthur was the Welsh version of Finn.

The characters do have much in common. Arthur had the Knights of the Round Table and Finn his Fianna. In both cases these bands contained heroes who had adventures of their own.

---

1   *The Conquest of Gaul*, II.4.

Both were born after their father's were dead and both had to prove themselves before being accepted as leaders of their respective peoples. Arthur and Finn had unhappy domestic lives. The story of Guenevere's affair with Lancelot is one of the most well known of all of the Arthurian legends. Finn's fiancé, Grainne, fell in love with his greatest warrior, Diarmaid. Just as in the Arthurian tale, the lovers ran off together and were chased by the jilted leader. In *The Pursuit of Diarmaid and Grainne* Finn and his men hunt an enchanted boar that was actually Diarmaid transformed into an animal. In a Welsh legend that did not make it into the Romances, Arthur has a very similar adventure. *How Culwch Won Olwen* is an arch-typical tale of the kind found all over the world. A young couple are in love, but the woman's father, in this case a giant named Ysaddaden, forbids their marriage unless the hero can perform a series of seemingly impossible tasks. Culwch employs the aid of Arthur and his knights to help him. The most significant of these tasks is the hunt for the great boar, Twrch Trwyth. This animal had once been a human being but had been transformed as punishment for his sins. The boar had a magic comb and razor or pair of scissors behind its ears.

On the face of it the evidence seems very convincing. Arthur would appear to be the Welsh version of Finn and derived ultimately from the ancient solar god Vin. The proponents of this theory often present the information much as it has been outlined here and leave it at that. Unfortunately there is a very important point that has not yet been mentioned. *How Culwch Won Olwen* mentions a great many characters. Suspiciously no fewer than eight of them are named Gwynn. Gwynn and Finn are the same name. One of these men was said to have been the son of Nudd. Finn was descended from Nuadu. Nudd and Nuadu are the same name. It means "Cloud Maker" and he was the king of the gods in the pagan mythology.

Once the importance of Gwynn has been accepted then it can be seen that the similarities between Finn and Arthur are not as striking as they first appear. In fact the two characters have more differences than similarities. Both Arthur and Finn had unfaithful wives, but so did King Mark in *Tristan and Iseult* and Mark was certainly not a god transformed into a hero. The love triangle was a common theme in Britano-Gaelic mythology and is not limited to stories of the sun god. Furthermore, Finn arranges for the death of his rival, something Arthur does not accomplish.

They had bands of heroes but that does not prove a mythological origin. There are legends about Charlemagne and his heroes, called the Paladins, which are not well known in the English-speaking world. This is probably because Britain was never in Charlemagne's empire. The men go on quests, rescue damsels in distress and encounter a wide variety of monsters. The monarch even had his own enchanter, Malagigi. The difference is that the eighth and ninth centuries are much better documented than the fifth and sixth. Not only can it be proven that Charlemagne himself was real but some of his Paladins are also known to have lived. The hero of the most famous of the stories, *The Song of Roland*, was the Emperor's nephew who was killed at the Battle of Roncesvalles in 778.

Although he was leader of a war band, Finn was not a king. The Irish hero was proficient at poetry, he could foretell the future and he gained insight into the supernatural world after eating the Salmon of Knowledge. All of these were skills beyond Arthur. Their endings were different as well. There are two versions of Finn's death. In one he died when, as a very old man, he attempted to jump over the River Boyne. He failed and fell to his death. In the other Finn was slain in personal combat with the sons of a man named Uirgreann because the hero had slain their father years before. Arthur died in battle, not personal combat. His slayer was his nephew/ son from an incestuous relationship with his sister. Mordred's motivations were political and the results of his personal ambitions. They have nothing to do with vengeance for a dead father-quite naturally since Arthur was his father.

It was Gwynn who was the Welsh equivalent of Finn and the story was altered to introduce Arthur. Gwynn must have been too well known to edit out completely, so he was pushed into the background and not even very far into the background since his name appears over and over again. A comparison of other Irish tales and Arthurian legends supports this conclusion. Certain stories that feature Finn in Ireland are associated with Perceval in Welsh tales. If Arthur were Finn, why are these stories about one of the Knights of the Round Table and not about the king himself?

Culwch and Olwen is part of a collection of eleven tales called *The Mabinogion*. An examination of other tales shows that characters named Gwynn are mentioned in three other tales.[2] That is not very many, but it does indicate that at one time Gwynn was more popular than the surviving material would indicate. The British versions went through a process of evolution in which other heroes usurped Gwynn's adventures.

Proving that Arthur was not Finn does not prove that he really existed. There are a great many more mythological aspects to the character than those that have been mentioned thus far. *The Spoils of Annwn* (*Preiddeu Annwn*) is a fragment of a poem attributed to Taliesin, one of the most famous bards of post-Roman Britain. It is included in the *Canu Taliesin* (*The Book of Taliesin*). Unfortunately the original manuscript is much decayed. The beginning and ending are missing; all that survives is part of the middle. It tells how Arthur led three ships to raid an Otherworldly island. There was a fierce battle from which only seven men survived. Among the loot that the men stole was a magic cauldron. It is at this point that the story breaks off. Another story in *The Mabinogion* is *Branwen Daughter of Llyr*. It is a much longer tale and it contains an incident very similar to the adventure recounted in *The Spoils of Branwen*. There is an attack upon an island, in this case Ireland, a magic cauldron and only seven survivors of a battle. Since they are obviously two versions of the same story it is essential to establish which of them is older. The dates of the manuscripts themselves are not conclusive. Dating the manuscripts will merely assign a time to an individual copy, it will not fix the timing of the composition of the story itself. The relative ages of the stories must be determined from an examination of the plots.

---

2 *Pwyll: Lord of Dyved, Branwen Daughter of Llyr* and *Gereint and Enid.*

As a general rule, the older a story is the greater number of supernatural elements it contains. This is because such tales originated as religious narratives from the pagan mythology. After the conversions to Christianity the stories continued to be passed down in the oral traditions. But they went through a long process of recomposition to edit out the overtly pagan elements; the more magical elements that remain, the less editing that has been done to the story. Both tales have magic cauldrons both have mythic settings: Annwn was one of the names of the land of the dead from Welsh mythology, while Bran led his followers to an enchanted land where they lived for eighty years without aging. It is in the figures of the heroes themselves that the answer lies.

Arthur may or may not have originated as a god, but Bran certainly did. Bran the Blessed was a sea god and part of a divine family of great importance. His father was Llyr who was remembered for many centuries. After a certain garbling of the mythology he eventually became Shakespeare's *King Lear*. In the tale under consideration Bran's true nature was obvious. He grew to giant size (Britano-Gaelic divinities were often depicted as giants) and walked across the Irish Sea. During the battle Bran was badly wounded and he ordered his men to cut off his head. This did not kill him. The head continued to give his followers advice. It stayed with them throughout the entire eighty-year period that they lived in the mystic land. Probably the most important factor in the episode is about the stealing of the magic cauldron. Bran owned a magic cauldron but Arthur did not. The adventure must have originated as an explanation as to how he got that special item. These are the only legends in which Arthur is the hero, but he was not an original character in either of them. It is a strange fact that although the tales are called Arthurian, Arthur himself is a minor character in most of them and many could be told without even mentioning him. How could he be a mythic character if he had no myths?

Another problem with the idea that Arthur was mythic in origin is posed by nomenclature. The name Arthur is either derived from the Latin *gens* (clan) name Artorius or the Old Welsh *arth* meaning bear. Artorius will be dealt with first. Britano-Gaelic deities were often referred to by Latin names in ancient sources. Since the Romans believed that everyone worshipped the same gods, the divine beings of conquered peoples were given the names of Roman deities with similar attributes. For example Apollo was a popular Roman god among Western Europeans. He was god of the sun and a patron of healing. One name for him was Apollo Vindonnus. The name Vindonnus means "clear light" and is an alternate form of Vin. If Arthur was a god and his name was derived from Latin it would be the same as, or at least similar to, the name of a Roman god. There are extensive records that preserve the names of even the most minor Roman deities. Although his name is similar to at least one minor, local god, this raises the question as to how so unimportant a figure could become the single most important figure in Welsh traditions. Nothing just happens, everything has a cause. If there is no cause, there can be no effect. An obscure god would not simply become the famous King Arthur by magic.

It has been suggested that the name Arthur comes from *arth*, Old Welsh for bear. Starting from the fact that ancient peoples were well educated in the field of astronomy, attempts have been made to link Arthur with the "bear constellations" Ursa Major and Ursa Minor (*ursa* is Latin for bear). In Wales today Ursa Major is often called "Arthur's Table," but there is no evidence that this connection existed in ancient times. The Britano-Gaels did not have the same constellations as the Romans and there is no evidence that they had the concepts as Ursas Major and Minor. They did have several bear deities, but the most important was a goddess, not a god. She was worshipped among the true Celts. Her name was Artio and the most important centre of her worship was Berne in Switzerland. Memories of her gave the place its name. Berne of course means bear in German. There was a version of the Roman god Mercury who was associated with bears. There is an inscription in which he is referred to as Mercury Artaios. However neither of these deities seems to have been worshipped in Britain. The bear cult on that island was very minor so again there is the question as to how the character could have become so important.

The bear deities were patrons of the hunt. Arthur does hunt in a few stories, but so do many characters in medieval stories. Hunting was an important pastime and it often figured in tales. No special connection can be found between Arthur and hunting. The places associated with the hero were supposed to have been areas that were dedicated to his worship. But no known bear cult locations in Britain are associated with Arthur. The bear cult was confined to what is now the north of England in areas like York. Most places with Arthurian connections are in Wales, Devon and Cornwall and southern Scotland. There is absolutely no correlation between Arthurian locations and bear cult locations.

There are a great many places that are connected with Arthur in districts as far apart as Scotland and Brittany. He could not possibly have visited them all. That does not necessarily mean that they were places that were sacred to the worship of Arthur the god. Locations can become linked to a real person in the minds of the populace without that person ever really coming anywhere near them. An obvious example of this comes from the New England area of the United States. America's first president supposedly visited many buildings that date back to the eighteenth century. The phrase "George Washington slept here" is so common that it has become a joke. He could not possibly have had enough time to lead his army and later govern the new nation and still have visited all of his supposed nap sites. Obviously locals who were proud of their communities attempted to bring greater fame to their areas by connecting them to an important person, the same phenomenon may be behind Arthur's association to so many different places. Another explanation for the Arthurian place names is that they were connected to different men with the same name. In the mid sixth century Arthur was a very popular name among the Britons. Places associated with one or more of these men could easily have become confused with the more famous figure in the popular imagination.

If Arthur was not a god transformed into a hero, then was he simply a mythic hero? Though he may never have been worshipped, was he a fictitious creation none the less? The story of his birth certainly suggests that this was the case. According to tradition, Uther Pendragon fell in love with Igrayne, the wife of Duke Gorlios (or Hoel) of Cornwall. The duke locked her up in his fortress at

Tintagel. Uther retaliated by invading Cornwall. Rather than leave the outcome to the fortunes of war, the king made himself look like the duke through the magic of the wizard Merlin. Uther was able to slip past the Cornish guards at the castle and spend the night with Igrayne. Nine months later Arthur was born.

Many mythologies have stories of gods who disguise themselves in order to sleep with beautiful women. Those born of these liaisons are always characters that are important to legends of the culture. The story of Arthur's conception bears a strong resemblance to the Greek myth of the origins of Heracles (better known today by the Latin form of his name, Hercules). In that tale Zeus, the king of the gods, takes on the appearance of Amphitryon so that he can seduce that man's wife, Alcmene. Britano-Gaelic deities were certainly able to change their shapes for similar purposes. For example, in Irish tradition the god Mannan took on the form of Fiacha, king of Ulster, in order to sleep with Fiacha's wife. Their son was Mongan, who became a famous ruler of his people. Stories of a miraculous birth do not necessarily mark a character a fictitious. In Greek tradition, Zeus was said to have been the father of Alexander the Great and Alexander certainly lived. A highly respected person was automatically believed to have some sort of connection to the supernatural world. Giving divine origins to a real hero was a way of explaining how that person was able to accomplish his or her extraordinary feats.

There is another argument against the "Arthur as fictitious hero" theory that cannot be overcome. Heroes go on quests, they fight villains or monsters and rescue damsels in distress. In the few cases in which Arthur participates in this kind of activity the story was originally about someone else then rewritten at a later date to feature Arthur, or a medieval writer not of the original tradition invented it. Aside from *Culwch and Olwen* and *The Spoils of Annwn*, Arthur's only other adventure of importance is the slaying of a giant at Mont-St-Michael. This story first appears in the *Historia Regum Britanniae* (hereafter referred to by its English title, *The History of the Kings of the Britain*) by Geoffrey of Monmouth. The book was written *c*1136. Although Geoffrey was Welsh he was ambitious and wished to impress people in power in England so that he could gain their help in furthering his career. The work in question was meant to gain the attention of King Henry I. By the time it was completed the king had died and England had been plunged into a civil war between his possible successors. In Geoffrey's attempt to ensure that he supported the winning side he wrote no fewer than three different dedications, the last one addressed to the victor, King Stephen. For this he used exactly the same wording that had appeared in an earlier dedication, he simply inserted Stephen's name in place of the original, Waleran of Beaumont[3].

It was Monmouth's intention to provide a history for the Welsh while at the same time popularizing Arthur's tales for the English. He failed in his attempt to be an historian, but in his role as publicist for the king he succeeded brilliantly. In order to accomplish this second task he deliberately inserted information that he thought his audience would like to hear. The adventure

---

3 Geoffrey's attempts to gain favour led to his named bishop of the see of St. Asaph in 1152.

of the slaying of the giant was just such an episode. The action took place at a famous location in Normandy. Ever since the Norman Conquest in 1066 many English aristocrats were also members of the Norman nobility. There were no earlier traditions of Arthur killing a giant and no other writer who worked from traditional sources mentioned the episode. Furthermore in Britano-Gaelic mythology giants were usually gods, not evil creatures that had to be slain.

Arthur cannot be located in the mythic tradition, but this is not conclusive. Britano-Gaelic mythology is not as well preserved as that of other Western European peoples. The Romans wrote extensively of their beliefs and such works as *The Metamorphoses* by Ovid and Virgil's *Aeneid* are readily accessible to modern readers. Norse tales were deliberately collected into a continuous narrative in a work called *The Prose Edda* by an Icelander named Snorri Sturluson (1178-1248). Many of the gaps that Snorri left were filled in by another work, the anonymous *Elder Edda*. These authors deliberately set out to preserve the old beliefs before they became completely forgotten. Britano-Gaelic myths had no such compilers.

Contrary to the beliefs of some researchers, the pagan Britano-Gaels were not illiterate, but very little of what they wrote has survived. All that remains are a few inscriptions on stones or carved into bits of metal that have rusted in many places. They were written in Latin or in one of their own languages using the Greek or Latin alphabets. They were forbidden to ever write about their religion. This stricture was caused by the fact that the belief system was based upon nature and writing is an artificial method of passing on information. Another factor was the elitist nature of their society. The religion contained "sacred mysteries" that were considered too holy to be known by the uninitiated who might happen to read them if they were written down. If the information was passed on by word of mouth then the druids could control who learned it. The restrictions regarding the religion were lifted after the conversions to Christianity. However there was no Britano-Gaelic Sturluson who decided to gather the myths into one collection. As was mentioned earlier there are seven areas of the Britano-Gaelic world. Of these seven only Ireland and Wales preserved their tales in written form. Neither made any systematic attempt to explain their religion; they simply wrote the stories that were the most popular. What is more the Welsh wrote very little until the eleventh century, (or at least very little of what they wrote before then has survived), by which time many of the stories had become confused and their meanings lost. The Welsh themselves were aware of this. One of the tales of *The Mabinogion* is *The Dream of Rhonabwy*. The anonymous author included an incident in which a bard recited a traditional poem that was so obscure that none of the characters knew what it meant.

All of this leads to the conclusion that simply because Arthur cannot be located in the surviving material that does not prove that he was not of mythic origin. He may have been derived from a group of tales that were not preserved in their earliest forms, but were passed down orally before being presented as medieval Romances. Since no definite answer can be obtained from the mythic material, then an examination of the historical sources is the next logical step.

The strongest argument against the existence of Arthur is the fact that there are no accurate histories that cover the time period he is said to have lived that make any mention of him. This is true. But it is only true because there are no accurate histories that cover the time period at all. The fifth and early sixth centuries are the worst documented period since literacy came to Britain. The information we have has survived entirely by chance and chance does not respect rank or reputation. The argument is a double standard. The lack of hard evidence is not supposed to prove that he was not mythical, but it is supposed to prove that he was not real. Three works are usually put forward as being the most likely to speak of Arthur if he really existed. These are *De excidio et conquestu Britanniae* (*On the Ruin and Conquest of Britain*, hereafter referred to as *De excidio*) written by a monk named Gildas *c*540; *The Historia Ecclesiastica Gentis Anglorum* (*History of the English Church and People*) written by the Venerable Bede in 731, and the royal genealogies which recorded the names of the monarchs of the different dynasties that ruled the various petty kingdoms of Britain. The most important of these works from the point of view of the Arthurian scholar is the first one.

St Gildas, also called Gildas Sapiens ("the Wise") lived around the time when Arthur is supposed to have been active. According to the *Annales Cambriae* (the *Welsh Annals*), Arthur won the Battle of Badon Hill in 517 and was killed in 538 at the Battle of Camlann. Gildas mentioned that he was born the same year as "the siege of Mount Badon" (*obsessio Mons Badoniccus*)[4] and *De excidio* was written roughly two years after the date for Camlann. It is logical to expect some mention of Arthur in the work. Gildas even mentioned five kings who ruled different districts of Britain in his time. But nowhere does he speak of Arthur. The usual explanation that is put forward by those who support the idea that Arthur was real is that Gildas held a grudge against him because the king had killed the saint's brother, Hueil. This story originated with *The Description of Wales* by Giraldus Cambrensis (Gerald of Wales). According to Gerald, Gildas had originally written several works praising the British rulers but he became disillusioned with them because of his brother's death and several other incidents. He destroyed these books and then wrote *De excidio* in disgust. Unfortunately Gerald was a bit naïve. He believed almost any story he heard, even tales with a liberal helping of magic or the miraculous. Since he lived almost five hundred years after Gildas and was certainly not an eyewitness, he must have been recording a tradition he had heard or read somewhere. The story may have been valid, or it may have been invented to explain Arthur's absence from the book, there is simply no way to tell.

The full tale of the death of Hueil was recorded in *The Life of St Gildas*, written *c*1125 by Caradoc of Llancarfan. According to the story Hueil rebelled against Arthur. The rebellion was initially successful, but Arthur killed Hueil by tricking him into believing he wanted peace talks and then ambushing him when he arrived to negotiate. Hueil's father Caw (Caius of Strathclyde, *fl*490's) was forced to abdicate. He and the rest of his family were relocated to Wales. If Arthur and Gildas really were on opposing sides in a civil war then that would make Gildas Arthur's

---

4 *De excidio*, 26.1.

enemy. Yes Gildas would have been Arthur's contemporary, but then again John Wilkes Booth was Abraham Lincoln's contemporary, which did not do Lincoln any good. The problem is that everyone on both sides of the debate is using the rule that says contemporary sources are always the most reliable. Unfortunately no one is taking into account another rule that says that no one can ever be truly unbiased. The contemporary rule is supposed to be used *after* the biases of the author have been determined. In other words no one has ever considered that Gildas deliberately lied. It has never actually been verified that Gildas told the truth; everyone is just assuming it. This leaves the "Arthur was real" camp to come up with explanations as to why the name is not in the book. But if the two men were enemies, then Gildas was biased against Arthur and there is no need to explain the absence of the name, only a need to show that Gildas is unreliable.

Since there is so little information on the fifth century the reliability of the author must be determined by examining earlier events for which there is more information. Gildas betrays a pro-Roman and anti-British bias that is so strong that it crosses the line into bigotry. Take for example his version of the rebellion of Boudicca in the late first century. "A treacherous lioness butchered the governors who had been left to give full voice and strength to the endeavors of Roman rule. On this the news was reported to the senate, which hastened to send an army with all speed to seek revenge on what were pictured as tricky foxes. But there was no warlike fleet at sea, ready to put up a brave fight for its country, no orderly square, no right wing or other apparatus of war drawn up on the beach. The British offered their backs instead of shields to their pursuers, their necks to the sword. A cold shudder ran through their bones, like women they stretched out their hands for the fetters. In fact it became a mocking proverb far and wide that the British are cowardly in war and faithless in peace."[5] This highly inaccurate account depicts the Britons as a bunch of murderous cowards who slaughtered unarmed civilians and were completely incapable of even trying to defend themselves against armed warriors. As for the so-called proverb, it is a boldfaced lie. In fact, no one ever called them faithless except Gildas and as for their reputation in wartime, it was the exact opposite, they were renowned for their bravery. So much so that Romans recruited large numbers of them for their armies, something they would not have done if the Britons were considered cowards. It cannot have been a mistake, as is generally assumed, since he said it was a proverb. A proverb either existed or it did not, and if it did not then he made it up. It is a lie.

This is not the only example of such talk in the book. Up until now, no one has thought much of this, after all Gildas was a Briton himself. At least so everyone believes. Actually he was not. His family was of Roman origin. There would have been three political groups: one pro-Briton and anti-Roman, one pro-Roman and anti-Briton and one in the middle. The relative size and strengths of these factions would depend upon a variety of factors that are simply unknown in this case. However it can be safely concluded that Gildas was not in the middle. Gildas was a liar and possibly a bigot. The fact that he lived in the sixth century is irrelevant. The issue is not chronology it is honesty.

---

5 Ibid 6.1-2.

Once his reliability is questioned, it falls to pieces. It is well known that his account of Britain in the Empire is not accurate. But it was assumed that he was making honest mistakes. But as the arguments already made have been designed to show, at least some of them could not possibly have been mistakes. Absolutely nothing he says about the period from the Roman conquest in the first century (the starting point for his historical narrative) until Britain gained its independence is right. But after it gained independence he is considered the single most reliable source we have. He is supposed to have gone from being completely unreliable to 100% reliable literally from one paragraph to another. The problem is the evidence does not support that assumption. With the exception of a handful of statements, everything that he said about the fifth century is contradicted by the independent sources, whether the sources are British, Anglo-Saxon or the archeological record. The assumption is that this is because of missing information, except in the case of the Arthurian material, where it is assumed that the Arthurian authors lied or at least made mistakes. But it does not look like missing information; it looks like the independent sources are telling a completely different story.

Arthur would not have been Roman. The Romans in Britain lived mainly in the south and the east, with the exception of a few military families (like Gildas' own family) in the far north. According to tradition Arthur was born in Cornwall in the far southwest. He would have been native aristocracy, a descendant of the chieftains of the Cornovii tribe. Viewed from this perspective the problem becomes simple-Arthur's name does not appear in a book written by a biased liar who would have been his enemy. It looks probable that the name is missing from the book precisely because Gildas is *not* reliable.

Gildas was a preacher, not a historian. Statements he made prove this. "I had decided to speak of the dangers run not by brave soldiers in the stress of war, but by the lazy."[6] He could not have been clearer if he tried. He was interested in live villains, not dead heroes. Gildas mentioned nine kings, but he actually named only six of them. He was mainly concerned with criticizing tyrants (or at least men he considered to be tyrants) who were alive at the time he wrote his book. That accounts for five out of the six. But that is no help to the Arthurian researcher. Arthur would not have still been alive by then. The date of 538 in the *Welsh* Annals for Arthur's death cannot be taken at face value. People in the fifth and sixth centuries were not very good about recording dates. Gildas himself included no dates in his entire book. Most dates that exist for this period are actually guesses made much later and are often out by as much as twenty years or more. The *Welsh Annals* was composed in *c*960 in St Davids in south Wales. Gildas was actually alive at the time and his account contradicts this date. It is impossible to date his birth with any certainty, but Gildas could not have been born as late as 517. He was born some time around the year 500 or a few years earlier.

Dionysus Exguus invented the current dating system in the early sixth century, but it was not widely accepted until the late seventh century. Even then it was considered the preserve

---

6 Ibid, 1.2.

of scholars and not ordinary people. Stating the number of years that elapsed after some well-known occurrence was the usual way of dating events. This means that when two events listed in a source are connected to each other and one has been given the wrong date, then the date of the other one is probably wrong. What should be examined is the interval of time between them. According to *The Welsh Annals* the interval of time between Badon and Camlann is twenty-one years. Since it has been determined that Badon was most likely in the 490's that would place Camlann in the five teens. There is an interesting mathematical coincidence in this approach. If it is assumed that *De excidio* was written in exactly 540, then Badon would have taken place in 497, because Gildas stated that he was 43 years old at the time he wrote his book, which would place the other battle in 518. This is only one year off from the date given in the *Welsh Annals* for the earlier battle. It is possible (but only possible) that whoever compiled that section of the *Annals* knew not only that the two battles were twenty-one years apart, but also that one of them had been fought in 517 but he dated the wrong battle to that year.

Whatever the actual dating, the course of events is straight forward and all laid out in Gildas' book.[7] Gildas was born the same year as the siege of Mount Badon. This is also known as the Battle of Badon Hill and is recorded in tradition as Arthur's greatest victory. Gildas lived in a time of constant civil warfare, but he grew up during a period of peace. This confirms the basic outline of the Arthurian traditions and places them into a time frame. Arthur fought his battles, the most important being Badon, he reigned over a period of peace, which he maintained with the Round Table, and then he was killed in a civil war. Since the peace lasted long enough for Gildas to grow up he would have been approximately twenty years old at the time of the civil war that ended the peace, the one in which Arthur is said to have been killed. But he was forty-three when he wrote his book. If Arthur really did exist he would have been dead for roughly twenty years when Gildas wrote his book.

Gildas' hero was Ambrosius Aurelianus. Although it is accepted by everyone that he was a hero, there is little evidence to support this. He is not in the *Welsh Annals*, there is no battle poetry for him nor is he in the *Triads*. The only other sources that mention him are the *History of the Britons* and *The History of the Kings of Britain*. The first contains both history and legend. He is barely mentioned in the history section. He had one legend, which he could not even hang on to, since it was rewritten in the twelfth century and turned into a Merlin story, while the author of the second was something of a storyteller who embellished his account with liberal doses of fiction. This creates a totally new wrinkle in the debate. Are the sources trying to pass off Arthur as a real person or Ambrosius as a hero?

Ambrosius Aurelianus is unique in *De excidio* for three reasons: he was the only dead king Gildas mentioned by name, he was the only king Gildas praised and he was the only one who was Roman. Gildas calls the other rulers tyrants. But that word had three meanings in this period. The word is Greek in origin and the first meaning was simply king. Since the kings of the other Greek

---

7 Ibid, 26.1-2.

states were hostile to the democracy at Athens and since most of the surviving Greek material was written at that same city, the term took on a negative connotation. In the sixth century it could still be used to mean king, it also meant what we mean by the term or it could mean usurper. Since Gildas was pro-Roman it is not unreasonable to argue that the only political authority that he recognized as legitimate was Roman authority. It is true that he attacked each tyrant for specific crimes, except for Vortigern. It is assumed that he was evil, after all the supposed hero Ambrosius killed him, but what if he was not evil at all? What if all that was simply pro-Roman propaganda?

Gildas stated that Ambrosius was not a Briton with a Roman name; he was a Roman living in Britain. He also stated that both of the king's parents had "worn the purple."[8] This term means that they were both members of imperial families. Since this is impossible, it is generally agreed that he changed the meaning of the term, but another interpretation is that he was establishing the man's credentials. Gildas criticized all of the other rulers as tyrants because they had no legitimate claim to the imperium. This means that Gildas could not have mentioned Arthur. He would not fit with the five tyrants because he was not a cruel ruler and because he would not have still been alive and he could not have been placed beside Ambrosius because Arthur would not have been Roman.

It could be argued that since the king's death brought about the end of an era, it would have been important enough to have appeared in the book anyway. This supposes that Gildas understood the significance of the events. The importance of many historical events can only been seen in hindsight. Gildas would have had no way of knowing that the Arthurian period would be remembered as a Golden Age by future generations. The full consequence of what happened at Camlann could only be appreciated in light of the disasters during the second round of Anglo-Saxon wars that began in the 550's.

Gildas may not have been an historian, but the Venerable Bede was. His book, *The Ecclesiastical History of the English People*, is still studied for the wealth of information it provides about the development of Anglo-Saxon England. But the title itself reveals the limitations of the work from the point of view of the Arthurian scholar. Arthur was a Briton, the descendant of his people are the Welsh, Cornish and Breton, not the English. As well informed as Bede was about his own people, he knew very little about the Britons (or the Scots or Picts for that matter). Even the best read English of his day seldom concerned themselves with Welsh material. His main source of information about the Britons in the fifth and sixth centuries was Gildas. Bede relied so heavily on *De excidio* that he actually copied part of it almost word for word. Since Gildas never mentioned Arthur, Bede new nothing about him. Even if Bede had not read enough Welsh material to find mention of Arthur, should he not have come across the king in Anglo-Saxon sources? The answer is no. The Anglo-Saxons did their best to forget all about the military reverses that they experienced in the late fifth century. For example both Welsh tradition and archeology indicate that the Anglo-Saxons suffered severe defeats in northern Lincolnshire

---

8 Ibid 25.3.

in the 490's. Not one single Anglo-Saxon source mentions anything about them. With very few exceptions, they wrote only of their victories, not their defeats. If the Anglo-Saxons would not even admit that they had been defeated, they would not have recorded information about the man responsible for those defeats. The concept that historians should record all information only dates back to the eighteenth century. It was the invention of Edward Gibbon and his contemporaries. Before that the belief was that the only information that should be preserved is whatever is useful or entertaining. By useful they meant something that could illustrate a moral point or be used for propaganda purposes. Contrary to what is usually assumed, there is no evidence that the English knew anything about Arthur until after the French Romances became popular in the twelfth century.

As for the third source, the genealogies are the least understood of all of the works. It is generally agreed that Britain was politically divided into a number of small kingdoms, each with its own dynastic families. Such lists were common to ancient peoples all over the world and are referred to by different terms: royal genealogies or king lists being the most common terms. In point of fact the two things are not identical. A royal genealogy records the names of the heads of a family back to the supposed founder. These founders are only "supposed" because genealogies often contained propaganda and families would claim descent from heroes they were not really related to, even mythic figures. Genealogies often stretch back before the establishment of the kings. A king list records the names of the rulers of a particular kingdom, even when they were not related to each other. The overwhelming majority of the British material is in the form of genealogies, but some are king lists.

A long time ago someone noted that Arthur's name was not on any of the lists. The side that says that Arthur was real usually explains this by citing a ninth century text that calls him a general with the rank of *dux bellorum*, "leader of battles,"[9] or by saying that he did not live in the last decades of the fifth century or first decades of the sixth. He needs to be pulled farther back or pushed forward. It has even been suggested that Arthur was his nickname, not his real name. There is another explanation as to why his name is not on the lists. We do not have all of the lists. In fact we do not have anywhere near all of them.

Anyone who takes a map and attempts to work out where all of the kingdoms were would have to give up in frustration. There is quite a bit of territory completely unaccounted for. There are kingdoms such as Elmet and Dent for which we have no genealogies and there are kings mentioned in various sources whose names are not on any of the genealogies we have. Ambrosius Aurelianus himself is one such king. The situation is far more complicated than anyone seems to realize. The Britons had divided inheritance; when a king died sometimes the territory was divided between his heirs. This means that the number of kingdoms would have been constantly changing. Not only would new ones have been created, but also every once in a while one branch of a family would die out, given that these people lived in an almost constant state of warfare that would have happened

---

9 *Historia Brittonum*, 50.

more often than under normal circumstances. When it did happen, their lands would be inherited by another branch of the family, uniting two realms. They would stay united only until someone decided to divide them again. Even in a well-documented time period it is difficult to keep track of all the changes to the map for a people using divided inheritance, in a badly documented time period it is simply impossible.

The genealogies themselves were not written down in this period. They were memorized by bards and passed down for generations before finally being written much later. The oldest manuscripts date to no earlier than the tenth century. There was never any attempt to collect them all. They did not think in those terms. The genealogies were propaganda and were recited at coronations and royal weddings. Later kings wanted to boast about how far back their families or kingdoms went and who their illustrious ancestors were. Then there was the phenomenon of sub-kings. A sub-king was a man with the title of king who did not actually ruler his own kingdom. The practice was widespread throughout Western Europe in this period and in fact it did not completely die out until the twelfth century.[10] The term sub-king was not always used for these men and even if it had been, it did not even exist in the fifth and sixth centuries. Britano-Gaels had a much larger number of sub-kings than any other people. The lists give absolutely no indication if the names recorded were rulers of independent kingdoms or sub-kings.

To sum up: the fifth and sixth centuries had a chaotic situation and the only documentation that can be used to keep track of it not only does not date to the period but also was never intended to be used to keep track of it in the first place. Practically any place could have been its own kingdom at practically any time and we would not know it.

According to tradition Arthur was born at Tintagel in Cornwall. Most researchers state that this was in the kingdom of Dumnonia. The genealogy for Dumnonia survives but Arthur's name is not on it. But there is no reason to insist that it should be. The idea that Cornwall was in Dumnonia is an assumption, not a fact. No sources ever say that Arthur ruled Dumnonia; they state he came from Cornwall. According to the legends, Arthur's branch of the family was wiped out and he had no surviving children. His heir was Constantine of Dumnonia, his cousin. This suggests that the two places may actually have been ruled by different branches of the same family until after Arthur's death.

There is proof that Cornwall had kings for at least part of the sixth century. Dumnonia was divided then reunited then divided again, a phenomenon that would not have been uncommon under these conditions. The "written stone" (*Men Scryfa*) bears the inscription "Riolbran son of Cunoval." The Britons used throne names, which means when a king came to power he sometimes changed his name. Riolbran means "Royal Raven" and can only have been the name of a king. Cunoval is an alternate form of Cunobelin, a royal name known to have been in use even before the Roman invasion. These were not sub-kings. The Church never put more

---

10   The last two recorded sub-kings were Angus mac Heth of Moray in Scotland (died in 1130) and the so-called Young King Henry of England (died 1183) the son of Henry II.

than one bishop in the same kingdom. The bishops for Dumnonia were at Exeter, but John Morris found a reference to a bishop with the double see of Bodmin and Padstow in the 430's.[11] Cornwall is supposed to have been in Dumnonia, which also included Devon. The Anglo-Saxon kingdom of Wessex conquered Devon in 710 but Cornwall held out until 936. The *Welsh Annals* records the death of King Dungarth of Cornwall in 875. Obviously the Cornish king list is missing. Cornwall was definitely in Dumnonia during the reign of Cunomorus. (r.*c*550-*c*570). His son Durstan was buried near Castle Dore in Cornwall. The place probably became divided upon his death. Cunomorus ruled a small empire that also included Brittany. This empire was divided with Devon going to Cador and Brittany to Waroch. It is possible that Cornwall went to someone else whose name has been lost.

If the king lists are in such bad shape, then why has no one noticed? The fact is that some have. John Morris pointed out that there was a serious problem as far back as 1973 and others have also mentioned it. But one of the main reasons why this debate survives is because most historians, whether amateur or professional, are working in virtual isolation with people trying to do virtually everything by themselves while missing important ideas from others. Another problem is the way the debate is being framed. Men who were used to the Anglo-Saxons defined the debate back in the nineteenth century. They took what they knew about a Germanic people in a well-documented time period and applied it to a different people in a badly documented period. Much of what they said has since been proven wrong. But many researchers do not know that and they keep repeating ideas that others have said before them. It is the tyranny of repetition.

Since there are explanations as to why Arthur is not mentioned in some written sources, the next step is to examine the sources in which he is mentioned. The first move when doing that is to determine exactly what are the oldest written references to him. The older the work the more likely it is to be accurate. Different researchers have suggested a variety of works as being the oldest, but an examination of all of the sources makes the situation very clear. The four oldest works that contain references to him are the anonymous *Geraint fab Erbin* (hereafter referred to as *The Eulogy for Geraint*), written *c*501, *Y Gododdin* written by the bard Aneirin (pronounced Anesin) in the late sixth century, the *Historia Britonum*, attributed to a monk named Nennius and compiled *c*820 and the *Welsh Annals*, which have already been mentioned. In each case there is an argument as to whether or not the Arthurian material is genuine.

There is some confusion as to when the first poem was written. The version that survives is not the original. It was written in Old Welsh but was probably transcribed from an older version that was Late Brythonic, the language spoken by the Britons in the post Roman period. For this reason it is not usually accepted as the oldest source to mention Arthur. In fact many people believe that the reference to him was added later and was not part of the original poem at all.

---

11 *The Age of Arthur*, pg.366.

It is a eulogy for a man named Geraint who came from Dumnonia who was killed at the battle of Llongborth. The poem is an eyewitness account and implies that Arthur was at the battle. The title of the work appears to refer to King Geraint I who died some time in the 550's. However ancient poems had no titles and the name was added later so it may not actually have been him. There is also another problem. Most men named Geraint in the surviving documentation had fathers named Erbin. It should not be forgotten that the king lists were passed down orally for generations before being written down. The formula "Geraint son of Erbin" seems to have been applied automatically, probably because of a man of that name who was famous at one time, but has since become confused with other men of the same name. The poem mentions horsemen in almost every stanza. This dates the battle to the fifth or sixth century. The Britons relied heavily on cavalry at first but by the late sixth century the Anglo-Saxons had captured the horse breeding areas so from that time onward most British warriors fought on foot. In the *Anglo-Saxon Chronicle* there is an entry for the year 501 that states that a chieftain named Port and his sons Bieda and Maelga attacked Portesmutha (Portsmouth) and killed an important British warrior, described as "a very noble man." It is usually agreed that this is the Battle of Llongborth. The problem is that Geraint I died in the 550's, which would make the date in the *Chronicle* a mistake and also place it after the Arthurian period. It has been argued that the reference to Arthur was actually poetic fancy. On the other hand John Morris stated that English tradition placed the battle to *c*480 and said that Geraint was mentioned in the lists.[12] He seems to have been implying that the subject of the poem was a man whose name appears on the list for Dumnonia as Gadeonnot. Linguistically it is possible that this could be a variant form of Geraint.

Was this an eyewitness account or poetic fancy? That depends upon the point of view. Either interpretation could be correct. Many of the dates in this section of the *Chronicle* are obviously wrong. It is known that in the early sixth century there was a rare period of peace between the Britons and the Anglo-Saxons, but the *Chronicle* places several battles in this period. Whether this particular battle should be pulled back or pushed forward in time it is impossible to say. There is also one fact that both sides have overlooked. There is no reason to believe that Geraint was a king. The poem never gives him any title at all. It presents him as an important hero, but not all heroes were kings. It is possible that both sides in the debate are wrong and the date of the battle should be left exactly where it is.

There is something else that needs pointing out. Although neither the poem nor the *Chronicle* specifically states which side won the battle, both provide good indicators of the victor. As was already stated the Anglo-Saxons very seldom admitted being defeated by the Britons so the very fact that they recorded the battle at all suggests that they won it. The British poem admits that Geraint was killed but never states that his death was avenged. This also suggests that the Anglo-Saxons won. If Arthur were an all-conquering hero from the mythology, why would the Britons associate him with a battle they lost? The Britons recorded two types of battles-victories and

---

12 Ibid, pg. 105.

tragic defeats. Llongborth falls into the second category. But the tragedy in this case is concerned with Geraint; it has nothing to do with Arthur. He is mentioned only in one of the seventeen stanzas of the poem. Llongborth diminishes the king's reputation. If he were fictitious then placing him at the fight would be an admission that the invaders were such powerful foes that even the greatest hero from legend was unable to defeat them-an extremely unlikely possibility to say the least and one that is flatly contradicted by the way in which Arthur is treated in all other accounts. On the other hand, very few real generals win every single battle. If he were present when Geraint was killed there would be no reason not to say so. The best explanation for including him is that he was actually at the battle.

Chronologically the next work to mention Arthur was *Y Gododdin*. The man who composed it, Aneirin, lived in the late sixth century. He was one of the two most famous bards of the period. In the thirteenth century all of the poems attributed to him were collected into one volume called the *Book of Aneirin*. Although he did not actually compose all of the works, the authenticity of *Y Gododdin* is accepted. King Mynyddawg of the Gododdin employed the bard to compose this particular work. Gododdin is pronounced Godothin-in Welsh a double "d" makes the same sound as "th" in English. This tribe lived in what is now southeastern Scotland and Mynyddawg's capital was Din Eidyn, modern Edinburgh. Mynyddawg was part of an alliance that gathered together as many warriors as it could in an attempt to crush the small Anglian kingdom of Deira. The two sides met at Catraeth, modern Catterick and the result was a disastrous defeat for the Britons. According to the account only one British warrior survived. The Gododdin never recovered and it was only a matter of time before their territory was overrun.

The poem survives in two forms, called A and B. The A version is more complete, but the B version is older and it contains the relevant passage in which a hero named Gwarwrddur is compared to Arthur. There are accusations that this line is a forgery. Whether or not it is a forgery is unimportant. The work does not claim that Arthur was at the battle; it merely likens him to a warrior who was present. If the king lived then it compares two real people, if he were fictitious then it compares a real person with a mythic hero. Both things happen all of the time. The poem is important for what it reveals about sixth century battle poetry, and about that particular battle, but from the standpoint of the Arthurian investigation it is useless. *Y Gododdin* has been included here only because of its position in the chronology of the written sources and because it is almost always included.

In 820 a Welsh monk, possibly named Nennius, compiled a book called the *Historia Britonum*. It is this work that many researchers use to support the idea that Arthur was a general with the title of *dux bellorum*. It also contains a list of twelve battles that are described as Arthur's victories. The list itself is copied from an older original, as the names and language are not consistent with the early ninth century. The argument from the side that maintains that Arthur was mythical is that the list was a forgery that was concocted to add authenticity to the idea that he was real. This is based upon the assertion that two of the battles were actually fought by other men-Ambrosius Aurelianus and Urien of Rheged.

In *De excidio* Gildas is supposed to have said that Ambrosius won the Battle of Badon Hill. Actually he did not say anything of the kind. Gildas mentioned a great many things that he assumed his audience was familiar with. So he did not explain them. He mentioned Ambrosius and Badon in the same section, but they are not even in the same paragraph. The passage begins with an account of the arrival of the Anglo-Saxons. It goes on to say that the war went badly for the Britons until the rise of Ambrosius Aurelianus. Then followed a period of seesaw warfare that came to an end with Badon. Gildas then stated that he was born the same year and added something about a period of time of forty-three years and one month. This is all it says. There is no real indication as to who commanded at the battle, the emphasis seems to be on the chronology of events, not the victory itself.[13]

The connection to Urien of Rheged (r.*c*570-590) is even more tenuous. In fact it is so weak as to be virtually non-existent. Urien's battles were recorded in a poem by the bard Taliesin. One of his victories was Brewyn while one of the battles attributed to Arthur was called Breguoin The two names are similar and are probably different forms of the same name, which is fine as far as it goes, but it does not actually go very far. Anyone who has studied military history knows that the same place can be the site of more than one battle. The thinking seems to be that when that happens then the battles are always numbered. This is not true. Battles are only automatically numbered when two or more battles are fought in the same location in the same war, when they are fought in different wars they are almost never numbered. Even if it is the same battle, that is still not enough evidence to prove a forgery. Medieval manuscripts were copied out by hand, sometimes copyists made mistakes sometimes they made deliberate changes. It is not unusual for different copies of the same work to contain discrepancies. Some versions of the battle list do not have Breguoin; they have Mt. Agned in that spot. A great deal of fuss is being made over a battle that may not have been originally attributed to Arthur anyway.

When the Britons did attempt to pass off a mythic character as a real person they never concocted a phony battle list or anything else of that nature. They simply placed the character into the historical account or the genealogy and left it at that. This is supposed to be the one and only exception. Exceptions are always suspect, especially when they fit a particular point of view. It is generally agreed that the list as it now exists is a Latin translation of a Brythonic poem. This means that if this is a forgery then someone not only gathered up twelve battles from different sources but also went to all the trouble to cast them into poetic form. This forgery theory also ignores the fact that if anyone wanted to attribute battles to a mythic character he could have done it much more easily simply by taking an already existing list a adding Arthur's name to it. It is possible that the list was originally that of Ambrosius, but the idea that it was a forgery is

---

13 *De excidio*, 25.3.

complete nonsense. Even the idea that it is the list of Ambrosius is weak and rests entirely upon an ambiguous passage whose exact meaning is unknown.

The two entries on Arthur in the *Welsh Annals* have already been mentioned. The first attributes to him the victory at Badon and the second is his death at Camlann. The entry on Camlann is assumed to be a forgery because the entry on Badon is assumed to be a forgery. They both have to be false in order to make the theory work. But this is interpreting evidence to fit the theory. The entries might be forged, but there is no evidence for it. There are a great many accusations of forgery, but no hard evidence to back any of them up. Any accusation of forgery in history should be treated the same way that it is treated in a court of law. In this case the whole mess would be thrown out for lack of evidence.

There is one final argument that is sometimes made by those who discount the idea of a historical Arthur. Some have said that if he were real it should have been proven by now, after all people have been trying to authenticate his existence for generations. Modern optimism insists that there is an answer to every question and a solution to every mystery. But no good historian believes that. The study of the past is based upon reconstructions from the surviving material. If not much has survived then very little can be reconstructed. It is an axiom that a person should not believe in something unless there is reason to believe in it. Arthur cannot be located in the mythology. Each of the four oldest references to him are concerned with historical events, specifically battles. These references may be forgeries, but then again they may not and insisting that they are does not make it true. There is no good reason to believe that Arthur was fictitious. It is now time to see if there is good reason to believe that he was real.

Chapter II

ARTHUR AS MAN

No Human being can be completely unbiased. Every idea we have is influenced by our own beliefs and desires. It is impossible to avoid this, but there are ways to mitigate the affects. The best way to proceed is to gather all of the evidence first and then to see were it leads. Unfortunately this is easier said than done. It is difficult to simply gather information without forming opinions about it. This causes us to work the other way around. It is natural to come up with ideas that seem good to us and then look for evidence to support them while downplaying or ignoring evidence that contradicts them. We are taught this approach in school. We are taught to present a thesis first and then support it. This is a technique of debate, not reasoning. It compels people to accept an idea, but it does not really prove that an idea is true. The problem is that the evidence is almost as malleable as wet clay and it can be shaped to suit a wide variety of ideas. You cannot find the truth if you think you already have it. The choice of the evidence examined and the way in which it is examined is coloured by the desire to prove the theory. Most researchers who believe Arthur was real use one or more of the following sources: linguistics, *The History of the Kings of Britain* by Geoffrey of Monmouth and/or a collection of medieval Welsh legends called *The Mabinogion*. The limitations of linguistics will be examined first.

Even within the same language words that are not related can be similar to each other. To, too and two are all pronounced the same but each has a different meaning. Such examples are obvious when the reader is familiar with the language. The Arthurian material is far more confusing because it was passed down in several different languages. The official tongue of Roman Britain was, of course, Latin. However the majority of the population spoke Late Brythonic. Unfortunately very little of it has survived into our own time. Latin may be a dead language but it can still be read by thousands of people all over the world. Late Brythonic is not only dead it is decomposed. Only scraps of it have survived and they were preserved mainly in the names of places and people. The common language evolved into three tongues-Welsh, Cornish and Breton. Only the Welsh wrote their legends, but the English largely ignored these stories. Except for some families along the English-Welsh border, the two peoples had virtually nothing to do with each other. The French, on the other hand, found the Breton oral traditions highly entertaining. It was the French, not the Welsh, who introduced the Arthurian legends to the English. This can be seen by the fact that many of the names that are familiar in the English-speaking world (e.g. Guenevere, Camelot, Lancelot, Excalibur) are actually in French forms. If the English had these stories they would have rendered them into English forms.

All of this combines to produce a linguistic quagmire in which it is very difficult to discern the true origin and meaning of many words. A simple example will serve to illustrate this point. Some researchers rely on toponymy, the linguistics of place names. When examining the Pennine mountain chain it has been argued that it contains the root word *pen*, which means "head," and can be found in the names of hills and mountains in many parts of Britain. All of this is true, but in this particular case it is only a coincidence. Pennine is not Brythonic it is Italic. The Romans named the mountains after the Apennine mountain chain that runs up the centre of Italy. There are so many place names in Britain that once an investigator has decided that he or she has located Arthur in a specific region it is always possible to find locations in more or less the right area whose names can be made to fit those associated with the king. With the example of the Pennines the truth can be discerned because the origin of the word is well recorded. In most other instances the origins are more obscure and investigators are free to guess as to the true meanings. But a guess may seem right and still be wrong.

The History of the Kings of Britain poses a different series of problems. Geoffrey of Monmouth claimed that his work was a translation of "a certain very ancient book written in the British language"[14] which had been given to him by Walter Map, Archdeacon of Oxford. A great many people believe that there was no such book. Opposed to this is the theory that the original was *Brut y Brehinedd* (*The Chronicle of Kings*). None of the surviving copies of this work predate Geoffrey's book so some people maintain that the *Brut* is really a Welsh translation of the *History*. These chicken and egg-type of questions may be important to the literary scholars but they have no relevance for the historian. The real issue is not where Geoffrey got his information, but whether or not it is accurate. Even a brief examination of other sources reveals the work's weaknesses. There are some passages that recount real events but there are also myths presented as history, pagan gods and Roman emperors turned into British kings, individuals taken from their proper time periods and moved to completely different centuries, all to suit the narrative purposes of the author. With all of these inaccuracies in other parts of the work it is amazing that so many researchers are convinced that the Arthurian material is accurate. There are a few kernels of truth within the work, but separating the wheat from the chaff is not easy. An examination of another medieval figure can illustrate the situation.

We are fortunate in that the story of Robin Hood first appeared in a literate period. The tale evolved over the centuries, but most steps in that process can be traced in the written records. The three oldest manuscripts that contain material about the romantic rogue are *Robin Hood*

---

14 *History of the Kings of Britain*, iI.

and the Monk (c1450), *Robin Hood and the Potter* (c1500) and *A Gest of Robyn Hode* (c1510). The stories were set in the reign of Edward II (1307-'27) or Edward III (1327-'77) and it is generally agreed that the surviving tales were derived from now lost works that dated from this period. This is much later than the modern versions that set the story during the reign of Richard I (1189-'99). The texts contain many familiar elements, but also many surprises. The setting is Barnsdale in Yorkshire as well as Sherwood Forest. Robin is a yeoman-a free commoner, not the deposed Earl of Loxley. The Sheriff of Nottingham is still the villain, but Prince John is missing, quite naturally since he died in 1216, over a hundred years before the story takes place. Robin's band is quite small; it is only a quartet. Aside for the hero himself, there is also Little John, Will Scarlock and Much the Miller's son. Friar Tuck and Maid Marian are conspicuous by their absence. The alterations to the Robin Hood story took place over a roughly five hundred-year period and can be traced through the preserved manuscripts. The Arthurian legends were passed down orally for a similar period of time before being written down. This means that it is impossible to even guess at what alterations may have been made before Arthur appeared in the pages of *The History of the Kings of Britain*.

At least Monmouth's book contains some recognizable history. The *Mabinogion* is a collection of legends, many of which originated in the pagan mythology. There is absolutely no evidence that even one of the stories is based upon a real event. Despite this many researchers simply assume that there is accurate material in the tales and then they set about reinterpreting them in order to use what they like as evidence that certain theories are true. There is a school of thought that says that all legends are derived from real events. This may be a convenient concept for those seeking to support a given theory but it makes no real sense. It is based upon the premise that our ancestors had no imaginations, they could not invent new stories, they could only rework tales about actual episodes. The imagination is like any other part of the human anatomy, the more it is used the stronger it becomes. In modern times most people have their entertainment created for them through motion pictures, television, novels, computer games and so on. In the Middle Ages there were certainly professional storytellers, but it was believed that anyone who had the talent for it not only could but should tell stories. An examination of the authors of the Arthurian manuscripts bears this out. There were professionals like Cretien de Troyes and Marie de France, but there were also amateurs such as the anonymous authors of *The Vulgate Cycle* (monks who sought to instill Christian values through entertainment), Wolfram von Eschenbach (an impoverished knight who took up writing to supplement his income), and Thomas Malory (another knight who wrote his book to pass the time while serving a prison sentence). These are only some of the known manuscripts, obviously the list cannot include works that have been lost or tales of those who worked orally and never wrote anything. Since so many people were encouraged to exercise their talents in this way peoples in Ancient and medieval times had better imaginations than we have today. As proof of this one need only look up at the night sky. When they viewed the stars our ancestors saw animals and monsters and fabulous creatures, we see a Big Dipper and a Little Dipper.

The main function was not to preserve accurate history but to entertain audiences. This means that even if a story were based upon reality it would be reworked by succeeding generations of storytellers. This phenomenon is observable even in our own society. Novels and motion pictures may be based upon true stories but they are always rewritten to make them more entertaining. Truth may be stranger than fiction but it is not as dramatic. The trick is to be able to see what is truth and what is fiction. Many researchers rely heavily upon *The Dream of Rhonabwy* one of the stories in *The Mabinogion* because it is the oldest legend that mentions Arthur. But its age is no guarantee of its reliability. There is no way to tell if it actually contains any accurate material and even if it does there is no way to determine what is true or what is fictitious or if the historical material really concerned Arthur. The way in which a legend is treated is determined by the needs of the researchers when it should be based upon the nature of the source itself.

The researchers who use linguistics and legends are making the same fundamental mistake. They are trying to find one source that can provide almost all of the answers. There is no such source. Every statement- whether from a history, or a legend or a battle list or any other source- must be examined on its own to determine its reliability and must also be examined in the light of other sources that concern the same events. There is no blueprint; it is a jigsaw puzzle with missing pieces and no box top to show what the finished picture should look like. It is with good reason that the word for the study of the past comes from the Ancient Greek *historia*, which means "researches."

The proper approach can be illustrated using *De excidio*. Gildas' statement that he was born the same year as the Battle of Badon Hill can be taken at face value. He had no reason to lie and he would not have been mistaken about the year of his own birth. On the other hand he was rather muddled in his understanding of the Roman military system. In the course of his narrative Gildas stated that the island was left unprotected several times, when in reality the Romans maintained a very large garrison until the late fourth century. So is the book accurate or not? That depends upon which part of the book is under examination. This illustrates the general rule that unless dealing with obvious accurate material no statement should be accepted unless there is at least one piece of independent evidence to substantiate it. The Arthurian sources must now be examined using these criteria.

Before any attempt is made to prove any aspect of Arthur's career, that career must be outlined so that we may define exactly what it is we are talking about. The information presented here is taken from the earliest traditions, with all of the obvious mythological material cut out. The first point to be made is that Arthur was very firmly set in a specific time period-the late fifth and early sixth centuries. Not only were all of the dateable battles in that timeframe but historical figures in the narrative (Caius of Strathclyde, Constantine of Dumnonia etc.) also lived then. In the second half of the fifth century Britain was a dangerous place. The Picts raided out of the Highlands, the Irish controlled several colonies along the west coast, but more threatening than these were the Anglo-Saxons. The term "Anglo-Saxon" was invented in the eighth century to distinguish between the Saxons of Britain and the Saxons of Germany. It is now used as an umbrella term to refer to a variety of Germanic tribes that settled in Britain. The two largest were the Angles and the Saxons, but there were also Jutes, Friesians, Swabians, Alemanni, Vandals and Varni. Their Britano-Gaelic enemies called them all Saxons. The Anglo-Saxons themselves used the two terms interchangeably, which is why although their kingdoms were eventually united by a Saxon dynasty (from Wessex), the resultant state was named after the Angles (England=Angle land). Throughout this work the term Anglo-Saxon will be used except when referring to a specific tribe or utilizing a quotation, as it is the more usual and slightly more accurate than simply saying Saxons or Angles.

Beginning in the fourth century Germanic tribes began to abandon their homelands and move westward into areas controlled by the Roman Empire. They did this to escape the military pressure being placed upon them by their Slavic neighbours to the east who were being crowded out by steppe nomads. The Huns, who had originated in the region along the Chinese border, had put the whole process in motion. The movement of so many peoples at one time is called the Great Migrations.

The homeland for the Jutes was the peninsula that is still called Juteland. Virtually the entire people moved to Britain leaving their territory open to be occupied by a people who were moving south from southern Sweden and the island of Zealand. These were the Danes, which is why Juteland is now in Denmark. According to Bede the Jutes settled in Kent, the Isle of Wight and the coastal area just opposite Wight. The Angles came from the coastal areas at the base of the Juteland peninsula. They also abandoned their homeland almost completely. They were the most numerous, eventually settling in all of northern England and roughly half of the south as well. The Saxons were actually the largest group, but many of their people remained on the mainland and did not come to Britain, they originated in the lands to the west of the Anglian tribal homeland. The Saxons campaigned in Gaul against the Romans in the fifth century and were Charlemagne's chief eastern enemies in the eight and ninth centuries. Those who came to Britain tended to settle in the south, not penetrating any farther north than the modern county (and ancient kingdom) of Essex. The settlements of the other tribes were too insignificant to be dealt with here.

As was mentioned earlier there is good evidence that there was a Germanic presence in Britain before the Roman conquest. This presence was slightly strengthened during the Imperial period as the Romans hired Germanic mercenaries to act as auxiliary troops in the defense of the island. After the Roman withdrawal the Britons invited more to come to help them against the Picts and the Irish. The newcomers were impressed with the wealth of the island and the weakness of its defenses. They decided to take advantage of this weakness to grab the wealth. They revolted against their paymasters and gained control of sections to the east and south of

Britain. By the 480's they occupied almost the entire eastern coastline from the mouth of the Humber River to the Channel. They had a colony along the south coast called Sussex and later another, smaller one, called Wessex.

The Britons were in grave difficulties. They were fighting a general's worst nightmare-a war on multiple fronts with the Irish in the west, the Picts in the north and the Anglo-Saxons in both the east and the south. But they were winning. According to legend this was because of Arthur. He defeated all of his people's enemies and reigned during a period of peace and prosperity, which was brought to an end by civil war. The general outline of the legend is corroborated by the facts. By the 490's all of the Irish settlements had been completely overrun. The Battle of Badon Hill was fought in the same decade. Gildas reported that it was such a crushing defeat for the Anglo-Saxons that even in his time, forty-three years later, the enemy still had not dared to attack again. Archaeological excavations have shown that the invaders abandoned some of their holdings and fled to more easily defended areas. This was especially true in Lindsey (now northern Lincolnshire). The kingdom of Sussex was almost completely destroyed, although it recovered in later centuries. Some of the invaders even fled the island altogether. A style of pottery that was invented by the Anglo-Saxons began to appear in graves on the mainland of Europe in this period. After the fighting was over there was a period of roughly twenty years of peace. This came to an end with a civil war, one that ushered in several decades of almost constant civil war among the Britons. It was during this period of warfare that Gildas wrote his book.

There are fourteen specifically named battles associated with Arthur: his twelve victories as recorded by Nennius, his defeat at Llongborth mentioned in *The Eulogy for Geraint* and his defeat and death at the Battle of Camlann as mentioned in the *Welsh Annals* and other sources. Llongborth has already been dealt with in the first chapter. As was stated there, many people believe that the reference to Arthur was poetic fancy, not literal truth. The argument revolves around determining the intentions of a poet who died fifteen hundred years ago. In the study of history the burden of proof rests with the side proposing the theory. This means that ambiguous material may be used to attack an idea but not to support one. *The Eulogy for Geraint* is inadmissible as evidence that Arthur existed. A similar problem is presented with Camlann. Although the civil war was certainly real, there is virtually no information about it. It cannot be shown that there actually was a Battle of Camlann, let alone that Arthur fought it. All that is left to be examined is the Nennius battle list.

Researchers on both sides of the debate concentrate on whether or not Arthur fought the battles, rather than on whether or not the battles themselves were real. The approach taken here is the reverse of the usual approach. The most important points to be determined about these conflicts are when and where they would have been fought if they were real. Unfortunately this kind of information is available for only some of the battles.

The first is the River Glein, which is probably the same as the River Glen in Lincolnshire. The second through fifth battles took place on the banks of the River Dubglas in the region of Linnuis.

Linnuis is almost certainly a variant for of Lindsey, the old name for northern Lincolnshire. The Anglo-Saxons had settled in this area in the second half of the fifth century. Little trace of these early villages survives except for the graveyards. These were abandoned in the 490's, indicating that the local populations had fled. Since there is no evidence of any kind of natural disaster the logical conclusion is that they were fleeing from their military enemies. If this were true than the Dubglas would be the Witham. The modern name is Old English and it means "the homestead (or village) in the river bend." The British name for it is unknown, but it could easily have been Dubglas. This means "blue-black" and was popular for the names of rivers among the Britons.

The sixth battle was on the River Bassas, which is unknown. The next took place in the Caldonian Wood. There is no doubt about this location. Caldonia is the old name for Scotland and the forest is the wood north of Carlisle. The eighth is another mystery. It was at Castle Guinnion.

Battle number nine was at the City of the Legion. There are three possible locations: Chester, Caerleon and York. The Romans stationed several legions in Britain over the centuries, but these three served the longest as legion headquarters. In fact the first two commemorate the Roman occupation in their names. Chester is the Old English pronunciation of *castra,* which is Latin for a fortified camp or fortress. Caerleon is a Welsh corruption of "Camp (or City) of the Legion." Although the name of York bears no indication of it, the city was actually headquarters of a legion longer than any other town in Britain. Some versions of Nennius' work specify Caerleon, which fits best linguistically.

The tenth, the River Tribruit, is another unknown. The eleventh is controversial. In some sources it is Breguoin and in others Mt. Agned. The first cannot be identified; the second is the old name for one of the mountains overlooking Edinburgh. It is now called Arthur's Seat.

The last name on the list is Badon Hill. There is more information about this battle than any other single conflict in Britain in the fifth and sixth centuries put together. It is a sad comment on the nature of the evidence that it must be admitted that we still do not know very much about it. Like the Linnuis battles, it can be dated, but not with certainty. In *De excidio* Gildas mentioned the arrival of the Saxons (*adventus Saxonum*), Badon, his own birth and period of forty-three years and one month. This passage can be interpreted in three different ways. The first is that the battle took place forty-three years after the *adventus*. Bede read it that way but that creates the problem of dating one event in relation to another event. It is usually stated that Bede dated the *adventus* to 449, a closer examination indicates that he did not know when it took place, but indicated that 449 was the earliest that it could have been. The second approach, which is the more widely accepted, is to conclude that Gildas was giving his own age as forty-three at the time he wrote his book. Since the work was composed some time around the 540, that would place the battle at roughly 497. The third idea is that he was referring to a coincidence-the same amount of time elapsed between the *adventus* and the battle as had passed from the battle to writing the book. Both Gildas and Welsh tradition indicate that a period of peace followed the battle. Archaeology indicates heavy fighting in Lindsey in the 490's. This means that Badon could not have been early in the decade, as that would not allow for enough time for these battles. This means that the battle was some time in the late 490's or early 500's.

Having established the time period for Badon it now becomes necessary to pinpoint the location. The manuscript in the Harleian Library, which contains the *Historia Britonum*, also has two other works. This was not unusual. In the Middle Ages books were not always tailor made to fit texts, often books were produced then texts were copied into them to fill them up. One of the other works was written by an unknown author and is called *Mirablia*. It details the "wonders of Britain" and contains a reference to a "hot lake where the Baths of Badon are, in the country of the Hwicce." The reference to the hot lake and the baths point to the town of Bath, the mention of the Hwicce removes all doubt. Hwicce is the Old English pronunciation of Gewesse. This was a term for a confederation of tribes, but in this case it referred to a specific group that had been established in the fourth century by a man named Octavius. He passed into legend as Eudaf or Eudes. Many dynasties from southern Wales and the southwest claimed descent from him.[15] The Anglo-Saxons conquered the Gewesse in the late sixth or early seventh centuries. They survived as a distinct group, but after the conquest a noble family of Mercian origin ruled them. In the ninth century Bath was not actually in their territory, however it was just over the border and surviving charters indicate that it had been in Hwicce land some time earlier. Besides Bath is the only location anywhere near the Hwicce that fits the description of having a hot lake.

What is most interesting is the way in which the author treated the name. Medieval copyists were well aware that language can evolve and names can change. If there had been an alteration the author would have indicated this in one of the usual ways by writing something like "Badon that is Bath." Instead he behaved as if he expected his audience to be familiar with the name itself but may have needed an explanation as to where it was. This suggests that in the early ninth century the Welsh name for Bath was still Badon.

All of this is fine as far as it goes, but none of it shows any kind of connection between the battles and the king. For that we must turn to the *History of the Kings of Britain* of Geoffrey of Monmouth. It has already been pointed out that this is not a reliable source. However it has also been argued that no source can be rejected in its entirety-each point must be examined individually and information from an unreliable source can be used if independent corroboration can be found to support it. The Nennius list and Geoffrey's account corroborate each other. Geoffrey presented Arthur's military career as part of a continuous narrative. The battles can be divided into three groups: his early career in Britain, the conquest of the Highlands and the war against the Romans.

---

15 According to tradition he was the father-in-law of Magnus Maximus, who was himself said to have been the father-in-law of Vortigern. Cynan, the first king of Dumnonia was said to have been his son. The first recorded ruler of Brittany, Cynan Meriadoc, was either his son or nephew, depending upon the sources, while Erb, the first ruler of Gwent was his grandson.

To deal with them in reverse order-the campaign on the continent was taken from the career of the Roman general Magnus Maximus. He made a favorable impression among most Britons and passed into folk tradition as Macsen Gwledig. This shows that although Geoffrey's book is not accurate, at least some of the material is based upon fact. The author changed the information but he did not invent it. The conquest of the Highlands was achieved in two battles, Alclud and Loch Lomand.

Alclud means "Rock of the Clyde" and it is now known by the Scottish name, Dunbarton (Fort of the Britons). It was the capital of Strathclyde. There is no information on a battle there in this period nor is there any corroboration for a fight at Loch Lomand. According to Geoffrey the Picts and Scots were defeated and accepted Arthur as their overlord. Since Strathclyde was a British kingdom Geoffrey clearly has his information muddled.

The earliest of the battles in Geoffrey are much more interesting and have names that are suspiciously familiar. The first is the River Douglas, which is obviously the same as the Dubglas. The next is York, one of the possible locations for the City of the Legion. The third is on a river outside the town of Lincoln. The only river that fits the description is the Witham, which archaeology suggests as the location of the Dubglas. The fourth is Caledon Wood, clearly the same as the Caldonian Wood. The final fight was at Bath, which has already been identified as Badon.

It is often assumed that the similarities between the two battle narrations are a product of the fact that Geoffrey used Nennius as a source for his book. But a comparison of the two suggests that this might not be true. Geoffrey mentioned only five battles, (seven if the two in the Highlands are included) not twelve; he placed them in a different order and used different names for most of them. Geoffrey also made a distinction between the Douglas and the river near Lincoln; he does not even seem to have known the name of the latter. It would have been impossible for him to get a battle on the Douglas and another on a river whose name he did not know from four battles on the river Dubglas. Whatever source Geoffrey used for his information it does not appear to have been the *Historia Britonum*. This suggests that the Welsh recorded at least two sets of traditions about the same battles and attributed them to the same man. This makes the idea of forgery much less plausible.

With all of the attention being paid to the battles, everyone is missing something else of much greater importance. After the fighting there was a period of peace that ended with a civil war. Arthur was not famous for fighting a battle. The Round Table was not assembled to fight Badon. Arthur was not only a war hero he was also a peacekeeper. The legends clearly recorded that he maintained the peace and then was killed in a civil war. Gildas referred to the peace in his book. He stated that the period of civil wars in which he lived was caused by "an age that had grown up ignorant of the storms"[16] of the previous period of warfare. In other words the peace lasted long enough for a generation to grow from children to adults. The *Welsh Annals* stated

---

16 *De excidio*, 26.2.

that the Battle of Badon Hill was fought in 517 and Arthur was killed at the Battle of Camlann in 538, twenty-one years later. That is long enough for a generation to grow up. This period of peace did come to an end with a civil war; it was the first of many.

There is a problem with the dates. As was already argued Badon did not take place in 517. Almost all researchers on both sides of the debate generally accept this. For some reason some people leave the date of Camlann at 538 but exactly the same source provides the dates for both battles. If the *Welsh Annals* was mistaken about Badon, what makes anyone think it was right with Camlann? Ancient peoples did not think in terms of exact dates. They would not have remembered that Arthur had been killed in 538; they would have believed that he had died twenty-one years after Badon. If the date for the first battle is moved then the second one must also be moved. This means that three sources: Gildas, the *Welsh Annals* and the Arthurian legends, record the same course of events. Both the legends and Gildas indicate a period of constant warfare. Gildas stated it came to an end with Badon, the *Annals* attributes that battle to Arthur, and the traditions credit him with bringing peace. The peace lasted twenty-one years, or roughly long enough for a generation to grow up. All three sources confirm that it came to an end with a civil war and both the legends and the *Annals* indicate that Arthur was killed in the war. None of the sources contradict each other, except in the dates and that was a very common mistake in this period. They provide different details but when the information does overlap it is consistent.

No one has paid much attention to this because they are looking for a war hero. The idea that Arthur was chiefly remembered as a peacekeeper is alien to the debate. But it is central to finding the truth. The kings were little more than a group of petty warlords, constantly fighting each other to try to increase their own power. They had their own private armies to fight their own private wars. However the kings and their war bands made up only a small percentage of the population. In pre-industrialized societies the warrior class was usually only about 3%-7% of the population. The overwhelming majority of the population was made up of ordinary people who were simply trying to live their own lives. They did not like the fact that at any time, virtually without warning, a group of marauding thugs could come sweeping through town, pillaging, raping and murdering. They were more interested in the peace, than in who won which battle. They were also illiterate. The only way to pass on the memory of the events that the people considered worth remembering was through oral traditions, which means that the history would automatically become tangled with the myths and legends.

Many historians make the same mistake of ignoring the peace with another Britano-Gaelic king. Brian Boru was considered the greatest of Ireland's medieval monarchs. It is usually said that this is because he defeated the Vikings at the Battle of Clontarf in 1014. Brian was killed at Clontarf. We do not judge a king's entire reign based upon the last thing he did. His reputation must have been based upon something other than the battle. Before the battle he maintained the peace for twelve years. It was the longest period of peace Ireland experienced throughout the entire Middle Ages.

War and peace were intimately connected to their concepts of kingship. A monarch was supposed to bring peace by defeating the enemies of his people. On Christmas day in the year 800 Charlemagne was crowned emperor of what he called the Holy Roman Empire. As the pope placed the crown upon his head he said "life and victory to Charles the August, crowned by God the great and *pacific* emperor of the Romans"[17] (italics mine). *The Councils of Cormac* was an Irish treatise on the proper conduct of good citizens in general and kings in particular. It was attributed to Cormac mac Art, a third century high king of Ireland. It contains the same kind of concepts of war and peace. The first entry says that kings should have "A hand wielding swords in defense of every tribe, attacks across borders." But he is also advised to "knit every peace treaty together."[18] Then there is also the fact that the Romans were praised for giving the Ancient World the *pax Romana*, the peace of Rome.

The usual interpretation of the peace in this period does not fit with the international situation. The Britons defeated the Anglo-Saxons at Badon and then stopped. According to the usual explanation this was because the invaders were contained. But the Britons did not want to contain them; they wanted to drive them off the island altogether. They had the advantage and they should have pressed it. A people do not end a war that they are winning unless they are concerned with something else. There was no other foreign enemy for them to be concerned with, so it must have been something domestic. The kings did not trust each other, but that should be self-evident. Everyone on both sides of the debate agrees that these kings were warlords. Warlords do not want peace; they have a vested interest in fighting each other. The more of their rivals they could defeat, the more wealth and power they could amass for themselves. Warlords are not impressed by negotiation, but they are influenced by intimidation. The ambitious kings were trying to defeat their rivals and force them to submit in order to make themselves high king. There is only one reason why they would stop doing that; there already was a high king, one too powerful to challenge. They would not have established a treaty or alliance to give them something they did not want. Warlords do not keep peace unless they are forced to, which means someone was forcing them to.

Let us say for the sake of argument that they did want peace and they set up an agreement to get it. The question then becomes: how did this agreement operate? According to the usual interpretation some sort of treaty or alliance maintained the peace. Historian after historian repeats the phrase of "some sort." But in fact there is only one sort of alliance and two sorts of treaty. The alliance shall be explained using some famous examples.

In the fifth century Gaul was one of the most fought over of all regions in the Roman Empire. Eventually most of it went to the Franks and became France. Like most other people in this period, the Franks were divided. Their king, Clovis, laid the foundation for their success. In 496 the Alemanni attacked the Ripuarian Franks. They made an alliance with another branch

---

17 *Frankish Annals.*

18 *The Councils of Cormac* I.

of their tribe, the Salian Franks. Clovis, king of the Salians, became commander-in-chief of the allied Frankish army and high king of the Franks. Clovis defeated the Alemanni at the Battle of Tolbiac. He then became involved in a Burgundian civil war (his wife, Clotilda, was a Burgundian princess). When this was settled he turned against the Visigoths. They made an alliance with the other branch of their people, the Ostrogoths. Theodoric, king of the Ostrogoths, became commander-in-chief of the allied Gothic army and high king of the Goths. In other words, when no high king existed before the establishment of an alliance, then the creation of the alliance itself would create a high king. The reason for this is obvious. All of the monarchs led their own troops on the battlefield. The supreme commander would have to give orders to kings. Kings do not take orders from just anyone. They only take orders from senior kings or emperors. A powerful king would have led an alliance.

Treaties are made between parties that are equal, or parties that are not equal. If, as most researchers insist, there were no high king in this period then it would have to have been an agreement between equals. That type of agreement in this period never involved more than two kings and even then in roughly half the examples on record it did not work. Either one king would break the agreement and war would start up again or one of the kings would murder the other. Something so small scale and so fragile could not have maintained peace among roughly three-dozen kings for twenty years.

An agreement between parties that are not equal would mean that there would have been a power at the centre. Since every state in this case was a monarchy, to say that there was a power at the centre would be another way of saying powerful king.

A high king was at the top of the system. Any other king trying to build up his power was a threat to the man at the top. He had a vested interest in peace. It is quite possible that he had allies, but he was the key. Without him there was no reason for peace, let alone a way to make it work. He would end the war with the Anglo-Saxons if he were smart. The more resources he expended fighting them, the fewer resources he would have had to keep the other British kings in line. Continued war would risk rebellion. None of this proves that the name of this king was Arthur, but Arthur is the only name we have. This is exactly the period Arthur is said to have lived and keeping the peace is exactly what Arthur was famous for.

Britain was divided into separate kingdoms for over five hundred years. Only roughly the first one hundred and fifty are badly documented. They did have periods of peace for which there is documentation. Ireland was also divided for many centuries; it too had peace in times that are well documented. Every documented example of peace from both islands had the same cause: a powerful king using either intimidation or a combination of intimidation and diplomacy to keep the troublemakers in line.

If a powerful king is the only way to maintain the peace, then that must be the way in which it was done. It would be highly unreasonable to argue that the Arthurian period was the one and only exception. No known king had that much power. So it must have been one of the kings whose names have not survived in the reliable documentation. In a badly documented time period the documentation is the problem. It cannot be allowed the final word, besides there is no documentation on a treaty or alliance either. Someone just made that up and almost everyone else went along with it. The answer has been arrived at through indirect evidence, but indirect evidence is perfectly valid and is often used by historians in a wide variety of investigations. The great mistake in the debate about King Arthur is that both sides are trying to find the answer using direct evidence, but that is virtually impossible given the state of the surviving information, which is exactly why the debate has lasted for so long.

This approach even explains why so much myth and legend became mixed into Arthur's story. The storytellers wanted to keep his memory alive, but their job was not to preserve history, it was to entertain audiences, and the sorry truth is that peace is boring. They had to fill up the story with something and the adventure tales provided a convenient answer. The more heroes they could attach to the king, the greater his popular reputation. Unfortunately these stories took him farther away from history and muddled the truth. But it is still there to see, for anyone who knows how to look. The biggest mistakes are that people are asking the wrong question. They ask, "who won Badon?" instead of "who kept the peace?" Most theories about Arthur involve changing the information. This one involves changing the way in which the information is viewed. It indicates that Arthur was never really lost, we were.

There is more evidence to back up the basic contention. The most powerful known king in this time period was Dumnagaul. The name means "World Ruler" and eventually evolved into Donald. He ruled two kingdoms. He probably inherited Manu Gododdin and then came to power in Strathclyde after his relative, Caius, was deposed. Since transportation and communication were very limited many names were unique to specific tribes. Dumnagaul was a rare name in this period, the only previous example in the king lists comes roughly two generations earlier in the kingdom of Bryneich. This was a Gododdin kingdom and it is probably no coincidence that the next appearance on the lists was a ruler of another of their realms. Since he was so important, why was he not better remembered in the traditions? Dumnagaul is so forgotten that even many historians do not know about him. The best answer is that another king who was even more powerful overshadowed him. But there is another connection to Arthur with this king.

There is a mystery as to how Dumnagaul came to rule Strathclyde, the other kingdom under his control. The only account of what happened comes from *The Life of St. Gildas*, because Gildas' father was Caw, or Caius, of Strathclyde. According to the account the family rebelled against Arthur, lead by Caw's eldest son, Heuil.[19] He was defeated and Caw was forced to abdicate. Most researchers agree that this is not what happened, but no one has ever suggested an alternative. Dumnagaul did become king of Strathclyde, so how and why was Caw deposed? Insisting that the traditional tale is wrong is not very productive unless an alternative explanation can be

---

19   Gildas was not yet born at this point. Caw had twenty-four children. Heuil was the eldest son and Gildas was one of the youngest so there was a significant difference in their ages.

produced. The best interpretation is that Dumnagaul was Arthur's trusted ally and was given the kingdom of the deposed rebel. This story is consistent with the battle list. The Caldonian Wood would have been in southern Strathclyde and the battle fits with the idea that Arthur put down a rebellion by the rulers of that realm.

On July 4, 1998, a team of archeologists from Glasgow University working at Tintagel discovered a stone inscription with the words PATER COLIAVIFICIT ARTOGNAU-"Artognau, father of a descendant of Coal." The name is pronounced as if written Arthnow. The inscription dates to the sixth century and originally served as the dedication plaque of a small building, probably a chapel that once stood outside the castle. Tradition names Tintagel as Arthur's birthplace and Artognau is linguistically similar to Arthur and might be a variant form of the name. This proves that a man with essentially the right name was associated with the right place in the right time period. It is agreed that Artognau was not a king, but that is based upon the assumption that we know Cornwall was in Dumnonia, when we do not really know that at all.

The argument about the similarity of the name is as far as anyone has gone. But Artognau is only one word. The Britons must have considered the whole inscription important, or else they would not have carved it into stone. It is incumbent upon the researcher to try and determine what the rest of the inscription means. The wording is very strange; in fact it is unique. Artognau himself was not descended from Coel, but his child was. This can only mean that his wife was. In Ancient Britano-Gaelic society women had equal rights with men, but hundreds of years of Roman occupation had given them male chauvinistic tendencies. They would not have directly referred to a woman in a stone inscription, except on her tombstone. Clearly they considered the connection to Coel to be important. Coel was the great king north of the Humber in the first half of the fifth century. Almost all of the northern dynasties claimed descent from him, including Dumnagaul's family. This means that we have the reference to the descendant of a powerful northern ruler in a monument found deep in the south. This suggests a dynastic marriage and in order to have a dynastic marriage, Artognau would have to have been a king.

This fits with other known facts. The Britons did trace descent through women as well as through men. Furthermore in monarchy the reigning monarch is always the centre of attention even if he or she is not the subject under discussion. Everyone assumes that the subject of the inscription is Artognau, when in fact it is his child. Artognau's name is there because he was the king, but the wording itself is clearly referring to his offspring.

Most of the popular image of the great king is derived not from dedication plaques or battle lists but from legends. There can be no doubt that there is a great deal of mythological material mixed into what is often called the Arthurian Cycle. There can also be no doubt that the Welsh did try to present fictional characters as if they were real. On the other hand it is also true that they incorporated real people into their mythic traditions. Geraint was a knight of the Round Table and Arthur's nephew; he was also an historical figure who was killed at the Battle of Llongborth. Another of Arthur's knights was Yvain son of Urien. Rendered back into the original

Welsh this would be Owain ap Urien, the son and successor of Urien of Rheged. There is also evidence that Bedivere and Perceval were derived from real men named Bodwyr and Peredur.

There are several points that should be made about these figures. The first is that they were all warriors, not bards or saints or any other type of person likely to have been remembered. The second is that they all lived in the sixth century. The most interesting point is how exclusive the list is. Not one individual from another time period was included in their number. The Welsh deliberately kept all of their sixth century war-heroes together-with Arthur. On the other hand it is also true that he has been linked to clearly fictitious characters like Gawain and Lancelot.

In order to find the truth every reasonable possibility must be examined to determine which is the most likely to be true. The earliest written references to him are said to be forgeries and poetic fancies. This may be true; on the other hand maybe they are genuine. The myths in which he appears were definitely rewritten. Arthur was dated to a specific time period with all of the battles taking place within a roughly twenty five-year period from the early 490's to just before 520. He was said to have been killed in a war that really happened and a stone baring a similar name and carved in the right period has been found at the very place he was said to have been born. The nature of the debate itself is suggestive. Each argument made by those who maintain that he was mythical can be countered by a closer examination of the evidence or by reasoned arguments backed up by examples. The greatest argument against Arthur's existence is his absence from Gildas' book. However Gildas is known to have lied about other things and if the story of the rebellion of his family were true, then he would have had a motive to lie about Arthur. It could be said that the entire debate is based upon the assumption that Gildas is reliable, but that is an assumption. He did live in the sixth century, but if he did not tell the truth in the first place then the century is irrelevant.

The idea that Arthur was real can only be countered by the constant repetition of the fact that this position cannot be proven. But failure to prove something does not automatically disprove it. Besides, much of what is generally accepted about the fifth and sixth centuries cannot be proven, but most of it is less controversial. It is human nature to prefer certainties, but real life does not work that way and with Arthur almost nothing is certain.

It is always maintained that the burden of proof rests with the side that says that Arthur was real. This is convenient, but not very practical. In a court of law the burden of proof rests with the prosecution because the court is not only trying to learn the truth, but also to protect the rights of the individual. The prosecution must prove its case beyond a reasonable doubt, if it fails then the defense gets the benefit of the doubt. Outside of a court of law to insist that the burden of proof rests with one side is to claim the benefit of the doubt, but by what right does anyone make such a claim? People debating King Arthur are not defending the rights of individuals. Socrates stated that to truly reason people must question everything, including their own assumptions. But insisting that one side has the burden of proof is not questioning assumptions; it is grasping on to assumptions with an iron grip and refusing to let go unless the other side can prove their case. The traditional account makes perfect sense. The people who say there was no King Arthur must prove what really caused the twenty years of peace and they must come up with something more convincing than the vague statement of "some sort" of treaty or alliance. They must prove that he is mythical, but they have failed to do this. Getting at the truth is not based upon shifting responsibility to the other side; it is based upon examining *both* sides to determine which one makes the more sense.

In the previous chapter it was stated that an idea should not be believed unless there is good reason to believe it. If all of the evidence is examined in an unbiased manner as possible there is certainly more reason to believe that he was real than to believe that he was mythical. Many people will not find this very satisfying, but it is the best answer that can be given in the circumstances.

Chapter III

THE HISTORY

S HOWING THAT Arthur probably existed is not enough. Most people want more than just a name and a few events; they want a recognizable person. Different scholars have come up with very different theories when trying to reconstruct Arthur's life, often revealing more about themselves than about their subject. Before the man can be examined, the world he lived in must be outlined. Often not enough time is spent studying the history and culture of ancient and early medieval Britain and this leads to mistaken conclusions about Arthur himself. The history will be outlined first.

Contrary to popular belief, Julius Caesar did not conquer Britain. He invaded it twice but was driven back both times. These attacks were an extension of his Gaulic campaigns. The actual conquest was in AD43-47. The reasons for the invasion are often misunderstood. Many researchers state that the Romans attacked Britain because of the activities of the druids. They were the elite of the religious classes. The main centre of druidic learning was on the island of Mona (now called Anglesey), off of the north coast of Wales. The druids of Gaul were also taught at Mona and according to an oft-repeated idea these druids incited the Gauls to rebel against the Roman occupation.

Whatever the druid activities may have been, they were not considered a real threat to Rome. The conquest was actually the result of completely different set of circumstances rooted in imperial politics. The emperor Caligula was assassinated in AD41, leaving no clear successor. This caused a serious political crisis. The Praetorian Guard, the emperor's bodyguard, realized that without a body to guard they would be out of a job and so they proclaimed Caligula's uncle, Claudius, as the new ruler. In order to secure his position Claudius needed the support of the army and the Senate. The Praetorians may have backed him, but they did not speak for the entire army. To the high command he was an unknown quantity-Claudius was a scholar, not a soldier. He had almost no friends in the Senate, where he was generally regarded as a fool. But the new emperor was wise enough to see a solution to his problem. The quickest road to promotion in the military was through distinguished service in wartime, so the officer corps wanted another conquest. The Senate was full of wealthy men who were always on the lookout for new investment opportunities, not to mention new ways to spread the tax burden and reduce their own taxes. The conquest of Britain would provide the generals with a new campaign and would add a wealthy province to the Empire. Some researchers have criticized Claudius for not taking an active role in the invasion. He came to Britain only once, for a ceremony to commemorate the surrender of several tribes. In fact he did exactly the right thing. Claudius may have been of the same dynasty as Julius Caesar, but he was not Julius Caesar and everyone knew it. The army did not want him involved in the war; they only wanted him to provide the resources they needed so that they could carry it out. This may not satisfy modern notions of a conquering hero, but it suited the actual political and military situation.

The invasion began in AD43 and took several stages. The relatively open lands of what are now England and southern Scotland were taken within a few years. The Highlands of the north were a different matter. The peoples living there were not defeated militarily and remained openly hostile to the Romans. There were actually several cultural groups that lived in the Highlands, but the Romans called them all *Picti*, the "Painted People" because they covered themselves in tattoos and their warriors also wore a blue dye called woad. Irish sources reserve the term Picts for the people who lived just to the north of the Antonine Wall. This ran from the Firth of Clyde to the Firth of Forth and it marked the farthest northern boundary of imperial influence.

There are several main reasons why the Picts and other northerners retained their independence. The most important factor was that the Romans did not feel they could spare the troops to capture and occupy so remote a land that had little or no material wealth to offer the Empire. What is more the mountainous terrain would have posed severe problems for the progress of the legions. Changes to the Pictish political structure would also have hampered a campaign. Originally they had been divided into many small, warring tribes. In response to the Roman threat these tribes organized into larger confederations. By the third century there were two such confederations: the Caledonii and the Maeatae. They are usually called simply the North and South Picts. These political changes gave them a measure of military strength that was useful not only in defending themselves, but for attacking others. With their lands free of threat from the Empire, the Highlanders were able to launch raids into Roman occupied Britain. With defensive responsibilities for one of the largest empires the world has ever seen, the Romans found themselves hard pressed to protect that far off corner of their domain. The Romans tried two solutions to this problem.

The Antonine Wall was actually the second such defensive work constructed by the imperial authorities. The first was the more famous Hadrian's Wall, named after the emperor who ordered it constructed in AD122. The walls in and of themselves were not enough. There were four tribes that lived between the walls. The Romans tried several methods to bring them to heel, or at least keep them friendly in order to create a buffer zone between the hostile Picts and Roman Britain. By the time that accurate histories were being produced these tribes had formed states that are usually referred to as the Northern Kingdoms.

The largest and longest lasting of these kingdoms was Strathclyde. Its capital was the fortress of Dunbarton Rock north of Glasgow in modern Scotland. On the east coast there was Manu Gododdin. Gododdin was the native pronunciation of the tribe the Romans called the Votadini. This people also created another kingdom just to the south called Bryneich, a name that was later pronounced Bernecia. This is most of the information that survives, but it is known that there was at least one more kingdom for which we have very little information. The borders of these kingdoms were ill defined and shifted over time.

Even before the buffer zone was established most of Britain enjoyed nearly three centuries of relative peace and prosperity as a Roman province. An inherent flaw in the Roman political system and the Great Migrations were to change all of that. The word emperor is derived from the Latin *imperator*. This was an honorary title bestowed on a popular general or civic leader by his followers. It literally translates as "he who has the right to command." In military terms it meant that his men felt the general was entitled to lead them by virtue of his abilities and was not simply some government appointee or beneficiary of the "old boys network."[20] The problem is that sometimes such generals came to believe that their abilities gave them the right to rule to whole empire. Of course the current ruler always disagreed, and civil war would ensue. Britain had the highest concentration of soldiers of any diocese in the Empire.[21] It was a testament to both the vulnerable position of the region and the importance that Rome placed upon it that no fewer than three full legions were stationed there. This meant that it provided an excellent source of soldiers for would-be emperors.

In 383 Magnus Maximus, the ranking commander in Britain made an attempt to seize the throne. He was supported by several of the western provinces. He was defeated and the victorious emperor, Valentinian II, forcefully established his presence on the island. This is the same Magnus Maximus or Macsen Gwledig[22] whose battles Geoffrey of Monmouth appropriated for Arthur. Maximus was not trying to gain control of the entire Empire. The Romans had become aware that their vast holdings could not be effectively administered from one location. The solution, as taken by Emperor Valentinian I (r. 364-375) was to split the Empire into two roughly equal parts. Britain, along with the Iberian Peninsula, Gaul, Italy and a large stretch of North Africa, made up the Western Empire. In 410 the capital was moved to Ravenna, on the Adriatic coast, as it was easier to defend against invading tribes. However Rome remained as one of the chief

---

20 In the Roman military system a rich man could literally buy a command.

21 The Empire was divided into diocese which were sub-divided into provinces. Although at first a province, Britain was alter a diocese of four provinces. The Church copied this basic structure, which is why diocese is now an ecclesiastical term.

22 There is some dispute as to the meaning of Gwledig. One theory is that it was a term of respect, possibly meaning "lord." Another is that it was a rank held by the man who held overall command of the militia in Britain.

cities of the Empire. Most of the Balkans, Anatolia, (modern Turkey), Palestine and Egypt went to the Eastern Empire, with its capital at Constantinople, modern Istanbul.[23]

Another Roman in Britain, Constantine III, followed Maximus' example and tried to make himself emperor. This was either in 406 or 407. In between this event and Maximus' bid for power and important development had occurred. The Great Migrations had begun and Germanic peoples were forcing their way into the Empire. The Germanic tribes were not trying to destroy the Roman Empire; they were looking for refuge within it. In exchange for shelter, support and the benefits of civilization, the Germans pledged to ensure that no other barbarians would cross the border in their sector and agreed that their warriors would fight Rome's enemies. This agreement never really worked the way it was supposed to. The Roman military system was breaking down. The Germans found that they were lords of their own areas, and there was good reason to believe that they could expand those areas. Instead of being clients of the Empire, they began to establish more or less autonomous enclaves. The situation got so bad from an Imperial point of view that a few years after Constantine started his campaign to become emperor, Aleric, king of the Visigoths (West Goths), laid siege to Rome itself.

Not all of the important action was taking place on the mainland. Anglo-Saxon pirates had begun sailing the Channel even before Constantine tried to realize his imperial ambitions. However the main threat to the Britons in the fourth century was not the Germans, the Romans had seen to that. They had created a series of forts all along the east coast from Hadrian's Wall down to the Channel. This was called *Litoris Saxonici*, "Saxon Shore." Since most of the regular Roman soldiers had been withdrawn in two failed attempts to seize the throne, many of the forts were actually garrisoned by Germanic mercenaries and local militia. The Picts, who managed to breach the Wall, and the Irish, who were not opposed by any important fortifications, both threatened the Britons. Unlike the others, the Irish were not merely raiders they were invaders. By the mid-fourth century they had established what were intended to be permanent colonies in many places in the west. Although they had been driven back in some places, it is known that they held Dumnonia (modern Devon and Cornwall), Demetia (roughly modern Dyfed in southwest Wales), and Venedotia (roughly modern Gwyedd and Clwyd in northern Wales). In 410 the Britons sent a letter to Emperor Honorius asking for help. With Visigoths tramping all over Italy (Aleric sacked Rome the same year), Honorius reluctantly had to reply that he had no help to give. Historians use this episode as marking the point at which Britain gained its independence from the Empire. However there is circumstantial evidence that people on both sides of the Channel believed that was only a temporary situation and that Britain would one day return to the Empire.

---

23 This was the most common configuration. In fact the Empire was divided several times in several different ways. To talk of the Roman Empire is a misnomer. It should actually be Empires, in the plural.

The fate of the Empire was settled in 476. In that year the Germanic tribal leader Odoacer deposed Emperor Romulus Augusulus and proclaimed himself king of Italy. The course of events in Britain itself is very difficult to follow. In 411 a bishop named Fastidius wrote a letter in which he commented that magistrates in Britain were being killed for their sins. Exactly what these sins were is impossible to say. It could have been corruption or treason. They may have been supporters of Constantine. The executions may also have been the result of a coup. Since normal contact with Rome had been severed, the magistrates had taken over the government of the diocese. Emperor Honorius' letter to the Britons in 410, telling them to fend for themselves, was addressed to the *civitates*, not to any single official. The *Anglo-Saxon Chronicle* states that in 418 the Romans in Britain fled to Gaul. This is an oversimplification. It is known that some stayed, in fact one would become a very important ruler later in the century. It probably meant that the civil government was overthrown for its inability to deal with the barbarian threats. The dates are not very accurate for this section of the *Chronicle* so it is difficult to tell if this is a reference to the same events mentioned by Fastidius or a different political upheaval.

Whatever shortcomings the civil government may of have, the Britons had a difficult time replacing it. Gildas indicated that a number of men quickly gained power and just as quickly lost it again.[24] These men are sometimes called "mini-emperors," rulers who tried to impose a copy of the Roman system of government in miniature on the province.

The first verifiable figure to appear on the political scene after the Roman period was Coelestius or Coelius. He was better known as Coel Hen ("the Old"). Regnal lists state that he was a king who ruled all of the land from the Humber to Hadrian's Wall. Almost nothing is known of him for certain, however a very famous legend about Coel has survived into our own time. His daughter Gwawl married Cunedda, a chieftain of the Gododdin. Apparently Coel the Old was a merry old soul and at the wedding celebration he had a little too much to drink from his drinking bowl, pulled out his bagpipes and sat in with the band. Whatever the truth of this story, he was almost certainly the same Coel mentioned in the stone carving found at Tintagel. He must have been highly respected as almost all of the northern dynasties claimed descent from him.

Although the earliest verifiable information comes from the north, the vast majority of the surviving material deals with the south. The period of instability lasted until *c*424. At that time southern Britain had come under the sway of a man named Vortigern. This is actually *vawr-tighern* which means "overlord," or "over king." Many researchers state that it was his title, while his name has been lost in the mists of time. But this ignores ancient British nomenclature. In their culture adults could change their names at any time in order to reflect a change in status or to commemorate some event in their lives. The names taken by rulers sometimes sounded like titles. Roughly one hundred years after the time of Vortigern there was a ruler called Vortipor. His name also incorporated the word for king, but it was his name. This is known because his

---

24 *De excidio*, 21.4.

tombstone happened to survive. If Vortipor could have been a name, then so could Vortigern. Even more telling is the fact that in the mid sixth century there was a king of the Gododdin whose name was Outigern. This is a variant form of Vortigern. This man was no high king. Furthermore all of the early sources treat it as a name, it is only modern researchers who insist that it must have been a title.

There is another mistake that is often (but not always) made in regard to Vortigern's nomenclature. Gildas is not supposed to have provided either his name or his title but to have called him only "the proud tyrant."[25] But Gildas spoke of five other men he called tyrants, all of whom he considered proud, so why was Vortigern "the" proud tyrant. What is more he simply started using the term, without any kind of explanation as to whom he was referring. The passage runs: "Then all of the members of the council, together with the proud tyrant..."[26] The exact phrase he used was *superbus tyrannos*. But *tyrannos* could mean either tyrant or king. Gildas liked to play word games so a word with a double meaning could easily have been used in a phrase with a double meaning. But the author and his audience were well versed in Latin. They could not help but notice that if the letter "b" is removed from *superbus*, then it becomes *superus tyrannos*, "superior king," which means essentially the same thing as Vortigern. Since he simply started using the term without explaining whom he meant, it is possible that it was actually a well-known piece of anti-Vortigern propaganda.

To return to the king himself, he must have been a remarkable man. The speedy rise and fall of his predecessors indicates that Britain was faction ridden. The mini-emperors had been unable to accommodate enough groups to retain power. Vortigern was to hold his position until the 460's. He must have done this by placating the factions, as tradition indicates that he had a long-standing struggle with another man. Despite this feud Vortigern lost power only after one of the greatest disasters ever to befall Ancient Britain. Most historians simply copy Gildas' assessment and call him a tyrant. But John Wilkes Booth called Abraham Lincoln a tyrant. Gildas was merely expressing an opinion and his word should not be accepted as final.

The threats facing the rulers of Britain were very grave. The Irish were trying to expand their holdings in Britain in the west, while the Picts became a much more serious threat from the north. The Picts had gained an able high king named Durst I. According to poetic fancy he reigned one hundred years and fought one hundred battles. Irish sources say that he actual reigned from 424-453. The reference to the hundred battles was a traditional epithet for a great warrior. One of the Irish high kings was called Conn of a Hundred Battles. Durst launched large-scale raids that caused massive devastation and he harbored ambitions to expand his territory. The attacks launched across Hadrian's Wall were the worry of Coel, but the Picts also built a large fleet and sailed south to attack Vortigern's territory. Vortigern's solution to the military situation was to invite in Germanic mercenaries. The year in which these men arrived is one of the biggest mistakes that are made by

25   Ibid, 23.1.

26   Ibid, 21.2.

researchers. Many (but not all) use the date of 449, which is supposed to come from Bede.[27] But Bede did not actually say that. What he said was in that year Martian became emperor and the Anglo-Saxons arrived sometime during his reign. The emperor Bede was referring to was actually named Martianus, who ascended the throne of the Eastern Empire in 450. So if they arrived during his reign it could not have been in 449. Another argument against that date comes from the activities of their leader, Hengest. He was known to have been involved in an incident called the Fight at Finnesburg before he came to Britain. Professor Tolkien, using Scandinavian sources, argued that this event could not have taken place any earlier than 450 and was probably later than that.[28]

Gildas quoted a letter sent to the Roman consol Aetius asking for help. The letter states that he was "consul for the third time."[29] Aetius actually held the post four times and his third term was 446-452. There is no record of his reply but it must have been the same as that of Honorius in 410, he could spare no men to help. This time it was because of the threat posed by Attila the Hun. It is reasonable to assume that the Anglo-Saxons were hired after the failure of the Britons to enlist Roman help.

The brothers Hengest and Horsa led the mercenaries. Hengest was the senior partner. They neutralized the Pictish threat and probably helped to liberate some of the lands conquered by the Irish, but the Irish were not completely driven out of Britain, at least not yet. The Anglo-Saxons may also have been deployed against domestic enemies. According to Nennius, in 437 a man named Ambrosius rebelled and fought against Vitalinus at a place called Wallop.[30] This passage raises certain questions that cannot easily be answered. The cause of the revolt is completely unknown, although there are a great many guesses. It can be assumed that Vortigern's side was victorious since he remained in power. As to the identity of Vitalinus, that is entirely unknown. There is some speculation that he was Vortigern's son, but Nennius provided a great deal of information about Vortigern's family and no Vitalinus was mentioned. Vitalinus may have been Vortigern himself, or at least the name his parents gave him. Another explanation is that he was one of the king's chief supporters who was famous in his own day, but has since been forgotten except for this one reference. Obviously this revolt took place before the Anglo-Saxons had arrived but it does indicate that Vortigern had British enemies who needed to be intimidated in order to be kept in line.

An attempt was made to send the Anglo-Saxons home. It must have been by some political faction, as Vortigern himself authorized an increase in their number and cemented his alliance to the foreigners by marrying Hengest's daughter Rowena and gave them Kent in payment for their

---

27   *A History of the English Church and People*, I.15.

28   *Finn and Hengest*, pg. 167.

29   *De excidio*, 2.20.

30   *Historia Brittonum*, 66.

services. Two of the colonies established by the Irish were liberated in the 450's. The increase in mercenaries was probably for this purpose. It is also possible that although his side won at Wallop, Vortigern still feared the rebels and tried to use the Anglo-Saxons as a counter-weight.

The king had other problems as well. During his reign a religious controversy that originated in Britain swept across Europe. A champion of orthodoxy, the bishop St. Germanus of Auxerre, arrived to attack the heresy at its source. He actually made two visits to Britain. The first time he came was in 428. Anglo-Saxons and Picts attacked the region he was visiting, (probably the Vale of Llangollen in Wales where in later times the bishop was highly respected). The bishop, who had been a soldier in earlier days, volunteered to help organize the defenders. In order to lift their spirits and scare the attackers he had his men give a loud cry of "Alleluia." The shout echoed through the valley and frightened the pagans so much that they fled. This is known as the "Alleluia Victory."

Germanus returned and according to legend he confronted the king directly about the religious situation; Vortigern could not afford such a controversy. He had both foreign enemies and local political factions to deal with; the last thing he wanted was a religious debate as well. The true resolution of the second visit is lost. Most of what has survived is miracle stories and religious propaganda. Supposedly one of Vortigern's own sons, Faustus, sided with the saint and became a monk. But the account is obviously fictitious. Nennius recorded that Vortigern had three sons, and then inserted Faustus as a fourth without any explanation for the contradiction.[31] The tale culminated in Germanus praying until God sent a miraculous fire from the sky that burned down the king's castle and killed everyone inside. This is recounted because some historians merely say that Germanus badgered the king until he died, without explaining the miraculous aspects. Since there is another version of Vortigern's death this creates the impression of two stories. This has led to some speculation that there were two Vortigerns, with the second having a much less successful career than the first. In fact there was only one and his later years were disastrous. The disasters were at least partially of his own making.

Vortigern's Britain was prosperous. Both Gildas' account of the period[32] and archaeological excavations show this. Its wealth was to prove its undoing. The mercenaries began to complain that they were not being paid enough and that the payments were late. These accusations were probably true. All sources agree that more men arrived just before Vortigern's marriage to Rowena and Vortigern probably found that they were more expensive than he had bargained for. In those days taxation was an emergency measure, it was not collected annually. Attempts to increase taxes in order to pay the mercenaries would have led to greater unrest in the general population. Vortigern simply could not afford to pay them. They decided to take matters into their own hands. At first the mercenaries had things pretty much their own way, quite naturally as they were the only soldiers in most of the areas in which they were stationed. However the Britons

---

31 Ibid, 48.

32 *De excidio*, 21.2.

rallied. Nennius recorded that Vortigern's eldest son, Vortimer, defeated the rebel mercenaries and drove them onto the island of Thanet.[33] The Anglo-Saxons enlisted reinforcements from their homeland and then invaded Kent.

Both Nennius and the *Anglo-Saxon Chronicle*, sources that viewed events from opposing sides, recorded that there were three battles. According to the British account they were: the River Daret, Set thirgabail, the English name for which was said to have been Epsford (both Horsa and Catigern, Vortigern's second son, were said to have been killed there), and a stone near the Gaulic Sea.[34] According to the *Chronicle* they were Aylesford in 455 where Horsa was killed, Crayford in 456, Wippedefleot in 465. The last battle was named for Wipped, an Anglo-Saxon chieftain killed there.

There are a great many problems with this information. The two sources gave them completely different names and put Horsa's death in different places, and both claimed victory in all three fights. The dates in the *Chronicle* are only approximations. Whatever the exact dates, the implication is that most of the fighting was small-scale raids with only a few large battles. Nennius recorded that Vortimer died of natural causes shortly after the third battle. One more point should be made. The surviving sources for both sides concentrate exclusively on Kent, but most researchers agree that there was fighting elsewhere as well.

The battles against the Anglo-Saxons were not the only conflicts afflicting the Britons. In 446, following an outbreak of the plague the Picts launched a large-scale raid into the north. The 450's also saw an escalation in the fighting against the Irish in the west. For the operations against the Irish Vortigern utilized a new strategy. The Votadini were a powerful tribe that ruled two kingdoms: Bryneich and Manu Gododdin. These kingdoms were in the northeast in what are now northern England and southern Scotland. Not in this period, but some time later the capital of Manu Gododdin became Dyn Eiden, modern Edinburgh. A chieftain named Cunedda, the same Cunedda who had married the daughter of Old King Coel, came south with his war band and drove the Irish out of most of Gwynedd in northern Wales.

It is often assumed that when the Picts launched their great raid in 446 they marched right through Cunedda's territory, apparently completely unmolested. A few years later the very same chieftain was moved hundreds of miles away into northern Wales. This is unlikely. Cunedda was probably the younger brother or other relative of a king and had little chance of inheriting his own land. Cunedda and Vortigern cut a deal. The chieftain would liberate Gwynedd from the Irish and the high king would grant him the land. Such arrangements were common in the medieval world. A very famous example dates from the eleventh century and led to Robert Guiscard, who was Norman French, becoming the ruler of Sicily. At that time both the Muslims of North Africa and the Byzantine Empire (the former Eastern Roman Empire) were attempting to conquer southern Italy. The Italian states, led by Pope Leo IX, were trying to drive out both

---

33 *Historia Brittonum*, 43.

34 Ibid, 44.

groups. Guiscard was the leader of a company of Norman mercenaries in the service of the Byzantines. He captured Leo in 1053 and then switched sides when the pope offered him all of Sicily. In order to claim it Guiscard had to conquer it from the Arabs.

The Picts did march through Gododdin territory, but it was unlikely that it was Cunedda's territory. If he was already a king in the north he is not likely to have abandoned that kingdom to establish a new one in Wales. The dynasty he founded became very powerful. The red dragon that is now on the flag of Wales was their symbol and was mentioned by Gildas in connection with Cunedda's great-grandson, Maelgwyn.[35] Gwynedd, which in this period was still called by the Latin form of its name, Vendotia, bordered the kingdom of Powys (the Latin name was probably Pagenses which meant a rural area). This was Cornovii territory. They were a powerful tribe. The Cornovii were the only tribe to maintain a unit in the Roman army when Britain was part of the Empire. At the same time that the Votadini were battling the Irish in Vendotia the Cornovii were doing the same thing in Dumnonia (Devon and Cornwall). It is not well known that the Irish were there, but it was confirmed by both Irish sources and archaeology. The operations in Gwynedd and Dumnonia must have taken place at more or less the same time and therefore they must have been part of a well thought out strategy directed from above. This means Vortigern and his military advisors planned them. It is probable that these operations took place before the Anglo-Saxon revolt and that the mercenaries were part of the liberating armies.

In *c*800 the ruler of Powys erected a monument known as the Pillar of Eliseg, which stated that Brittu was founder of the kingdom, he was said to be Vortigern's son (really grandson). After his death Vortigern had only one surviving son, Pascent. Part of southern Powys was detached from the kingdom and given to him as his own kingdom called Gwerthrynion, which is actually a variant form of Vortigern turned into the name of a place. Pascent would only have had a claim on territory that belonged to his own family. These facts prove that Vortigern came from Powys. Cunedda was moved into territory right beside Vortigern's homeland at the same time that the high king's followers liberated Dumnonia. These cannot be coincidences. Geoffrey of Monmouth stated that Vortigern himself was a Gewesse, part of the confederation established by Octavius. There are indications that there were connections between this group and the Cornovii. The Cornovii might actually have been part of the confederation in this period.

It should be pointed out that there is a counter theory. According to legend a tyrant named Benli ruled Powys. During a storm he refused refuge to St. Germanus, but a slave named Cadell took him in. A heavenly fire fell from the sky, burned down the king's castle, killing him. The saint then elevated the slave to the kingship. The story of Benli and Cadell is obviously fake. It follows a very common type of religious story from the ancient world. A saint/angel/god/goddess (it varies depending upon religion) who is often in disguise arrives in a place where s/he is not well known and is roughly treated by the locals but is helped by a humble person. A miracle transpires, the villains are punished and the virtuous are rewarded. This particular tale

---

35 *De excidio*, 33.1.

seems to have been inspired by the tale of Sodom and Gomorrah. In both cases the punishment was a miraculous fire from heaven. The tale also bears a suspicious similarity to the other story of divine regicide in which Vortigern is killed by miraculous forces. It cannot be a coincidence that both feature the same saint and the same punishment. In later generations Vortigern had a terrible reputation. No doubt the Cadell story was invented as propaganda so that the dynasty could distance itself from its infamous ancestor. It was such obvious propaganda that even some members of the family did not believe it. The Pillar of Eliseg made absolutely no mention at all of Benli or Cadell.

Although Vortigern founded the dynasty, his successor, whose name was Brittu according to the pillar, was not his son. The Pillar says son, but according to the Harleian Genealogies he was actually the son of Categrin, Vortigern's second son. Discrepancies such as these are common in the genealogical material.

The liberation of north Wales and Devon and Cornwall was the high water mark of Vortigern's reign. It was not to last long. It should be remembered that both the Britons and the Anglo-Saxons claimed victory in the last battle in Kent, suggesting that it was a draw. Hengest decided to break the stalemate by repeating a trick he had used before he came to Britain. There are very few surviving manuscripts written in Old English. No fewer than three of them contain references to an incident known as the Fight at Finnesburg, which indicates that it was very famous at one time. The poem *Widsith*[36] mentions it, there is a summary of it in *Beowulf*,[37] and there is a fragment of a poem about the battle itself called *Fight of Finnesburg*. The details are sketchy, but what is clear is that Hengest was the leader of the bodyguard of a Danish king called Hnaef. Hnaef's sister had married a Frisian ruler named Finn. One year Hnaef decided to spend the winter with them. Some sort of a fight erupted between Hnaef's men and Finn's men and the visitors were besieged in one of the halls of the fortress. Although the attackers lost more men, Hnaef himself was killed. Finn and Hengest then came to some sort of an agreement that seems to have led to Hengest joining the Frisian king's war band. Some of his followers criticized Hengest for not avenging their lord's death. In the spring more Danes arrived and Hengest masterminded an ambush in which Finn and his bodyguards were slaughtered. It may have been to escape retribution for this act that he came to Britain in the first place.

Hengest's actions have been defended in that they fit with the ancient Germanic code of honour that held that avenging the death of a fallen lord took precedence over promises and oaths to his killers. Be that as it may, it cannot be denied that Hengest also broke his oath to Vortigern in a similar way. The leaders arranged a treaty. A feast was held to celebrate the end of the war. The Britons came unarmed, but the Anglo-Saxons concealed knives in their clothing. At a command from their leader the mercenaries turned on their guests and killed all of them except Vortigern himself. The term Night of the Long Knives is sometimes used to refer to an episode

---

36 *Widsith*, line 27.

37 *Beowulf*, lines 1066-1159.

of betrayal. This was the original Night of the Long Knives, so named because the Anglo-Saxons used a distinctive knife with a long blade. According to the accounts the king was spared out of consideration for Rowena, Hengest's daughter who had married Vortigern. In reality it was more a case of ransom. Although all of the surviving sources deal with Kent, the Anglo-Saxons held almost all of the east coast south of the Humber River. Hengest forced Vortigern to recognize their rights to much of this land. He gave them Essex, Sussex and Middlesex.[38] The Britons held the Thames area, including London, but to the south the Anglo-Saxons held much of Kent, which went to Hengest himself.

The Anglo-Saxons must have thought that they had achieved a major coup, but they were wrong. Vortigern had powerful enemies within Britain. With most of his supporters slain the king could not maintain his position. Ambrosius Aurelianus, who is believed to have been the son of the Ambrosius who rebelled in 437, followed in his father's footsteps, but more successfully. He and his followers chased the king to one of his castles and burned it to the ground. The date of this revolt is unknown and almost all of the information that has been preserved of its leader comes from Gildas. Both of his parents were born to the purple.[39] This was a technical term that meant they were both related to emperors. His parents were both killed in the war by Anglo-Saxons. It is not known where he was based. Odds are it was somewhere in what is now southern England rather than Wales as that area had a larger Roman population. According to Gildas Ambrosius himself fought the Anglo-Saxons in a seesaw kind of war. It is at this point that the details become sketchy and speculation takes over. According to tradition Pascent hired a Saxon woman to poison Ambrosius. In the 490's the Anglo-Saxons were pushed out of northern Lincolnshire and suffered a crushing defeat at the Battle of Badon Hill. What is not known is whether Ambrosius was killed before or after these victories.

Following Badon there was roughly twenty years of peace. This peace came to a sudden end with a civil war. To distinguish it from all the others it will be referred to as the Great Civil War. It marked the end of stability and a return to constant conflict with the kings battling each other, each trying to dominate the others. Gildas accused the five tyrants of a variety of crimes. The crime that incensed him the most was fighting civil wars.

The most important ruler to emerge after the Great Civil War was Maelgwyn of Gwynedd in north Wales. The region the Romans had called Venedotia. Maelgwyn was a direct descendant of Cunedda and of Old King Coel. He seized power by killing his own uncle in battle. Although a great deal has been written about Maelgwyn being a powerful ruler, his sons actually surpassed him. Some time around 560 a dispute arose between Maelgwyn's son and successor Rhun, and Elidyr of Rheged. Elidyr was killed. In order to avenge him, and also because of fear that Rhun was becoming too powerful, a coalition of northern kings raided Caernarfon. In retaliation Rhun marched north, through Rheged, swung eastward to York and then turned northward

---

38 *Historia Brittonum*, 46.

39 *De excidio*, 25.3.

again and marched to the border of Pictish territory. With the exception of one battle early on, this march seems to have been completely unopposed. He had a reason for going to the Pictish border. The Picts had a ruler named Brude mac Maelcheon, technically he was their high king, but he was having difficulties with certain rebellious lords. Although Brude is a Pictish name, Maelcheon is not. It is a corruption of a British name. It is generally agreed that the original form was Maelgwyn. In other words Rhun and Brude were brothers, probably half-brothers. No dynasty would rule so much of Britain again until the sixteenth century when King James VI of Scotland became James I of England.

The sources grow strangely quiet about Rhun after this expedition. It is to this period that the Anglo-Saxon conquest of most of the south should be dated. It fits with the archaeological record. There are no dates on the southern conquest until the *Anglo-Saxon Chronicle* records the Battle of Dyrham in 577. With this victory the Anglo-Saxons took Gloucester, Cirencester and Bath. They had reached the west coast. Rhun is said to have died *c*580, so the dates are consistent. He was not actually at that particular battle, but the south was lost in his time. If his reign began well but ended badly it would certainly explain why the sources suddenly stopped talking about him.

It may also have been at this time that the Gododdin were defeated at the Battle of Catraeth as commemorated in the poem *Y Gododdin*. This battle is often dated to the reign of the high king Owain. There is an Owain who is mentioned several times in the poem, but it was a very common name and he was Owain son of Marro, but the high king's father was Urien. Besides the high king Owain was not a Gododdin. The poem is about the defeat of that specific tribe which is why it bears that name. Rhun is not mentioned, but he was a Gododdin and the poem specifically states that a contingent from his kingdom of Gwynedd was at the battle.[40] Rhun was not to blame for the deteriorating military situation. Britain had been swept by a horrible plague in the 440's. Maelgwyn himself was killed by it. The Anglo-Saxons, on the other hand, were virtually unaffected. The two peoples hated each other so much that they had virtually no contact, except when they were killing each other. The Britons had not fully recovered from this disaster when they were hit by another plague, or perhaps a return of the same one. One of the reasons the Britons could hold the Anglo-Saxons in check was because the invaders did not have the resources to capture the walled towns, which could be easily defended with small numbers of troops. After two plagues in quick succession they did not have the manpower to do this anymore. They were also weakened by their own inheritance system. Since they did not have primogenitor every generation some of the kingdoms were divided between the heirs so they became smaller and weaker.

After Rhun's death the high kingship passed to the kingdom of Rheged, the land of his old rival. During Urien's time the Britons recovered some territory. Almost all of the surviving information for this period deals with the north, so the course of the wars in the south cannot be followed. Urien concentrated his efforts on recovering Bryneich, which the Anglo-Saxons

---

40   Stanzas XIX and LXXIV

called Bernecia and which had not been in Anglo-Saxon hands for very long. In *c*590 Urien led an alliance of kings against this kingdom, which at first met with some success. The Britons were on the verge of wiping out the defenders at the siege of Lindisfarne when a lord named Morcant became jealous of Urien. At least that is the version in the surviving sources. There is no way to tell for certain the real reason for Morcant's animosity towards Urien. He hired a man named Lovan to assassinate the high king. Without its leader the alliance fell apart and the Anglo-Saxons won the war. This disaster removed the only real figure that could maintain unity among the Britons. Urien's son, Owain, tried to revive his father's dream of a northern alliance, but he was killed in battle against the Anglo-Saxons in *c*595.

With the collapse of Rheged the territory of the Britons had become physically cut into three. Devon and Cornwall were isolated in the south, the Welsh kingdoms were in the centre and Strathclyde, which had annexed part of Rheged before the Anglo-Saxons could get all of it, was in the north. Most of Britano-Gaelic Britain had become Anglo-Saxon England.

When placed into context it is easy to see why the period of peace in the early sixth century was considered so important. It was in fact the last hurrah of the Britons. They still held the majority of the island and for once their leaders were held in check and prevented from trying to slaughter each other. It was a time unique in their history. The Romans had maintained the peace of earlier times. Before the Imperial conquest tribal warfare was endemic. The Arthurian period is the only time they were both independent and peaceful. There should be no wonder that the man responsible for it was remembered as their greatest king. He *was* their greatest king.

Chapter IV

His World

THE ARTHURIAN period has had more written about it than almost any other era in British history. Ironically it is also one of the least studied. Most of what is written about the period involves supporting or attacking various theories, most of them about Arthur himself. Studying a badly documented time period is like trying to make a multi-thousand-piece jigsaw puzzle while having only a few hundred pieces. Certain researchers do not spend enough time going over the information we have and have too little regard for how much we do not have.

There were many more cultural groups living on the island in those days than is generally realized. The far north had the most variety and is the worst documented. Most of what little written information there is for the Highlands and Isles comes from Ireland. Archaeology provides more information, but it cannot always be fully understood. The far north contains archaeological remains of unknown invaders. Given the geography of the area, they probably came from Scandinavia. They constructed tall stone towers now called *brochs* to overawe the local inhabitants. By the fifth century these towers were abandoned and the invaders had merged with the local inhabitants. The locals, who not only lived in the region of the *brochs* but also the area south of it, were the Atecotti. This means "the Ancients." It is probable that they were the last remnants of the prehistoric inhabitants of the island, but another theory maintains that they were an offshoot of the Picts. The Atecotti are known to have participated in at least one major raid against the Britons but little else is known about them.

A people who originated in Ireland occupied the northwest. When they first arrived they defended themselves by building a type of fortification known as *duns*. The Irish called their territory *Iardomnan*, which means the "western lands." The name must have originated in the Highlands themselves, since the territory was actually northeast of Ireland. By the fifth century they had become well established and the duns were abandoned. Farther south, in the area of the Highlands directly across from Ireland, lived more recent Irish arrivals. They lived in a kingdom called Dal Riada.

Then there were the Picts. Although it is often argued that they were Britons who had never been conquered by the Romans, the traditions of both the Picts themselves and the Welsh say that they originated in Ireland. If this were true it would explain what happened to them. The Scots conquered the Picts and within a relatively short period of time their language and culture disappeared. But since the Scots also originated in Ireland it may be that their culture did not really disappear at all, but merged with that of the Scots. They lived in small tribes and had a cattle-based economy. Their inheritance was matrilineal, that is any position, including kingship, could be claimed through a mother or other female relative. The son of a sister rather than their own sons succeeded many Pictish kings.

The southern boundary of Pictish territory was the Antonine Wall. South of this lived several British tribes that were nominally allied to the Romans, but whose loyalty was sometimes suspect. There were four main tribes-the Damnonii (probably originally a branch of the Dumnonii who lived in Devon and Cornwall), the Novantae, the Selgovae, and the Votadini. They formed at least four kingdoms: Strathclyde, Manu Gododdin, Bryneich and an unnamed realm for which little is known. We have the names of five kings from two different dynasties. The last was Gwenddolau, who was killed at the Battle of Arfderydd, dated by the *Welsh Annals* to 573. South of them lay Hadrian's Wall. Everything from this wall to the Channel formed the Roman diocese of Britannia. The overwhelming majority of the population of Britannia was peasant farmers. Each farm had a mixture of crops and livestock. In the Lowland areas crops predominated, especially wheat. In the mountainous regions of the Pennines, Wales and Dumnonia the emphasis was on animals: cattle, pigs and in some areas, sheep as well. There was no money. There had been no Roman coinage since the fourth century and the Britons did not mint any themselves. The poor paid tribute in the form of food and items that they had made and they also owed labour to their lords. In exchange the nobility protected their lives and legal rights. Contrary to popular belief, the peasants did have some rights; they were not slaves. But those rights were few and limited.

The poor had a sense of belonging to the British nation. They called themselves *Cymbrogi*, "fellow countrymen," a word that evolved into *Cymry*, which is what the modern Welsh call themselves. There are many place names in England that incorporate this term, the most famous being Cumbria on the west coast. The word Welsh is derived from the Old English *wylisc*, which means "foreigner." A more obvious illustration of the "us and them" mentality would be hard to find. Despite their animosity to the invaders, the peasants had little love for their own lords. Their own kings treated them so badly that they had no reason to support one side over the other. This was a key factor in the Anglo-Saxon conquest. There were times, most notably in 633 when Cadwallon of Gwynedd overran much of Northumbria, when the Britons retook land that had been lost to the Anglo-Saxons. But there were never any popular uprisings in support of the "liberators." As far as the farmers were concerned one tyrant was as bad as another, the fact that some of them happened to speak the same language meant very little and they were not about to massacre their English neighbours just because a Welsh warlord asked them to.

A debate rages as to what happened to the native peasant population. There are accounts that large numbers of people were killed or driven off. Some historians take these statements at face value while others think that they were exaggerations and propaganda. John Morris provided the best evidence when he pointed out that English institutions (governments and guilds) made laws and rules about the Welsh communities in England as late as the eleventh century.[41] They would not have made such rules if there were no Welsh communities in England. They could not all have been drive off or killed. Another piece of evidence comes from a people called the Hwicce. Although they lived in the Anglian kingdom of Mercia, their inheritance laws were Welsh, not English. Not far to the west of the Hwicce territory there lived a Welsh tribal confederation called the Gewesse or Gewissei. This suggests that the Hwicce were originally conquered Gewesse who retained enough of their original culture that they continued to be recognized as a distinct people. These facts can be easily reconciled with the accounts of peoples being slaughtered. In Ancient times it was common for conquerors to use terror tactics to overawe the conquered. Communities that resisted the invaders were butchered while those who accepted the new rulers were left untouched. The idea (which often worked) was to frighten people into surrendering by showing them what would happen if they resisted. The Anglo-Saxons probably used this tactic.

Not all of the commoners were farmers. There were towns, but they were in decline. The economy that supported many of them had been destroyed. Some survived, but much smaller than they had been, others disappeared altogether. None thrived. The towns did have one advantage over the countryside. The armies of this period were too small to assault the average walled town. It was difficult to try to starve the towns into submission because they all had gardens that had fruits, vegetables and even grains and cereals. The citizens also kept livestock such as chickens ducks and pigs. The inhabitants could not produce all of the food they needed, but the attackers would have to surround the town completely to prevent fresh supplies from being taken in. This required a large number of men to essentially sit around and do nothing for months on end, not something that armies of the period could afford to do. They made much of their income from plunder. Towns had to be taken by force. As long as the Britons had enough men to guard the walls the Anglo-Saxons could be held in check. The plagues of the mid-sixth century changed all of that. Since the two peoples had almost no contact, the Anglo-Saxons were virtually untouched by the diseases. When they were over not even the two largest cities, London and York, could be held against the invaders.

The society was elitist. The only institution that allowed any upward mobility was the Church. It is common today to view the Church of the Middle Ages as being cut off from the people with the bishops and cardinals having no understanding of, or sympathy for, the common people. This is a gross oversimplification. Of course the Church had wealthy bishops, but it also had poor parish priests, monks, and nuns. In reality the Church was the *only* institution in the Middle Ages that cared about the poor at all. Certain modern researchers make it appear as if there was a clear separation between pagan and Christian. Although this was true for the religious leaders of each group, it was not true for the population at large. The average peasant farmer knew little

---

41 *The Age of Arthur*, pg. 134.

and cared less for the intricacies of the different theologies. In reality the people believed in a mixture of ideas from both faiths. As with all time periods very few people were well versed in theology and the majority of the population simply took the ideas they liked from both religions.

Modern pagans also talk about the poor following the Old Religion and staying loyal to the village druids. This is simply not true. The pagans had three levels of cleric: druids, vates (called filidh in Ireland) and bards. Only members of the aristocracy could join any one of these groups. There was no such thing as a village druid. This is what gave Christianity the advantage; it was the pagan clergy who virtually ignored the poor. The Christian monasteries were one of the few places of refuge from marauding war bands and their inmates provided free medical treatment and practical help for those whose homes had been burned and possessions looted. The people responded by supporting the religion. Britain was the first place in Western Europe to have a dominantly Christian population. It also began exporting the faith to other lands.

St. Patrick, the patron saint of Ireland, was a Briton whose name was Patritius. He was born somewhere on or near the west coast around the year 385. Irish pirates captured him when he was sixteen. He escaped but later returned to bring Christianity to his former captors. The tradition that St. Patrick introduced the religion to Ireland is not true, although the number of Christians before was quite small. Patrick was chosen to be the first bishop, but his mission was delayed because of a doctrinal dispute in Britain. Rome wanted another bishop who was a good theologian to represent its side. Since there was no justification for creating a new bishopric in Britain itself, their candidate, a man named Palladius, was made bishop of Ireland instead. He is known to have visited his see only once and to have spent the rest of his time in Britain. Patrick was the first true bishop of Ireland.

Another important Christian to come from Britain may have been St. Helen. There is some debate as to whether or not she was actually from the island; the general consensus is that she was born in the Balkans. Although her origins are in doubt, her later life is well recorded. She married a Roman officer who later became the Emperor Constantius Chlorus and she was credited with discovering the True Cross. Although Constantius later ended his marriage to Helen, they did have a son together who was named Flavius Valerius Constantinus. He commanded the Roman forces stationed at York and his men proclaimed him emperor in 306. He is known to history as Constantine the Great. Constantine not only ended the persecution of Christianity but he also made it the state religion.

Not all of the Christians from Britain aided in the development of their religion. One caused a very serious split among its ranks. In 380 a theologian from Britain named Pelagius put forward the doctrine that people found salvation through faith and good works. This ran counter to the teachings of St. Augustine of Hippo in North Africa who postulated the theory of predestination. Augustine's idea was that even before birth, God marked a person for salvation or damnation. Those who were to be saved naturally acted in a good way because they had the blessing of God's Grace. Augustine had several advantages over his opponent. He was a well-known author; his books the *Confessions* and *On Christian Doctrine* are still readily available in modern translations in bookstores and libraries across the Western world. This notoriety gave him the ear of the papacy. Augustine argued that the only way for people to purge themselves of the taint of original sin was with an established clergy, if salvation could be obtained through faith and good works alone, there was no need for the Church. This argument convinced the papacy to condemn Pelagianism as a heresy in 416.

Many researchers make too much of this religious debate. Modern peoples hear the word heresy and assume that there was oppression, torture, and victims burned at the stake. Such things simply did not happen in the fifth century. The Church at that time was much more open-minded. A heresy was simply a mistake that could be corrected by reasoned argument. It was to combat Pelagianism that Palladius was sent to Britain. But he was a theologian, not an Inquisitor. He engaged his opponents in peaceful debate and won them over to his side through argument, not force.

Hagiography, accounts of the lives of saints, was very popular in Wales during the Middle Ages. Arthur appears in four of these books-the lives of saints Cadoc, Carannog, Gildas and Pardarn. The king is never depicted in a good light. He is usually shown as a lustful and greedy tyrant. Some scholars have taken this as an indication that Arthur was a Pelagian. Since Catholics wrote the Saint's Lives, they argue that the tradition of animosity between Arthur and the monasteries was preserved and manifested itself as attacks on his character in these books.

This is a clear example of what could be called "historical projecting." That is the process by which a thinker takes a modern idea and projects it back onto another period where it does not belong. Needless to say the historians who support the "Arthur as Pelagian" theory are not Catholic. The Catholic Church is not very well liked by many in the modern world; some historians would prefer to disassociate the popular hero from the unpopular institution. This approach can be seen to be unrealistic by the way in which the religious debate is presented. According to such scholars it was a clear-cut argument between Pelagians and Catholics. But that is an oversimplification. The real argument was Pelagians on one side and St. Augustine and his followers on the other, with Rome acting as referee. It is true that the Church condemned Pealgius' ideas as heresy, but it took them thirty-six years to decide to do so. Furthermore Rome did not wholeheartedly embrace Augustine's doctrines. Its final decision on the matter was a compromise between the two theologies. Augustine's ideas of original sin and that salvation may be obtained only through God's Grace were modified to include the concept that God's Grace was open to any who wished to take advantage of it. The way in which one took advantage of it was Pelagious' concept of faith and good works.

The Saint's Lives were not biographies in the modern sense of the word. They certainly contained biographical material, but they were also written to teach the laity about the glory of the saint and, by extension, the glory of God. Since this was the case they were not overly concerned with ensuring that all of the information was factual. The authors developed a number of conventions that were used in most of the texts. One of these conventions was to bring the saint into contact with a powerful secular ruler. The ruler was always cast in a bad light to contrast with the holiness of God's servant. Often the king would set the saint a difficult or even impossible task, which would then be completed through the use of a miracle, much to the embarrassment of the monarch. This showed the reader that even the most humble of God's servants was mightier than the most powerful secular ruler. It should be noted that, with one exception, none of the traditions of Arthur's conflicts with the holy men could be based on accurate material. Except for Gildas, none of the saints were born until after the Arthurian period. Furthermore it is significant that the only story that could possibly be based upon a real event is the only one that does not present Arthur as lustful and greedy.

Even if the Saints Lives do preserve an accurate tradition it does not necessarily follow that the tradition concerned Arthur's religious beliefs. The accusations made against him were routine in the Middle Ages. Similar charges were made against such kings as Richard I (lustful) and his brother John (a greedy tyrant). Neither one of them were heretics. In a time period that is so badly documented as post-Imperial Europe it is essential to stick to what the evidence actually tells us and not to give into the temptation to read too much into things.

The elite of the Church maintained close connections with the political elite. There was little separation of Church and state. Members of royal dynasties often joined the clergy and naturally they continued to have contact with their friends and family in the secular world. Gildas himself was the son of a king and he deliberately tried to use his connections with the rulers to get them to rule the way he thought they should. It was a good idea, but personalities cannot be changed with words. The high king of that time, Maelgwyn of Gwynedd, had studied to be a monk[42] but changed his mind and decided he would rather be a king instead.

The kings were the capstone of a pyramid of society. Artists, jewelers, bards and others who provided luxury items depended upon royal patronage for their livelihood. The bards had originated as a class of cleric in the old pagan religion. Their exact function is unclear, although part of it was to compose magic incantations in verse. After the conversions, they became the court poets, singing the praises of individual rulers and their dynasties. Some of their surviving compositions have already been mentioned: *The Eulogy for Geraint, Y Gododdin* and the battle list for Urien of Rheged are all examples of the kind of works they composed. Although the bards are the best known today of the members of the royal entourages, the most important group was the king's *comitatus*, his war band. The political situation in Britain was both chaotic and bloody. A ruler needed bodyguards to defend him against rivals within the kingdom and an army he could use to raid his neighbours. These men had to be paid, not with money because they did not have a moneyed economy. They were given swords, slaves, expensive clothing, land, cattle, jewelry, and many other things of that nature. After a successful attack all of the spoils would be handed over to the king himself. He would then divide them between his followers. Kings who

---

42 *De excidio*, 33.4.

kept little for themselves and gave away most of the loot naturally attracted the largest number of followers. Such kings gained the epithet *hael*, "the generous."

The armies of this period were quite small. A good approach to take to try to understand the situation is to think of these kings as dukes or counts. In later centuries these nobles had their own armies, but the sizes were restricted based upon the resources of the individual lord. Large armies, especially in an alliance of several kings, could number in the thousands. On the other hand, a ruler of a small kingdom might be able to call upon less than one hundred men. Certain kings, those who were good generals and generous in their pay, could attract larger numbers of followers. The warriors themselves utilized Roman style weapons and tactics. This was only natural since Britain had been in the Empire for over three hundred years and even after it became cut off there were many people in Britain who had served in the Roman army. A system of fortifications was utilized. Old Roman forts were repaired or rebuilt, using stone the way the Romans had, but with poorer quality mason work. Pre-Roman forts were also rebuilt and new forts were constructed. These were either made of wood or a combination of wood and stone. The many references to castles in the documentation are actually talking about these forts.

The army itself had both infantry and cavalry. Many armies of the period fought on foot, however written sources emphasize mounted warriors. The *Eulogy for Geraint* makes repeated references to the hero as riding into battle. There are also many other accounts in poetry and folktales of cavalry. Mounted fighting men fit with what is known of Britano-Gaelic warfare in general. Julius Caesar was highly impressed by the way in which the Britons handled horses, while Irish tales often told of the great horsemanship of the heroes. The Roman and Irish sources refer to charioteers, but by the sixth century there were few chariots left. They had been largely abandoned in favour of individual mounts. The Britano-Gaels were a people who had a long tradition of horsemanship and they easily made the transition from chariots to cavalry.

The use of cavalry should not be overemphasized. It has even been suggested that entire armies were made up of mounted warriors. This is unrealistic. Cavalry needs wide areas of flat terrain in order to operate at its full advantage. Neither Britain itself nor Western Europe in general has the right topography everywhere. European warfare has always required foot soldiers to slog through hills, and marshes and other areas unsuitable for horses. For example Charlemagne attempted to maintain an all cavalry army, but quickly abandoned the idea and established elite units of infantry as well. The exact mixture of infantry and cavalry would vary from kingdom to kingdom, depending on the terrain and the availability of mounts in the area.

Among the warrior class the Britons created what is usually called a heroic society. They idealized the fighting prowess of individuals. To become a leader a man had to prove himself a great warrior. They were concerned with their own reputations and boasted of military prowess. The bards were little more than propagandists and their poems exaggerated the exploits of their patrons. This is an important point. More than one researcher has tried to discredit the Nennius battle list because it claims that Arthur himself killed nine hundred and forty Saxons.[43] Since that is clearly impossible, this is taken as evidence that the list is a forgery. In reality it is only evidence that the list originated as a poem, something that linguists had already determined because of the meter and word choice. The claim is quite in keeping with the exaggerations of ancient battle poetry.

In Arthurian Britain the bards were the propagandists for the heroism and Gildas was the critic. He was the champion of the Latin concept of *piety*. Although it is the origin of the Modern English word, when the Romans used it they did not just mean religious devotion, they also included dedication to family and society. When speaking of the previous generations he wrote: "kings, public and private persons, priests and churchmen, kept to their own stations, but they died."[44] This is an example of a concept that was widespread in the Ancient and medieval worlds. The gods, or God, had ordained that every person had a specific role in society. As long as everyone fulfilled their role, society was in balance and all was well. Gildas believed that many of the people of his generation were failing in their duties and it was part of his job as a leader of the clergy to remind them of their obligations. It was this sense of responsibility that led him to write *De excidio*.

The most famous section in the book is the attack on the five tyrants. It is worth summarizing in detail because it reveals a great deal of information about a variety of topics. Each of the tyrants was compared to an animal. This was not just fancy imagery. Each ruler used a specific badge so that he could be identified on the battlefield. Over time these symbols eventually acquired specific regulations of design until, by the late eleventh century, they became coats of arms, governed by rules of heraldry. In the Arthurian period there were no rules, so they were not heraldry as such, just armorial symbols.

Constantine of Dumnonia (Devon and Cornwall) was dealt with first.[45] He was described as the whelp of a filthy lioness. Was Gildas calling Dumnonia itself a lioness, or was this a reference to Constantine's mother? Unfortunately nothing is known about her, not even her name, so there is no way to understand the reference. This is not unusual, very little information about women has survived from this period, and the majority of what does exist only concerns who they married and what children they had, rather than what they did themselves. The same year Gildas wrote the book Constantine disguised himself as an abbot so that he could sneak into a church and slay two princes and their two guardians. He divorced his wife and committed parricide, Gildas did not indicate which parent had been killed but the most likely victim was his father, Tudvawl, as that would have allowed Constantine to seize the throne. Gildas also stated that he knew the king was still alive. Some people have interpreted that to mean that

---

43 *Historia Brittonum*, 50.

44 *De excidio*, 26.2.

45 Ibid, 28.1 ff.

Constantine had been deposed and was in exile. That is possible but it might also mean that Constantine had been ill. Since medical science was not very advanced, serious illness usually brought to mind thoughts of death.

The next king was Aurelius Caninus.[46].His name is significant. The first part probably indicates that he was a descendant of Ambrosius Aurelianus. The second part is the Latin word for dog used as a name. It must be Britano-Gaelic in origin. The Romans never called anyone a dog except as an insult, but the Britano-Gaels emphasized the bravery and ferocity of the animal. They also believed that dog saliva could be used to cure wounds and it was thought to have mystic properties. There is a mystery as to the kingdom Caninus ruled. There has been speculation that he was the same as the Cynan mentioned on the king list for Powys. Cynan is the Welsh form of the name that appears in Ireland as Conan. It is usually translated as "wise" or "exulted" but some linguists argue that the name means "dog." Every time the name Cynan was written in Latin it was translated as Caninus, which pretty much settles the debate. However showing that it is the right name does not show that it was the right man.

There is more evidence against the idea that he was from Powys than for it. Ambrosius was supposed to have been a popular hero who passed into oral traditions, but the royal house of Powys never claimed descent from him, they claimed descent from his archrival Vortigern. Furthermore it is agreed that Gildas mentioned the kings in geographic order from south to north, which means that the ruler of Powys should come after Vortipor of Dyfed, but Aurelius Caninus comes before him. He probably ruled one of the lost kingdoms, most likely around Avon and/or Gloucestershire. The king himself was described as a "lion whelp" that was guilty of parricide, fornication, adultery and starting civil wars. Gildas also mentioned that the tyrant's brothers were all dead, but whether or not he meant to imply that Aurelius had killed them is uncertain. As for the accusation of patricide, again the most likely victim was his father, but this time we do not know who that was.

Vortipor ruled Dyfed in southwest Wales. He was said to be "spotted with wickedness"[47] like a leopard. He committed adultery, murder and raped his own daughter. Although the woman herself was described as "shameless," unlike many other medieval moralists, Gildas did not blame the victim. Her lack of shame, whatever the monk meant by that, did not justify her father's attack in Gildas' eyes.

The next king, Cuneglasus,[48] has several mysteries surrounding him. First there is the name itself. Gildas stated that in Latin it would be *lanio fulve*, "Red Butcher." Actually it means "Grey Dog." This might be a word game, but if so it must depend upon a similarity of words in Late Brythonic and too much of that language has been lost to explain the connection. The next difficulty is determining the kingdom that he ruled. It has been suggested that he was the

---

46 Ibid, 30.1 ff.

47 31.1 ff.

48 32.1 ff.

monarch of Powys. This argument is overly simplistic. It merely states that since Aurelius Caninus was not the ruler of this kingdom, Cuneglasus must have been. But that assumes that Gildas included the king of Powys on his list of tyrants. It should never be forgotten that he singled out certain specific kings for criticism and if the king of Powys was not a rapist or murderer like the others, there would have been no reason to include him in the book. The reason two completely different kings have been suggested as ruler of Powys in this period is because there is a gap in the actual king list. We do really know who ruled Powys in this period.

Cuneglasus was a member of a cadet branch of the ruling house of Gwynedd. He inherited the region that had been ruled by his father, Owain Whitetooth. The theory runs that Gwynedd conquered Powys either in the time of Owain, or his father, Einion Girt and set members of its own ruling house upon the throne of the other kingdom. There is no evidence to support this aside from the rather chaotic state of the king list. Powys was a large and powerful kingdom. Gwynedd was a large and powerful kingdom. If Gwynedd conquered the other than this would have created the strongest known power block in Britain and would have secured the high kingship for its ruling house. Instead the high kingship went to Ambrosius Aurelianus and then, according to the usual interpretation, no one. The only clue as to where Cuneglasus ruled is that Gildas called him "charioteer of the Bear's Stronghold." This is Dinarth, which means "Fort Bear." It was deep in Gwynedd. This was obviously his capital. If Cuneglasus ruled Powys he would not have placed his capital in Gwynedd.

The king list for Gwynedd provides the clues to what really happened. Cunedda founded the dynasty and was succeeded by his son Einion Girt, both of Einion's sons, Owain Whitetooth and Cadwallon Longhand succeeded their father. In the Britano-Gaelic political system sometimes sons of kings were established as sub-kings, or royal governors, of regions within a kingdom. But they did not actually use the term sub-king in the fifth and sixth centuries. They called them kings. The most likely explanation is that Cuneglasus and his father before him were sub-kings based at Dinarth. Titles follow rules. Gildas knew the rules, as he was an aristocrat. A man is always referred to by the highest rank he holds. King of Powys was much more important than sub-king of Dinarth. Gildas would have connected him with the kingdom, not the sub-kingdom. Roughly two hundred years later the descendants of Cuneglasus raised a rebellion and tried to seize power in Gwynedd. At the time of the rebellion they were sub-kings with their capital at Dinarth. That is all they ever were.

Another mystery revolves around the fact that Gildas stated that this king waged war "with arms special to" him alone. There is no real explanation as to what this meant. An attempt has been made to say that his army was mainly cavalry while those of the other kings were foot soldiers, but this is unrealistic. The true meaning will probably never be known. Compared to the other tyrants, Cuneglasus comes off lightly in the list of his sins. He fought civil wars, divorced his wife and took up with her sister even though she was "promised to God in perpetually chaste widowhood," which probably meant that she was a nun, although that was not usually described as widowhood.

The last tyrant on the list was also the most powerful. He was Cuneglasus' cousin, Maelgwyn of Gwynedd.[49] Maelgwyn was the high king of that period. Gildas called him the "dragon of the island." This is the oldest reference to the Red Dragon, the badge that would be used by the kings of Gwynedd for centuries and is now the flag of Wales. Gildas deliberately utilized a double meaning here. Dragon was a synonym for prince or ruler. So Gildas was not only referring to his dragon badge but also to his position as high king. He was attacked more viciously than any other monarch in the book. The other kings are dealt with in only one paragraph Maelgwyn gets more than a page.

Gildas believed that every person had a role to play in society. When people kept to their stations and did their jobs, society worked according to God's plan. *De excidio* itself was a product of this thinking. As the most famous Churchman in Britain of his day he believed that it was his duty to remind the powerful, both secular and religious, to do their duty. Since Maelgwyn was the mightiest of the kings he had the greatest opportunity to do good and his evil was the most harmful.

The king seized power in his youth by killing his uncle in a civil war. Given the dating this must have been the Great Civil War, or one not too much later. It is sometimes assumed that the uncle he killed was Owain Whitetooth. This is based entirely upon the fact that he is the only uncle for Maelgwyn we know about, but it is highly unlikely that he was the only uncle he actually had. It does not fit the facts. Owain's son, Cuneglasus, inherited part of Gwynedd. If his father had been defeated than Cuneglasus would have been sent into exile and gotten nothing. The only way it could work is if Cuneglasus had betrayed Owain and sided with Maelgwyn, but such a breach of family loyalty would certainly have merited comment by Gildas. Furthermore he had more to gain by supporting his father. If Owain won, Cuneglasus stood to inherit all Gwynedd, why support Maelgwyn and settle only for Dinarth? The evidence suggests that it was a completely different uncle. Exactly who it was will probably never be known.

The death of this relative seems to have shocked Maelgwyn and he decided to become a monk. Gildas said he had the greatest teacher in Britain. This was almost certainly a reference to Illtud, who had also been Gildas' teacher. Maelgwyn broke his monastic vows and returned to secular life. This raises some interesting questions: who was ruling Gwynedd while Maelgwyn was a monk? Why did this person just step aside when Maelgwyn changed his mind? Unfortunately there is no way to learn the answer to these questions. Like the others, Maelgwyn fought civil wars, but being the most powerful king he was more successful than the others. He killed some of his rivals and exiled others. In his personal life the king murdered his first wife and his brother's son so that he could marry his nephew's widow. This passage is a good example of the limitations of the surviving information. No other source records that Maelgwyn even had a brother, let alone a nephew. The names of these people have not been recorded.

---

49   Ibid, 33.1 ff.

We should be careful not to read too much into these accusations. All of the men were guilty of terrible crimes, with the two most common being murder and starting civil wars; they were only the five worst offenders out of a much larger group of rulers. The fact that Gildas concentrated on the kings of the west probably means that this was the region that he knew the most about. His family had originated in the north; according to the genealogies his ancestors had been the kings of Strathclyde. Tradition stated that his father and brother had rebelled against Arthur before Gildas was even born, the rebellion had failed and the family had been deposed and resettled in central Wales. Gildas knew of events from the history of the north, but he showed no firsthand knowledge of the contemporary situation of the region. And he seems to have known almost nothing of the territory that is now southern England. His lack of knowledge colours our understanding of Britain because his book is our main source of information.

From what he did report about society certain generalizations can be made. Latin and Brythonic culture were jumbled up together. The name Aurelius Caninus is the most obvious example. This is important to an Arthurian investigator because of the question of the origin of the name Arthur itself. Some argue that it is Latin, derived from the name Lucius Artorius Castus a prefect of the VI Victrix Legion, headquartered at York. Others maintain that it is Brythonic, being derived from *arth*, which means bear. Since the Britons did mingle Brythonic and Latin there is no reason why it could not be both. A bilingual people could easily choose a name that had significance in both languages.

These passages provide more than just evidence of the mix of cultures. There is also an illustration of a very serious political problem. Three out of the five kings were accused of starting civil wars. Gildas was not against the concept of war itself, but he believed that the fight should be taken to the Anglo-Saxons. When introducing the section on the tyrants he wrote: "Britain has kings, but they are tyrants…they wage wars-civil and unjust."[50] He was right. In this period the Britons still had the advantage of numbers. Had the rulers set aside their petty feuds and personal ambitions and worked together they could have changed the course of British history and the history of every place affected by Britain. They could not have won a quick victory, the Anglo-Saxons were too well entrenched for that, but a sustained war of attrition could have gone in their favour. But the kings could not see this and their lack of vision led to the loss of the island. It is easy to see the course of events in hindsight but Gildas had at least some inkling of what was to come before it happened. That is one of the main differences between intelligence and wisdom. No question in history can be understood unless it is placed in its proper context. The context has been outlined. It is now time to examine the question of King Arthur himself.

---

50 Ibid, 27.

Chapter V

A Solution

To REVIEW the ideas about Arthur that have been presented; the investigation has centred upon the roughly twenty years of peace that followed the Battle of Badon Hill. It was argued that only a powerful king could have prevented the petty warlords from fighting each other. Historians insist that no king of this period had that much power. But that is based upon the idea that we have the names of all of the powerful kings. But there is no reason to believe that is the truth. An examination of the material for over five hundred years of British history and longer than that in Irish history shows that the only way the peace could have been maintained was with a powerful king. In the generations that followed this period the ordinary people who lived under the constant threat of the war bands of plundering kings looked back upon the period of peace as a Golden Age. They exaggerated it into a type of Utopia and turned the man responsible for it into their greatest hero. The memories were passed down in the oral traditions. The storytellers were not only trying to preserve information, but also to entertain an audience. The peace may have been welcome, but it did not make for very good entertainment. The storytellers incorporated myths in order to keep the attention of their listeners.

There is one source that appears to contradict this theory. Many people argue that the real reason Arthur's name does not appear on the king lists is because he was not a king. This idea comes from the *Historia Britonum* attributed to Nennius, which specifically states that he was not a king, but a general with the title of *dux bellorum*, "leader of battles." The argument runs that this bears a strong resemblance to the Roman rank of *dux Britanniarum*, the title of the highest rank of general of the Roman garrison in Britain. The *Eulogy for Geraint* gives Arthur the title of *amerauda*, which is Old Welsh for "emperor." It is essential to determine which of these two passages is correct. Although most investigators who accept the idea of a real Arthur champion the idea that he was a general that is actually the less likely possibility.

Nennius' book is the only source that ever denied Arthur a royal title. The passage is usually written: "Then Arthur fought against them in those days along side the kings of the Britons, but Arthur himself was not king, he was leader of battles."[51] But this is a mistranslation. The words

---

51 *Historia Brittonum*, 50.

"not king" do not actually appear in the original and the real meaning could be that he was the highest-ranking king and he had the right to command them in battle. This interpretation is supported by a number of arguments. The first is the concept of the chain of command. The passage clearly indicates that Arthur was the one giving the orders, and who gives orders to a king? Only a senior king or an emperor could do that. This is the same work that contains Arthur's battle list and the two are usually examined separately. But they are not separate. The *dux bellorum* passage serves as the introduction to the battle list. After the statement that he was leader of battles, the text states: "the first battle was…"[52] There is no brake; the two sentences are part of the same paragraph.

It is generally agreed that the list originated as a poem written in Late Brythonic. Logically the introduction probably originated as part of the same poem. This means that the similarity between *dux bellorum* and *dux Brianniarum* is just a coincidence, because the passage from Nennius was not written in Latin anyway, it was written in Late Brythonic. Since it started as a sixth century British battle poem then it should follow the pattern of sixth century battle poetry. Such works did not emphasize titles. A great many nobles are mentioned in *Y Gododdin*, but only of them, King Mynyddawg, was referred to by his title. This makes the precise nature of the definition of Arthur's title highly suspicious. There is something else suspicious in the title. While the similarity between the Latin phrases is often pointed out, there is another similarity that is overlooked. In the *Eulogy for Geraint* Arthur is called "leader in toil,"[53] meaning toil of war. It is even sometimes translated as "leader in battle toil." This looks a great deal like "leader of battles" but in the *Eulogy* it is a poetic epithet, not an actual title. Again there is the problem of the twenty years of peace. Modern generals might take on the role of peacekeepers, but sixth century generals certainly did not. All things considered the idea that Arthur was a general should be discounted.

These theories are fine as far as they go. They do not contradict any known facts, nor do they call for a radical reinterpretation of the evidence. The problem is they do not go very far. Arthur is left in a kind of limbo. He lived but where he came from and the other details of his life remain mysteries. The matter could be left there, but there are indications that the search can be narrowed down far more than to just leave him as one of many missing kings. The traditions were correct about the peace and the civil war, so perhaps they were also correct about where he came from. Geoffrey of Monmouth named Tintagel as Arthur's birthplace.[54] Many Arthurian researchers brush this aside as propaganda, saying that Geoffrey's patron was Robert, Earl of Gloucester, whose brother Reginald owned Tintagel. But everyone who says this has a vested interest in trying to discredit this idea because they all place Arthur somewhere else. The fact is Geoffrey's statement actually makes perfect sense.

---

52 Ibid, 50.

53 *Geraint fab Erbin*, stanza 8.

54 *History of the Kings of Britain*, viii.20.

First of all, Robert was not Geoffrey's patron because Geoffrey did not have a patron. He was desperately trying to get one in order to secure a promotion to bishop, which is why he dedicated his book to no fewer than three different powerful men. Even if the patron argument were true that would still not prove the statement was propaganda, only that it *could* be propaganda. Tintagel is in Cornwall. There are a surprisingly large number of different sources that connect Arthur to Cornwall or to its neighbouring county of Devon. The Geraint who was killed at Llongborth, Arthur's nephew according to tradition, came from Devon. The poem about him certainly predates Geoffrey's book. In 1113 nine canons from the French town of Laon travelled through Devon and Cornwall. One of them, Herman, wrote about their journey in a book called *De Miraculis S Mariae Laudenien*. In Devon they were shown natural rock formations called Arthur's Oven and Arthur's Chair. At Bodmin in Cornwall one of their servants had an argument with a local over whether or not Arthur was still alive. This is the oldest known reference to the legend that the king did not die and will one day return to lead his people. This was some twenty years before Geoffrey wrote his book.

The Welsh bards were required to memorize a large number of stories. As aids to the memory they grouped stories together based upon similar themes or plots. Since the vast majority were grouped into threes they were called the *Triads of Britain (Trioedd Ynys Prydein* in Welsh). Fittingly there are three main collections of *Triads*. They are the only sources to give a location to Arthur's court and all three of them place it in Cornwall. The different manuscripts were written in different centuries, each contains entries that are not in the other two and when the entries are the same, they are listed in a different order. This means that each compiler was unaware that the other manuscripts existed. They did not copy each other; they used oral traditions from different parts of Wales. In the Middle Ages all of the Welsh believed that Arthur was based in Cornwall Modern researchers who place him elsewhere do not seem to realize that it is highly significant that the inhabitants of Wales should be so unanimous in placing their greatest hero in Cornwall. Why not somewhere in Wales? If he did not come from Cornwall, why did they put him there? If there were other ideas about Arthur's origins, we should expect to find them in the traditions.

Traditions are all very well and good as far as they go, but none of this is hard evidence. Ironically some of the best evidence to show he came from Cornwall come from another county. In the second half of the fifth century someone built a very large fortress at Cadbury in Somerset. Archeologists call it Cadbury Castle, local tradition says that it was Camelot. Cadbury is not the original name of the place. It is Old English and it means "Cadda's Fort." The Brythonic name is not known, but the fortress is not far from the River Cam and the village of Queen's Camel. Camel is Brythonic and it means "Winding" and is found in the names of many rivers named by the Britons. Those who say that there was no Arthur argue that this in nothing more than a linguistic coincidence and there is no reason to believe that the fortress was built by anyone other than a local ruler. This is not an answer. The average fortress in this time period was built to hold a garrison of roughly one hundred men. Cadbury Castle was built for a garrison of roughly eight hundred. By their standards it was huge. The answer a person gets to a particular problem often depends upon the way the question is worded. Many people are asking: did Arthur build it? A better question would be: who built it? The accepted idea is that a king arose out of nowhere, amassed eight times the average power, built this palace and then disappeared into oblivion without leaving any other trace of his existence. Whoever built it, whatever his name was, it was automatically a powerful king whose name is not in the supposedly reliable sources.

The logical conclusion is that we do not have the names of all of the powerful kings. This does not prove that the name was Arthur, but it does suggest that it might be. Although not in Cornwall itself, this was in the territory of the same tribe, the Cornovii.

There is proof of kings in Cornwall in the sixth century. Historian Peter Beresford Ellis drew attention to a memorial stone at Men Scryfa in Cornwall with an inscription about Rialbran son Cunoval. The names mean "Royal Raven" and "Hound of Bel." Only a king would have a name like Royal Raven. Ellis also found a reverence to St. Padernus meeting a king of Cornwall.[55] Approximately twenty years earlier John Morris pointed out that the Church never placed more than one bishop in the same kingdom. Morris found that in what was supposed to be the one kingdom of Dumnonia there were two bishops. One was at Exeter in Devon; the other had a double see of Bodmin and Padstow. He even uncovered the name of one of the bishops, Wethenoc.[56] Two different historians, using different evidence, came to the same conclusion; Cornwall was its own kingdom.

There is more evidence than that. The last king of Dumnonia was Geraint II who was defeated in battle and presumably killed in 710 and Devon was conquered by Wessex. But Cornwall was not conquered until 936, as part of King Athelstan's campaign to unite the kingdoms. There are other written references to some of the Cornish kings who lived after 710. One of them is in the *Welsh Annals*. Under the date 875 there is an entry stating: "Dungarth, king of Cernyw, that is the Cornish, was drowned."[57] All of this makes it quite obvious that the king list for Cornwall is missing. Such men are assumed to have been Geraint's descendants, but if that is true the names should have been on the Dumnonian king list. A reduction in the size of the kingdom should have had no affect upon the list itself. A king list only records the existence of a kingdom, not its size.

---

55   *Celt and Saxon*, pg.75.

56   *The Age of Arthur*, pg. 366.

57   A cross that was found at Penlee House near Penzance bears the name of King Rictus. The cross dates to *c*900. King Hywell is recorded as paying homage to the English king Aelthelstan 27 July, 927. Although this is usually said to have been Hywell Dda, the most powerful king in Wales at that time, the passage clearly said that Hywell ruled the West Welsh, the Old English name for the Cornish. Finally there was Cynan, who rebelled against Aethelstan sometime in the 930's. He was the last known king of the Cornish.

This leads back to the plaque found at Tintagel with the inscription "Artognau, father of a descendant of Coel." It is obvious that Artognau (pronounced Arthnow) is linguistically similar to Arthur. It is also obvious that the plaque was found at Tintagel, Arthur's birthplace. It was argued in the second chapter that this was a king and one who had contracted an important dynastic marriage. This can now be linked to what has been said about Cornwall, and this king has a kingdom. Having shown that this was "a" King Arthur still does not prove that this was "the" King Arthur, although the circumstantial evidence is certainly starting to pile up.

Firmer evidence comes from the political system itself. It is always assumed that the Britons used the same system of high kingship that was used by the Anglo-Saxons. Among the Germanic peoples, power was dependant upon the resources of individual kingdoms and the abilities of individual kings. A ruler needed a power base. He needed a population from which to recruit his army and a strong economy with which to equip and supply that army. The two most important power bases in Britain in this period, and for over a thousand years to come, were London and York. The status of London is difficult to determine, Anglo-Saxons may have conquered it, however it is more likely that it was still in the hands of the Britons. The archeological record shows that there are no Anglo-Saxon artifacts in London until the second half of the sixth century. It should be expected that most, if not all of the high kings of Briton, controlled either York or London. In fact none of them did. How is it possible that the kings who had the greatest advantage over their rivals were *never* able to actually dominate the others? There is also the fact that the British kingdoms tended to be smaller than Anglo-Saxon kingdoms, giving each king fewer resources. One example illustrates the point.

Gwynedd in northern Wales produced two sixth century high kings: Maelgwyn and his son Rhun. In later centuries Gwynedd had difficulty in dominating even the rest of Wales. And most of the time it could not do it. Through much of the medieval period Wales had no high king and when it did he did not automatically come from Gwynedd. Even if the Anglo-Saxons are granted as much land as they could possibly have conquered, this very same kingdom would have to have dominated not only Wales, but at least half of what is now southern England, most of northern England and all of southern Scotland for roughly sixty years. How could a kingdom be so powerful that it could dominate that much territory for so long and never dominate anywhere near that much territory ever again?

It is assumed that the Britons used the same system of high kingship as the Anglo-Saxons because they used that system in later centuries. But what they were doing in later centuries is irrelevant. Tradition always maintained that their original political system collapsed because of the Anglo-Saxon conquest. This is quite possible. It would not be the first time or the last time that a political system collapsed due to intense pressure.

With many small kingdoms each king would have had limited resources and many competitors. There should have been very few high kings, or even none at all. Historians often remark that the Britons had an unusually large number, exactly the opposite of what should be expected under these conditions. Actually that is not what they had. Welsh tradition and an analysis of the historical information both indicate that the main phase of the wars came to an end with the death of Cadwaladr of Gwynedd. He was the last Welsh king to launch a major offensive to try to recover lost lands. From his time onwards the Britons were almost always on the defensive. This defines the time frame very precisely from 410 when the Britons became independent of the Empire until Cadwaladr's death, which was either 664 or 682. The following is a list of high kings for that period: at first there was an unknown number who rose and fell quite quickly in the early fifth century, then Vortigern, Ambrosius Aurelianus, then the time period in which Arthur is said to have reigned, then Maelgwyn, Rhun, Urien, Owain, Meurig, Cadwallon, Cadfael, Cadwaladr. That is not an unusually large number; that is a straight list with only one gap in it, a gap that exists only because people insist that it exists. The period of several rulers who did not last long indicates that it was not the Germanic system because that is impossible under the Germanic system. A king would either dominate or he would not. If no one could dominate, then they just did not have one. The only way to get several in a row who did not last very long is if no one could dominate but they kept having them anyway.

There are other arguments against this system as well. Ambrosius Aurelianus came to power in a coup. It is impossible to launch a coup in an Anglo-Saxon style high kingship. High kingship was based upon gaining the support of the other kings, either through respect or intimidation. But a man with popular support would not launch a coup; he would stage a rebellion. There is no example on record of any high king ever seizing power that way. Killing Vortigern would have created a gap at the top of the political pyramid, but it would not have filled that gap. Ambrosius could have seized power in Vortigern's kingdom and used that as a power base to make himself a high king, but that did not happen because Vortigern did not have a kingdom. It has been said that he came from Powys, which he did. In the ninth century the ruler of Powys erected a monument to commemorate his ancestors-the Pillar of Eliseg. It begins with the name Brittu and everyone agrees that this means he founded the kingdom. He is then described as son of Vortigern. Britons sometimes used "son of" to mean "descendant of." According to the genealogies Brittu was actually Vortigern's grandson. The kingdom does not go back far enough. The royal houses of both Builth and Gwerthrynion also traced descent from Vortigern, but they do not date back even as far as Powys. In fact they were both carved out of it. Vortigern did not have a kingdom.

Why would a Britano-Gaelic people who had been in the Roman Empire use the same political system as a Germanic people with virtually no Roman influences? Instead of comparing the Britons to the Anglo-Saxons, it would be more instructive to examine the Irish and the Romans. It is reasonable to conclude that they used either an Irish type system, or one patterned on the Roman model or perhaps a combination of the two. In order to illustrate the salient points it would be useful to examine both the Empire and Ireland.

The Irish are the only people to actually use the title high king (*ard ri*). In Ireland the high kingship was an institution. It is impossible to know exactly how far back it stretched. The list of rulers stretches well back before the Irish were literate so the early part is derived entirely from tradition. The accuracy is suspect since the very first name is Nuada, the king of the gods. The first verifiable king was Niall of the Nine Hostages, founder of the O'Neil clan. He lived in the late fourth and early fifth centuries and he died some time around 405. Although he was the first high king whose existence can be proven, it is probable that the position already existed before his time. Neill himself claimed descent from a late second early third century high king, Conn of the Hundred Battles. Tradition holds that the high kingship had been inaugurated at Emain Macha, now Navan Fort. Archeology indicates that *c*100 B.C. a very large fort centred on a sacred oak was constructed on the site. Some time later the capital was moved to Tara in county Meath. Tradition attributes this shift of location to Conn, in the late second century.

Unlike the Anglo-Saxons the Irish always had a high king. His position was often contested, or even ignored by some kings, but regardless of how much or how little power he actually had, someone could always at least claim seniority over the others. Beginning in the eleventh century (1002 to be exact), the leaders of Ireland would assemble at the capital and choose the high king. Before that, the kings of Tara, the heads of the O'Neil clan, usually claimed the high kingship. In pagan times the kings of Tara were chosen in a ritual called *tarbhfhess* "bull sleep." A sacred bull was sacrificed and the arch-druid would eat its flesh and drink the broth in which the bull had been cooked. He then went to sleep, while four other druids took up positions around him and chanted. The best choice of king would then be revealed to the sleeper in a dream. According to legend the choice would be confirmed by four magic tests. The last of these is that he would lay his hand upon the Stone of Destiny, which supposedly cried out when touched by rightful king. According to mythology one of the four magic treasures brought to Ireland by the gods was Lia Fail, the Stone of Destiny. The kings of Scotland were always crowned while they stood or sat upon the sacred Stone of Scone (also sometimes called the Stone of Destiny). Scone was Scotland's ancient capital and it was said that the stone had been taken from Tara in Ireland. The Scottish Stone was captured by England's King Edward I in the thirteenth century and brought to London, where it formed part of the throne used for the coronations of British monarchs until being returned to Scotland in 1996.

When they said destiny they meant it. They believed that divine forces had chosen these men. All ancient peoples used mythology for propaganda purposes. The candidate could prove he was the chosen one by passing a test or series of tests. The rulers had to prove themselves worthy. The most obvious way in which they could do this was through victory on the battlefield. The Romans had similar ideas.

The emperor was the man who could gain the support of the army and the approval of the Senate. The flaw in the system is that the army was spread out over literally thousands of miles of territory. Different units could support different candidates, which would lead to trouble in the case of a hotly disputed succession. The system was inherently unstable and Roman dynasties were short lived in comparison to the dynasties of most other peoples. The word emperor is derived from the Latin *imperator* and it literally means "he who has the right to command." It was originally an honorary title bestowed upon a popular politician or military leader and only gradually came to be confined to the ruler himself. It was believed that the emperor had to prove himself worthy of the position.

Although the details in the systems are different, there are similarities in concepts. The first is that the rulers were chosen. This was not something that the Irish learned from the Romans. It was actually a very widespread practice in Western Europe in ancient times and quite in keeping with ancient concepts of kingship. The Germanic peoples had the same idea. With the exception of the bretwalda himself, a council of nobles called the *witena gemot*, the "council of the wise", elected Anglo-Saxon kings. After the unification of England a national *witan* was established that elected the rulers of all England. The last king chosen by this system was Harold Godwinson; the man killed by William the Conqueror at the Battle of Hastings in 1066.

It appears as if there was always a high king of Ireland, but this is a disputed point. If it is true, then it appears as if the later Welsh were the exception rather than the rule in not having any kind of regular authority. The list of the high kings of the Picts has survived. It is continuous, with no gaps in it. This suggests that they were using the same type of system as the Irish. Over the course of the centuries the high kings of the Picts gained authority over the Scottish kingdom of Dalriada. In 839 the Vikings killed the Pictish high king, Eoganan, and most of the Pictish aristocracy in battle. In the political chaos that followed the Dalriadic ruler Kenneth macAlpin was able to overcome most of the other rulers and found the Kingdom of Scotland. What is usually ignored is that Kenneth was actually a high king. The high kingship was monopolized by one dynasty, but that was not unusual. In Ireland the O'Neils held a virtual monopoly on the title for five centuries while among the Picts all of the high kings before Kenneth macAlpin were from the ruling house of Caithness. MacAlpin's descendants actually maintained authority over three kingdoms. Aside form Scotland itself there was also the last surviving of the Northern Kingdoms of the Britons, Strathclyde, which was annexed by the Scottish crown in 1058. And there was also Moray, which had been a Pictish realm. Its rulers held onto the title of king until the dynasty died out in 1130. Brittany was also divided into three kingdoms and it too had institutionalized high kingship, with the rulers being chosen from the royal house of Domnonia.[58]

There are several variations on the list of the high kings of the Britons handed down in the traditions. This is not unusual. Most ancient king lists have variant forms because of the problems inherent in transmitting the information. What is unusual is the way in which this one is treated. Historians just assume that it is wrong. They add and subtract names from the list based upon their own interpretations, without any real relation to the information as it actually exists. There are a variety of names that are added, but the two most common are Coel and

---

58 This is an alternate form of Dumnonia and different branches of the same family ruled both places.

Riothamus. It is usually argued that Coel ruled the north while Vortigern was high king only of the south. The north was one kingdom, and the south, being politically divided, could not muster enough strength to dominate the region north of the Humber. The problem is there is no evidence that the south was divided that early. An examination of the dates of the founding of the known southern kingdoms shows that Gwent might date back to the 430's, but that is debatable. None of the other kingdoms appear before the 440's. There is not enough evidence to be certain, but it would appear that the original divisions simply followed the lines laid down by the Romans. Coel's kingdom corresponds to the old Roman province of Britannia Secunda.

Coel figures prominently in the northern king lists, but not in the accounts of the period. Gildas presented a picture in which Vortigern made the important decisions and neither he nor Nennius mentioned Coel at all. This has been explained by saying that they were following southern propaganda, but that is special pleading. Coel may have been very popular in the north, but the balance of power in Britain has almost always been in favour of the south. The south has the majority of the wealth and the population. In a Britano-Gaelic system of high kingship the south would have had the most votes in choosing the high king, which would have made Vortigern the senior king.

The other king was Riothamus, which means "Most Royal" and is assumed to have been the title of a high king. In 470 the Emperor Anthemius asked him for help against the Germanic invaders of Gaul. Most of our information about the campaign comes from the *Gothic History* of Jordanes written in 551. Riothamus was described as a king of the Britons who came form across the ocean to battle the barbarians, but he was betrayed. The Roman prefect of Gaul, Arvandus, harbored ambitions of his own for the province. The last thing that he wanted was to strengthen the central government. He wrote to Euric, king of the Visigoths, informing him that the only real imperial power in Gaul was Riothamus and his followers and urging him to attack it. Arvandus' letter was intercepted and he was placed on trial for treason. The letter was made public during the trial. Euric learned of its contents and ambushed the Britons. Their army was destroyed and the survivors fled to Burgundy, which was friendly to Rome.

It all seems straightforward until attempts are made to fit Riothamus into the chronology of Britain. There is no mention of him in traditional sources, a very strange omission for a man who was supposedly a high king powerful enough to receive a request for help from an emperor. It is agreed that he ruled in the south, but the date of his campaign places him at the same time as Ambrosius Aurelianus, which is impossible. By definition the same region could not have had two high kings at the same time. Gildas and Nennius both confirm that Ambrosius held that honour.

The answer is actually quite simple and has been pointed out by several historians. There were several times when Britons fled their homeland and settled in Brittany. These were not leaderless routes, they were carefully planned migrations with leaders to guide the people and warriors to protect them. They were also conducted with Imperial approval. The Romans were not in the habit of giving away land. They allowed others into the Empire if their warriors fought in the Roman armies in what were called federates (*foederati* in Latin). They had their own units and served under their own commanders. As the Empire collapsed the Romans relied more and more heavily on federates. The Franks were settled in northern Gaul under the federate system. Eventually, of course, they conquered most of Gaul and turned it into France. The Riothamus campaign looks like another example of the Romans utilizing federates. His people were called Britons because the word Breton did not exist yet and there was no linguistic distinction between the inhabitants of the island and the peninsula. He did cross the ocean, just as Jordanes said. But that writer failed to point out that Riothamus came to stay. Riothamus was not a ruler in Britain itself, he ruled Brittany.

It has been argued that Brittany would not have been militarily powerful enough to come to the attention to the Imperial authorities. First of all it would not have come to their attention since they would have to have negotiated the agreement that gave the land to the Breton in the first place, they already knew about Brittany. Secondly Brittany was actually surprisingly powerful for such a small place. In the wake of Rome's collapse, the Franks were the dominant power in the region. Despite several attempts, the Franks never conquered Brittany. Even Charlemagne failed twice. Brittany only became incorporated into the Kingdom of France through intermarriage. In the chaotic period of the fifth century with Franks, Saxons, Romans and Goths (to name the largest groups) all fighting over Gaul it is conceivable that they were able to do more than just defend themselves and that they did launch an offensive. After all that is what federates were for.

An examination of the rituals, concepts and terminology of Britano-Gaelic high kingship shows that they permeate the Arthurian tales. Arthur's father was Uther Pendragon. But this is not a name; it means "terrible head of the rulers." It is widely agreed that pendragon probably originated as a term or title for the man at the top of the system. Another term was "King of all the Britons" which was applied to Arthur himself many times in the Romances. The *Eulogy for Geraint* calls him *amerauda*, which is the Old Welsh word for emperor. Both Irish and Anglo-Saxon high kings sometimes used that title. They meant it in the sense that these men had authority over kings, but they might also have had in mind the original Latin meaning emphasizing the right to rule. The most striking similarities appear in the story of the sword-in-the-stone. There was no king of all the Britons so candidates came from all over the land to prove themselves worthy of the post. The rightful king would be known because only he could draw the magic sword from the stone. In other words once it was determined who had proven himself the best leader, the *imperator* could be crowned while he stood beside the Stone of Destiny. Much like the Irish story.

The stones for the Irish and Scots are well known. The Scottish Stone of Scone is now on display in Edinburgh Castle while the Irish one still stands where it has always been, stuck in the ground at Tara, the ancient capital. There is evidence that the Britons had one as well. In 1450 a man named Jack Cade raised a rebellion against Henry VI. Cade and his followers captured

London, where he is said to have taken a sacred oath and then struck his sword against an object called the London Stone. This was a pillar of stone with smooth sides. It was stuck in the ground and centuries later it was broken in order to widen Cannon Street. The top is behind a grate on the north side, while the base is buried beneath the pavement. In the sixteenth century, the antiquarian William Camden suggested that this was originally a Roman milestone, but modern opinion rejects that idea, although no clear consensus on an alternative has been reached. It was certainly considered of great symbolic importance in the fifteenth century, it had far more importance than would have been attached to a mere milestone and one school of thought argues that it was the Stone of Destiny for the Britons.

Royal stones signified many things to the Britano-Gaels. They represented the strength of the kings, both physical strength and strength of character. They also symbolized a connection to the land and the people who lived on the land and a link with the past. It cannot be proven that the London Stone was the British Stone of Destiny, but it is a reasonable assumption. There is a problem. Although the Irish and the Scots had Stones of Destiny, there is no evidence that the Picts or the Breton did. So the use of such things was not automatic. In the case of the Britons, the evidence is reasonable but not quite conclusive.

If there was always a king who claimed authority over the others, even if that authority was often theoretical rather than real, then that was the beginnings of a central government. Among the Scots and Breton this system evolved into a more conventional type of central government. In Ireland it was actually too weak to achieve this status. The high kings held seniority, and if not for the English conquest the system might have evolved into a true central government. There is not enough information to tell the true situation among the Picts, but some have argued that they did not use high kingship at all but actually did have a central government. The traditions maintain that the Britons themselves had a central government. The first person to suggest that the traditions were right was John Morris.

According to the usual interpretation Britain fragmented into little kingdoms shortly after becoming independent from Rome. This is supposedly proven by the fact that the sources record many kings. But by the original definition of the word "king" was only a chieftain, or more vaguely simply a leader. The basic meaning was essentially the same in all the known languages of ancient Britain (the unknown languages of course, being those of the Atecotti and the Picts). Whether it is the Latin *rex*, or the Brythonic *vawr* or *rix* the Old Irish *ri*, or the Old English *cynge*, they all had similar origins. Kingdoms were actually very rare in Ancient Europe. There were some, such as Macedon, but most polities were city-states, empires or tribes.

It has already been mentioned that Gildas treated Vortigern as the sole ruler, even though there were other kings. The only other political authority Gildas mentioned for this period was some sort of council. In the section that deals with the plan to invite the Anglo-Saxon mercenaries into Britain, he wrote: "then all of the members of the council together with the proud tyrant…"[59] Gildas

---

59 *De excidio*, 23.1.

stated that the council was convened specifically to deal with the crisis of the period, suggesting that it was not a permanent body. The letter Honorius sent to Britain in 410 was addressed to the *civitates*, the city based-councils that existed throughout the Empire. Unfortunately not much can be determined from two short references that might not even be about the same thing. Gildas may have been writing about a national council that survived at least long enough for the peoples of the first half of the sixth century to be familiar with it, or it may have been some sort of royal council of the type that any king might have. The wording yields no concrete conclusions. Closely examining the course of events of the fifth century yields better results.

In the 450's the Irish were driven out of Gwynedd, Devon and Cornwall. The examinations of these conflicts always centre on Cunedda of the Gododdin moving into Gwynedd. But the two campaigns were conducted at roughly the same time. That type of operation indicates unity of command, which needs some sort of central authority. The Cornovii drove the Irish out of the southwest, but this makes no sense if Britain were really politically divided. The Cornovii came from Powys. One look at a map shows that Gwynedd bordered Powys to the north and Dyfed bordered it to the southwest. Later the small kingdoms of Ceredigion and Gwerthrynion lay in-between, but neither of them existed in the 450's. Dumnonia (Devon and Cornwall) was the one Irish colony that did not border their lands. Why would the ruler of the independent kingdom of Powys attack the only Irish colony that was not a threat to him? One possible answer is that the other areas were too strongly defended so he attacked the place that he had the most chance of taking. That is contradicted by an examination of the topography. Gwynedd and Dyfed both had mountainous regions, but also flat open terrain. Devon and Cornwall were (and still are) moorland and hills from one end to the other. The terrain would have favored the defender. Since the campaign would have been difficult, why undertake it at all? Why not pick an easier target? Cunedda, who marched hundreds of miles into a completely different part of the island, drove the Irish out of Gwynedd. The founder of the Dumnonian royal house did the same thing at the same time. The use of these two specific tribes is interesting. They were two of the most powerful tribes. Had the Cornovii taken Gwynedd they would have created the largest holding in Britain. This would have seriously altered the balance of power, which the other tribes would not have tolerated. The whole operation looks like a trade-off. The Cornovii received more territory, but it was far away from their homeland, and the Gododdin received the same, which maintained the relative status quo of those two tribes. This suggests a central government, which needed to balance the concerns of different groups, not independent campaigns fought by autonomous kings.

The third Irish colony was Dyfed in southwestern Wales. It was not liberated when the other operations took place. In fact the situation there is very mysterious. All of a sudden in the late 480's the Irish leadership just disappeared from Dyfed, as if by magic. There continued to be an Irish-speaking population in the region for at least another century, but the rulers were British. The new king of Dyfed was named Tryffin. The problem is that Tryffin is not a name; it is the Old

Welsh pronunciation of tribune, a Roman military rank. It has been pointed out that ancient Britano-Gaelic rulers took names that often sounded like titles, but when they did that they took royal titles that incorporated *vawr* (king) or *rio* (royal), or some similar word. They did not use military ranks, at least not if they were kings in the modern sense of the word. The Tribune's grandson was Vortipor, the same Vortipor who was mentioned by Gildas. A memorial stone to him was found in the churchyard at Castell Dwyran. It says: MEMORIA UOTEPRIGIS PROTICTORIS. Protictoris is a variant of Protector. Many historians interpret this to mean that he was a great defender of his people, but in fact it is another Roman military rank. A simple protector was a member of a guard unit, but the word was also incorporated into the ranks of a couple of different types of staff officer. It is impossible to know exactly what was meant here, because not enough is known about the British military system. It is interesting to note that when the definition of the word king began to change and local chieftains were forced to take new titles, they used duke and count, which were derived from the Roman military ranks *dux* and *comes*. The titles were different but the basic idea may have been the same.

Some researchers believe that Tryffin was the son of the Irish king Aed who embraced Latin culture. The evidence contradicts this. In the tenth century one of the greatest rulers in Welsh history, Hywell Dda (Hywell the Good), had many genealogies put together into one collection. There were thirty-three lists altogether and the house of Dyfed is List 2. It clearly indicates that the family was Romano-British, not Irish. Tyffin's father was not Aed; his name is given as Clotin (Claudius) and the family claimed descent from no less a person than the Roman emperor Constantine the Great.

The suggestion that these men were Irish lords who copied the Britons does not explain why they took military ranks instead of royal titles. Furthermore the name Vortipor is neither Irish nor Latin, it is British. Gildas called Vortipor "tyrant of the Demetae."[60] This type of designation was very precise. The population of Dyfed was mixed Irish and British. Gildas mentioned only the British tribe. If the two groups had equal rights they would both have been mentioned. For example Kenneth macAlpin was called "King of the Picts and Scots." When only one was specified it was the dominant group. An Irish dynasty would not have made the Demetae dominant. The dynasty had to have been British.

There is at least one other suspicious title in this period. We have the name of only one ruler of Elmet, Gwallawg, son of Llenauc, who lived in the late sixth century. He is not called a king. The title is actually magistrate. These titles suggest that the rulers of the different regions in Britain were not kings in the modern sense of the word, they were nobles, men who in later centuries would have been called dukes or counts or some similar title. They did not even all have the title of king some had civilian or military ranks taken from the Romans.

The most compelling evidence comes from the agreements that Vortigern made with the Anglo-Saxons. When they first arrived he gave them Kent as partial payment for their services,

---

60 Ibid, 31.1.

against the objections of the local king Gwyrangon. A kingdom is a sovereign state, even if it is a vassal kingdom. It does not matter whether it is the Germanic system or the Britano-Gaelic system, a high king could not have done what Vortigern did. He is supposed to have deposed a vassal king without any kind of legal justification, disinherited the rightful heirs, confiscated land he had no claim to and handed it over to someone else who also had no claim to it. The name of the ruler of Kent is given as Gwyrangon or Guoyrancgonus, in the nineteenth century there was a school of thought that said that this was not a name. It was actually a garbling of a title for governor. Although this idea lost out to the mainstream idea of high kings, it must be the truth. The only way Vortigern could have done what he did is if the position of ruler of Kent was appointed.

Several historians have pointed out that what Vortigern did was to follow the Roman policy of treating the mercenaries as federates. This is true, but the only way he could have followed that particular Roman policy is if they had an essentially Roman style government. Later Hengest ambushed Vortigern and forced him to hand over more land. Hengest knew how the different political systems worked. He had served Germanic kings before coming to Britain and had acted as Vortigern's military advisor for some time before the rebellion. Hengest would not even have tried to get Vortigern to give him title to land ruled by vassal kings. The system simply did not work that way and Hengest would have known it.

The usual explanation of events is that all of the old Roman administration was swept away in the years of political chaos that came after Britain was cut off from the Empire and before the rise of Vortigern. That is not realistic. There would have been attempts to retain the Roman style of government because that was the only type of government the Britons knew. To be more accurate what they knew was a combination of Roman and British. The Romans did not uproot the old tribal structure of society. They laid down their administration side-by-side. This is an oversimplification, but generally the Roman administration was in the southeast and the towns throughout the island, while the chieftains held sway through most of the north and west but were answerable to Roman administrators. In the late Imperial period Britain was divided into four provinces, with the tribal areas being Britannia Prima in the west and Britannia Secunda in the north. A comparison of the maps shows that all of the men with the title of king lived in one or the other of these two regions. Elmet, with its magistrate, was in Flavia Caesariensis and Kent, with its appointed governor, was in Maxima Caesariensis, the two Latin provinces.

The political dynamics of the tribes would have been of secondary importance as long as the island was a far off corner of the Empire, but that would have changed in the early fifth century. Instead of the Roman apparatus and ways of doing things simply disappearing, it is more likely that the alterations were more gradual. With the collapse of the Empire, no new Romans came to Britain and the ones who were there fled or were gradually absorbed as a cultural group by the native population. With each generation the government became a little less Roman and a little more tribal. It is probably no coincidence that the strongest evidence for a central government comes from the fifth century. But even as it evolved from a Roman style administration with British influences to more of a British style kingship with Latin influences it would always have been a central government, that is until it fell.

Central governments do not just collapse under their own weight; they are torn down. In this case the forces tearing it came from within and without. The local kings wanted their own autonomy. This was not unusual it was actually quite common. Charles the Rash (r.1467-'77), duke of Burgundy, launched several campaigns to gain his independence from France. In Germany, Henry the Lion (r.1142-'80), duke of Saxony (and from 1156 also duke of Bavaria), tried to turn his lands into an independent realm. While in 1721, Frederick III, elector of Brandenburg-Prussia succeeded where the others had failed and was crowned King Frederick I of Prussia. This was a major step in weakening the power of the German emperors, which came to a head in 1806 when Napoleon officially dissolved the Empire. These are only a few examples, there are many more.

In post Roman Britain the problem would have been compounded by the nature of the central government itself. There would have been a royal family, but Britons had a very broad definition of family. A ruler's son did not necessarily succeed him; someone as distantly related as a second cousin could succeed him. And the Britons traced descent through women as well as through men. Many prominent, ambitious men could make a bid for power. This means that any pendragon would have to have dealt with what historians usually call "over mighty barons" and also rivals for their own position at the top of the political pyramid. Add to this the fact that they were under attack from foreign enemies from three sides and it is no wonder that the central government collapsed.

Most modern historians simply assume that the tradition of the central government is wrong. Medieval writers are supposed to have made a mistake and to have applied central government because they did not understand high kingship. The problem is they did understand high kingship. The title was used in Ireland on a regular basis until the mid-twelfth century. Even after that kings often claimed the title, even when they could not make good on that claim. Spain was politically divided for centuries. Although the Spanish did not use a special title, they were acquainted with the idea that there could be a senior king. The first to hold that distinction were the kings of Leon, but when the balance of power shifted to Castile, the rulers of that kingdom held the distinction until the unification of Spain in the late fifteenth century. The Crusaders established five autonomous realms in the Holy Land. Because of the way in which they were set up, there was a clear hierarchy among them at all times. The most important was, of course, the Kingdom of Jerusalem. The rankings of the others were apparent in their very names: The Kingdom of Armenia, the Principality of Antioch, and the Counties of Edessa and Tripoli. The titles in these examples are different but the basic concept is always the same. The peoples of medieval Europe knew what high kingship was and they knew that Arthurian Britain did not have it.

There are arguments against the idea of a central government, but they can be easily explained. The kings had their own armies and they battled each other to further their own ambitions. In later centuries the dukes and counts of France and Germany did exactly the same thing. The leadership shifted from one family to another, which certainly appears as if they had no ruling dynasty. But appearances can be deceptive. Since neither Ambrosius nor Arthur appear in the surviving genealogies, there are problems tracing the families for the rulers of the fifth century, but examining what is known of these rulers from Maelgwyn onward reveals something very interesting. He was succeeded by his son Rhun, who was followed by his nephew Urien, then came his son Owain, then his first cousin Meurig, then his second cousin Cadwallen (who was also a direct descendent of Rhun), then another usurper Cadfael, then finally Cadwallen's son, Cadwaladr. Which means that except for the usurper, this is all one dynasty by British law. It seems a little bit too much of a coincidence that these high kings should have all been related. Leadership did bounce around to different branches of the dynasty, but Britain was unstable. As the Anglo-Saxons gained land, branches of the family that had been important were conquered, shifting the balance of power within the nation.

A Roman system needed a standing army, since the emperor had to gain the support of the army. The Britons did have an army. When the island became cut off from the rest of the Empire there was still a Roman garrison there. It was not as large as it had been in previous centuries, but it was still there. The appearance of Roman military ranks over one hundred years later might mean that some sort of standing army did survive, although this is far from conclusive since Roman military ranks were adopted as title for nobles. The sources speak of men like Vortirmer and Vitalinus commanding troops on the battlefield, but never mention what kingdoms their warriors came from. Rhun supposedly led an alliance of kingdoms against rebels in the north. The sources record the kingdoms of the northern rebels-Rheged, Strathclyde and Manu Gododdin. But there is no mention of what kingdoms supplied warriors for Rhun's army. Normally under these conditions there would have been a list of the high king's illustrious vassals. In this case there is nothing, suggesting that he did not use any vassals but marched at the head of a standing army.

Once it has been established that there was a central government, it can be shown that contrary to popular belief, Gildas did mention Arthur, just not by name. Gildas stated that Maelgwyn seized power by killing his uncle in a civil war. Then feeling remorse for what he had done, he went into a monastery, after a time he came out of the monastery again and took over power.[61] It is now time to return to the question that was raised earlier in this book-who was ruling Gwynedd while Maelgwyn was in the monastery and why did that person step down when Maelgwyn changed his mind?

This situation is not unique. There were other occasions when such things happened. Based upon these examples it can be concluded that Maelgwyn left the monastery because he was

---

61 Ibid, 33.4-34.1.

asked to. In the other cases there was some sort of political crisis and it was believed that the man in the monastery could solve the crisis. According to Geoffrey of Monmouth there was a political crisis. After Arthur's death there were three pendragons in a row who did not last very long. The interesting point is that according to Geoffrey their names were Constantine, Aurelius Caninus and Vortipor. Obviously these are three of the same kings criticized by Gildas. Two points immediately present themselves from this information. The first is that all of these men were still alive during Maelgwyn's reign. This is not a problem. Britano-Gaels usually did not kill deposed kings, as that would have caused blood feud. Geoffrey indicates the total length of their reigns as only eleven years.[62] If this information is true, then chances are they would all have still been alive. The second point is that Cuneglasus is conspicuous by his absence.

Cuneglasus seems to have been Maelgwyn's right hand man. Gildas said he had an unfair advantage in the civil wars of the period, "waging war with arms special to [himself]."[63] Because of the violence of the period if anyone had an unfair advantage it would have to have been the pendragon, that is the only way he could have stayed in power. After all Cuneglasus could have used these weapons to make himself pendragon. If the weapons were not held by the pendragon himself then it stands to reason his lieutenant held them. This idea finds further support in two ways. The first is that Cuneglasus was Maelgwyn's cousin. The Britons emphasized extended families. If Maelgwyn had been accepted as head of the family (which he would have been if he was pendragon), Cuneglasus would have been honour bound to support him. Then the there is the question as to what these unique weapons were.

Normally if someone had unique weapons then they did not remain unique for very long, as others would copy them. This duplication would not happen only if the weapons could not be copied. The only answer that makes sense is that the weapons were the siege engines. These would have been extremely expensive, beyond the resources of most nobles. They would have been grouped into one unit called the siege train and this unit would have been commanded by one of the ruler's most trusted supporters.

Once this adjustment is made it becomes clear that the usual interpretation is incorrect. Gildas did not criticize rulers of different kingdoms in geographic order from south to north he criticized pendragons in chronological order. This leads inevitably to the conclusion that the unnamed uncle Maelgwyn killed was Arthur. Gildas states that Maelgwyn killed not only the uncle but also almost all of the uncle's warriors. According to tradition only one of the Knights of the Round Table survived Arthur's last battle. At first glance this would appear to contradict the tradition that he was killed by his own son, in fact it actually clears up another problem.

According to the *Triads* one of the "Three Unfortunate Councils of Britain" was when Arthur divided his army with Medraut at the Battle of Camlann. Medraut is the original form of the name Mordred and Camlann was Arthur's last battle. This passage does not mean what

---

62   Four years each for Constantine and Aurelius Caninus and three for Vortipor.

63   *De excidio*, 32.2.

it appears to mean. It looks as if Medraut was Arthur's trusted supporter but dividing the army was some sort of tactical error that led to defeat and it would have been better to have left the army in one piece. Dividing the army could not have been a tactical error because it was standard operating procedure. Every single army in Europe in this period and for hundreds of years to come was automatically split into divisions. There were usually three: right wing, left wing and centre with the commander-in-chief in the centre. In fact the triad does mention three divisions. The problem was not that the army was divided; it was that it was divided with Medraut. It was not unusual for a man who was going to betray his lord to do it on the battlefield because the lord was very vulnerable on the battlefield. A very famous example was when Richard III was killed at the Battle of Bosworth Field when Lord Stanley, commanding the right wing, switched sides and attacked Richard's division instead of the enemy. In this case it would mean that Arthur and Medraut marched to Camlann to fight someone else.

Who was this someone else? According to legend the enchantress Morgan used her magical powers to trick Arthur into sleeping with her. Nine months later Mordred was born. Making him Arthur's son. But Morgan was Arthur's sister, making Mordred also Arthur's nephew. This suggests that he is a composite figure made up of Medraut the son and Maelgwyn the nephew. According to Geoffrey of Monmouth Arthur had one of those prophetic dreams that medieval authors loved so much. In the dream a dragon arose out of the west and slew a bear after a fierce fight.[64] Arthur means bear and Maelgwyn ruled Gwynedd, which was symbolized by a dragon and which was in the west. This idea also has ramifications for the idea of the central government, since it places Arthur into the line of succession by making him Maelgwyn's uncle.

The ideas about King Arthur that have been presented in this chapter are theories based upon the evidence, as it is known. Nothing is contradicted by the facts and no interpretations have forced the rewriting of evidence. The fact that Cornwall was its own kingdom (or province) is not widely known, but two different historians have already published the idea. The concept of the central government has also been presented before. What is more other theories about Arthur either emphasize the battle traditions or the legends, but not both. This approach reconciles the two. Arthur was present at Llongborth, he did fight the battles on the Nennius list and he was killed at Camlann. He was also chosen rightful king of the Britons and he maintained the peace, being killed in the civil war that ended it.

---

64 *History of the Kings of Britain*, x3.

Chapter VI

THE ARTHURIAN GEOGRAPHY

ARTHUR IS associated with a great many places in both the historical record and the legends. Only the most significant locations will be dealt with here. The places named in the Arthurian geography can be divided into two categories-real places that are believed to have had a connection to him and places mentioned in traditions and tales that cannot be found on any map. The actual locations will be dealt with first. The logical place to start is his birthplace. According to Geoffrey of Monmouth, Arthur was born at Tintagel.[65] Most researchers who accept that Arthur was real reject this idea. Their arguments are never based upon firm evidence, they stem from the need to move the hero to fit some preconceived theory. If Arthur really had been born somewhere else then there should be traditions that point to another location. Tintagel is the only town that the traditional material has ever suggested as his birthplace.

The name is derived from *din tagell*, which means "fort by the neck of land." There is no record of the name any earlier than *c*1137. At that time a new castle was built on the site. The name itself must be far older since it is Brythonic and by the twelfth century the English ruled Cornwall and an English aristocrat who spoke French built the castle. Tintagel was a very different place in the sixth century from what it is today. The town is small and the ruins of the twelfth century castle overshadow it. In the Arthurian period there was a Romano-British fortress, and a small building which was probably a church. The town was a busy port. Since the Anglo-Saxons held most of the east and south coasts and their pirates sailed the Channel, most foreign trade flowed in and out of the Britano-Gaelic territory by the western ports. Tintagel was one of the largest in Cornwall and it would have greatly benefited from the local economy. Although the mines are tapped out today, in ancient times Cornwall was a major producer of tin. It was sold all over the known world, even as far away as the Holy Land. The town was a royal residence and exactly the kind of place one would expect a future king to have been born.

He may have been born at Tintagel, but Camelot was his capital. It was the seat of the Round Table and the location from which most of the adventures started in the legends. There is a problem

---

65 *History of the Kings of Britain*, vii.20.

when dealing with the capital cities of Britano-Gaels. There would have been one place that would have been used for religious and political ceremonies for the entire nation, in the case of the Britons this was probably London, at least until it was captured by the Anglo-Saxons. These places tended to have very limited administrative authority, although in this case the administrative importance would have depended upon how much of the Roman bureaucracy had survived. They were sometimes more symbolic than functional. Tara, the capital of the O'Neil clan, and the closest thing that Ireland had to a national capital, was not even a town it was a royal fortress. Each region had its own capital and a pendragon could hold court in any town at all, turning it into a temporary capital. Nevertheless there would still have been one place, usually a fortress, which was the main residence for the ruler. The Irish word for such a place was *rath* and the Britons called it a *pen lys* (head court). So Camelot should be thought of in terms of a pen lys rather than a town.

In the previous chapter it was suggested that this was South Cadbury Castle. John Leland, King's Antiquary to Henry VIII, first made this suggestion. It was a hill fort that was originally built in the Neolithic era and rebuilt on a larger scale in the late fifth or early sixth century. It is near the River Cam and the towns of Queen's Camel and West Camel. The arguments in favour of this location usually consist entirely of linguistics, but they can also include the process of elimination.

Since it was eight times the average size of a fort, then the average king could not have built it. Given the time period of its construction the only two possibilities for the builders are Ambrosius Aurelianus or Arthur. A fortress of this size would have been a pen lys. But we know the pen lys of Ambrosius, it was Dynus Emrys in what is now Snowdonia in northern Wales. The name even means Fort Ambrosius. With only two possibilities and one eliminated, that leaves the other. However there are other suggestions for the site.

Another contender for Camelot is Colchester, which the Romans called Camulodunum. This is unlikely as it was almost certainly in the Anglo-Saxon kingdom of Essex. If the castle was in Cornwall the most likely location is Camelford. The name dates from at least the thirteenth century and is actually a hybrid of Brythonic and English. Roughly translated it means: "ford of the crooked river." Welsh tradition names another important location called Celli Wig. It was said to have been in Cornwall, but there is no indication as to where.

Nothing can be reconstructed of Arthur's early life. Nothing is known until he started his military career. The difficulties in identifying most of the battle sites have already been mentioned. The problem is made worse by investigators who try to force interpretations to make the evidence fit the theories. This often leads to conjuring up hypothetical conflicts in order to make the theories work. This examination will take the opposite approach. Suggestions for the locations of the battles will be based entirely upon linguistics and known wars, with corresponding evidence where it is available. Unfortunately this means that some battles cannot be identified. It is better to admit ignorance than to insist upon the truth of an idea that is actually wrong.

Arthur was said to have fought fourteen important engagements. Twelve are his victories, as listed by Nennius, one is a defeat recorded in the *Eulogy for Geraint* and the last is his defeat and death at Camlann, as mentioned in the *Welsh Annals*. Since medieval manuscripts were copied by hand there are usually different versions of the texts because copyists sometimes made mistakes or deliberate changes. In the case of Nennius' book there are two main versions. The differences in the relative passages are small but important. The quotation that follows is from the manuscript that is in the Harleian library: "The first battle was at the mouth of the river Glein. The second, third, fourth and fifth upon another river which is called Dubglas, in the district of Linnuis. The sixth battle upon the river which is called Bassas. The seventh battle was in the Caldonian Wood, that is Cat Coit Calidon. The eighth battle was in fort Guinnion in which Arthur carried the image of St. Mary, ever virgin, on his shoulders and that day the pagans were turned to flight and a great slaughter was upon them through the virtue of Our Lord, Jesus Christ and through the virtue of St. Mary the Virgin, his mother. The ninth battle was waged in the City of the Legion. The tenth battle he fought on the shore of the river that is called Tribruit. The eleventh battle took place on the mountain Breguoin. The twelfth battle was on Mount Badon, in which nine hundred and sixty men fell in one day from one attack by Arthur, and no one overthrew them except himself alone. And in all the battles he was the victor."[66]

Several points should be made before examining the battles themselves. It is generally agreed by linguists that the list originated as a poem, so not everything in it should be taken literally. Arthur could not very well have carried an image of Mary on his shoulders during the Battle of Guinnion. It should also be pointed out that according to the *Welsh Annals*, Arthur carried the "Cross of our Lord Jesus Christ" at Badon. Most scholars believe that the original meaning must have been that the image was on his shield. Warriors were often said to have slung their shields on their shoulders. Equally impossible is the idea that he killed nine hundred and sixty men all by himself. But this is common medieval exaggeration. There is an eleventh century account that states that William the Conqueror commanded fifty thousand men at the Battle of Hastings. But the battlefield is too small, both armies added together could not have amounted to more than about twenty thousand at the most, and many historians believe that estimate is too high. Exaggerating numbers was a common part of medieval propaganda.

Moving to the battles themselves, the first was along the river Glien. *Glien* means pure or clean. Linguistically the best guess for the river Glien is the River Glen in Lincolnshire, but other rivers are possible. When the Anglo-Saxons conquered territories, they sometimes changed the names, so the modern name may be quite different. The second through fifth were all on the river Dubglas in Linnuis. *Dubglas* means blue-black and like glien it could apply to several rivers. Most investigators agree that Linnuis means the area around Lincoln. This also places it in the modern county of Lincolnshire. The Romans called Lincoln *Lindum* and the Anglo-Saxons called the whole district *Lindisse*, which later became Lindsey. Archeology indicates that Anglo-Saxons settlements in Lindsey were abandoned in the 490's, which would be consistent with the area being unsafe because of heavy fighting. The battles need not have been fought in the same

---

66 *Historia Brittonum*, 50.

place, merely somewhere along the banks of the same river. They may not have been fought one after the other. It is possible that the poet grouped them together for convenience. The best candidate for the Dubglas is the Witham.

Battle number seven in the Caldonian forest took place somewhere in or just south of the northern kingdom of Strathclyde. The List is written in Latin, but this entry is repeated in Old Welsh. *Cat* means "battle" and Coit Celidon referred to the region to the north of Carlisle. Carlisle is now in England, but at that time it was in British territory. The big question here is who was he fighting? It was almost certainly the Strathclyders themselves. If the tradition of the rebellion of Gildas' family is genuine then this was almost certainly the battle in which they were defeated and deposed. Gildas' family ruled Strathclyde.

The site of the ninth conflict was the City of the Legion. Early Welsh sources call two places City of the Legion: Chester and Caerleon. Some manuscripts specify Caerleon, but both were important military centres in Roman times. The XX Legion had its headquarters at Chester and the II was quartered at Caerleon. A third alternative is York, headquarters of the VI Legion. No one except Geoffrey of Monmouth ever called York "City of the Legion" and he is not reliable. Since the site of the battle cannot be ascertained, then no firm conclusions can be reached. If York is meant, then the enemy was the Anglo-Saxons. If it was either of the other two, then the most likely enemies were the Irish or an unknown rebellion by a local British ruler.

No one has ever come up with a likely candidate for Bassas, although there have been several attempts, none are convincing. It has been suggested that Guinnion was Vinovia, which is near the Antonine Wall in Scotland. The *Black Book of Carmarthan* contains a poem about a battle Arthur fought at Tryvrwyd, near the Firth of Forth. It is generally agreed that Tryvrwyd is probably an alternate form of Tribuit, in which case the enemy would have been the Picts. Breguoin is another place that cannot be identified with any certainty, but it was most likely in the north since Urien of Rheged fought a battle there and he was based in the north. An alternate version does not have Breguoin it has Mt. Agned instead. It has been suggested that they are the same place, but the evidence is inconclusive. According to Geoffrey of Monmouth Mt. Agned was Edinburgh. The *Triads* also mention a battle at Eidyn, which is definitely Edinburgh.

In order to achieve peace each of the foreign enemies would have to have suffered a major military defeat. The Britons were fighting on three fronts at the same time and the Anglo-Saxons were the main enemies and therefore most of the military would have been deployed in the east. Furthermore the lands of the Picts were mountainous and mountains favour the defender. The Britons are not likely to have launched a major offensive against them, but to have defended against a major Pictish offensive. The question that must be answered is: what was the most likely target for a Pictish attack? The answer is obvious-Edinburgh was by far the largest British town anywhere near the Pictish border. If Geoffrey is right then Mount Agned is the same place then Arthur's battle was on the site that is now called Arthur's Seat. The identification of these places is highly speculative and there is not enough evidence to be certain.

Badon is the only battle definitely confirmed by independent written sources. Gildas wrote that he was born the same year that the "siege of Mount Badon" took place. He also confirmed that it was a major victory for the Britons. The Anglo-Saxons were so badly beaten that they could not seriously threaten the Britons again for over half a century. The *Welsh Annals* date Arthur's victory there to 517, but that date is contradicted by what is known of the life of Gildas and should be pushed back to roughly 500. The *Annals* also record a second Battle of Badon that took place in 665. Unfortunately no details of this conflict were included. One theory states that Badon must have been in an area that bordered the Anglo-Saxon lands in the late fifth century but was still held by the Britons in the mid-seventh. Supporters of this theory usually choose either Badbury or Banbury as the site of Badon. Of the two, Badbury is more likely, not only because its name is closer to that used by Welsh records, but also because it had the more impressive defensive works, making it a more strategic location. Unfortunately for supporters of this idea, it is contradicted by linguistics. Both names are Old English, not late Brythonic. The suffix "bury" is Saxon dialect and it means fort. The exact translation of Banbury is disputed, but Badbury means "Badda's Fort." As Badda is an Old English name, it is impossible that it could be the origin of Badon.

The argument that Badon must have been in an area that was along the border in both the early sixth and mid-seventh centuries is flawed. Armies of the period were relatively small. They did not advance along wide fronts the way armies would in later centuries. A force could actually penetrate very deep into enemy territory before it met with any serious resistance. Border areas were certainly the most vulnerable, but few places in the lowlands were truly safe. For example, in the 630's Cadwallon of Gwynedd ravaged all of Northumbria, even capturing York. In the Arthurian period the Anglo-Saxons enjoyed complete naval superiority. Just like the Vikings of later centuries, they could have sailed anywhere around the coast or up the navigable rivers to locations deep inland. The only areas that were relatively safe were the large walled towns, as the Anglo-Saxons were not very skilled at sieges, and they tended to avoid these places until the second half of the sixth century, when the Britons had been ravaged by plague and did not have enough men to man the walls.

A fort on a hilltop would command the countryside for miles around and an enemy could be intimidated into abandoning an entire region if they lost control of such a strategic position. The fact that the two battles of Badon were over 160 years apart argues against a border area and suggests that the first battle was something of a gamble, an attempt to grab as much land as possible with as little fighting as possible. It failed and the Anglo-Saxons were not in a position to make another attempt until much later. If Badon was on the border they could have attacked it again much sooner. The reference to the second battle is of no help in determining its location. Since that is the case then other information must be used to solve the mystery.

More than one historian has pointed out a coincidence between the probable date of Badon and the death of an important Anglo-Saxon king. Under the year 829 in the *Anglo-Saxon*

Chronicle there is a list of the bretwaldas. The first name on the list is Aelle of Sussex who is recorded as having founded his kingdom in 477. The last action he is known to have taken was in 491. That year he and his son Cyssa were reported to have engineered the massacre of the Britons defending the old Roman fort of Anderida near Pevensey on the south coast. There was no further mention of Aelle or his deeds. In fact there was no further mention of Sussex until the year 607. How could the land have gone from producing the first Anglo-Saxon high king to being a political nonentity virtually overnight? The best answer is a major Anglo-Saxon defeat in which Aelle and a sizable portion of his army perished. This would place Badon in the south; a conclusion that is supported by the fact that Peter Berresford Ellis found evidence that Oisc of Kent was also at the battle. Depending upon the source, Oisc was either the son or grandson of Hengest.

Historians have pointed out that Sussex was actually too small and weak to dominate the other Anglo-Saxon kingdoms, so it has been suggested that Aelle was chosen in some way. The next questions would be why and how? The late fifth and early sixth centuries provide two examples of Germanic rulers being chosen overlords of different groups. This was mentioned in the second chapter, but now needs to be looked at again in slightly more detail. Clovis was chosen *brytwalda* of the Franks in 496 and Theodoric was made ruler of all the Goths some time around 509. In both cases they were picked for military reasons. The Alemanni attacked the Ripuarian Franks. They placed themselves under the protection of Clovis, ruler of the Salian Franks. But the Salians were the smaller of the two groups, so the parallel with Aelle is obvious. Clovis had already established a reputation as a good military commander, so he was chosen for his military abilities, not the size of his armies. After this he became involved in a civil war among the Burgundians. His wife was a Burgundian princess and the leaders of the opposing factions were her uncles. Clovis withdrew after receiving a promise from both men that whoever won the victor would accept him as overlord. They did this because both sides were afraid that Clovis would use the intervention in the civil war as an excuse to conquer Burgundy. Clovis then attacked the Visigoths. The pattern repeated. The Visigoths submitted to Theodoric of the Ostrogoths. In both cases the men were chosen to deal with a specific threat. Clovis had to deal with the threat posed by the Alemanni and Theodoric to the threat posed by Clovis. It is reasonable to assume that Aelle was also chosen to deal with a specific threat, and a good guess is that it was the threat posed by Arthur.

The best guess as to the location of the battle is Bath. Badon was fought on a mount. To the northeast of Bath lies a large hill called Little Solsbury Hill. There was a fort at its summit during the Arthurian period, confirming that it could have been the site of a siege. Furthermore Geoffrey of Monmouth states that Arthur won an important victory on a hill outside Bath. Both the chronology of the narrative and the importance Geoffrey placed upon the battle indicate that he was talking about Badon.[67] The evidence from the text on the wonders of Britain has already

---

67 *History of the Kings of Britain*, ix.4.

been mentioned. To repeat the information, the passage refers to a "hot lake, where the baths of Badon are, in the country of the Hwicce." Any mention of a hot lake in Britain automatically leads to thoughts of Bath and the mention of the Hwicce clarifies the situation beyond doubt. This territory included what are now Worcester, Gloucestershire and part of Avon, where Bath is located. The author made one mistake. In his day Bath was actually in Wessex and Hwicce was a Mercian sub-kingdom but charters indicate that it had been in Hwicce territory earlier. Bath is the only place anywhere near the Hwicce (the same name applies to both the people and their land) that fits the description of having a hot lake. Bath as the location for Badon also makes sense from a military point of view.

Under the date of 501 in the *Anglo-Saxon Chronicle* there is an entry boasting of a victory at Portsmouth. As was already mentioned, this corresponds to Arthur's defeat as recorded by the *Eulogy*. If the Anglo-Saxons held Portsmouth on the south coast and Bristol on the Bristol Channel then Devon and Cornwall would have been cut off from the rest of Britain. Bath is roughly midway between the two and control of its fort would have been essential for the plan to work. The *Chronicle* says a man named Port won the battle, but this was not a name and was clearly taken from Portsmouth itself. The reconstruction suggested here (and it is only speculation) is that Aelle sailed to Portsmouth, won the battle and then struck northward (actually northwestward) for Bath, intending to head for Bristol after he had taken the fort. He was stopped and decisively defeated at Bath.

Although Bath is the most likely candidate for Badon, it is not the only one. Of the other possibilities the only other one that is worth mentioning is Mynydd Baedon in Glamorganshire in southeast Wales. Two large burial mounds attest to the fact that a battle was fought there some time in its long history. However it would take an archaeological excavation to determine if the conflict dated from the right period and at present no such excavation is even in the planning stage.

The only battle site left is Camlann. It was first named in the *Welsh Annals*, which state that both Arthur and Medraut died there. It is also listed in the Welsh *Triads* as one of the "Three Futile Battles of the Island of Britain" and again under the "Three Unfortunate Councils of Britain." On the border between Powys and Gwynedd there is a field called Camlan. This would be consistent with the ideas suggested in the previous chapter that Arthur was a Cornovii (Powys was their heartland) and that he was killed while trying to deal with a rebellion launched by Maelgwyn of Gwynedd. Other theories have placed the battle at the Camel River near Camelford in Cornwall, at Cam near Cadbury and at the old Roman fort at Birdoswald near Hadrian's Wall. In Old Welsh Birdoswald was called Camboglanna. Without any information on the course of the war itself it is impossible to draw any firm conclusions. The main point to be learned from this battle tour is that Arthur's career took him to a great many places around Britain. Since so many cannot be identified it also underlines one of the problems with the source material. Even when sources record accurate information it is not always possible to decipher what it means.

There are many places associated with Arthur that are not battlefields. An examination of them moves in the opposite direction from the one taken thus far. These places are easy to locate on a map, but the connection to the hero is not necessarily clear. This tour begins at an unlikely place-Modena, Italy. On the northern portal of the city's cathedral there is an archway with a most interesting carving. It depicts a number of people whose names are inscribed near them. A woman called Winlogee (Guenevere) is a prisoner in a castle. The castle is at the centre of the carving. To its left three men are riding to rescue her. The first is unnamed. The second is called Isdernus (Yder) and the third is Artus de Bretania (Arthur of Britain). A man called Burmaltus (Durmart) is threatening Artus with an axe. To the right of the castle a man named Mardoc (Marrok or Mordred) is standing, holding a pole, while Carrado (Caradoc) rides out to fight Galvagin (Gawain), Galvarium (Galeron) and Che (Kay).

The scene is obviously taken from a story about King Arthur and his knights rescuing Guenevere. There are several interesting features. The first is that all of the names on the carving are in the Breton forms. The names given in parentheses here are the more familiar forms found in the Romances. The second point is the date when the carving was created. It was completed *c*1120-'40. Geoffrey of Monmouth's *History of the Kings of Britain*, the oldest known important Arthurian work written for a non Britano-Gaelic audience was completed *c*1136. This means that even as Geoffrey was writing, Arthurian stories had already reached Italy. Since the names are Breton the story could not have been known in the area for very long. It they had the names would have been rendered in a way more pleasing to an Italian ear. This means that for an explanation as to why Arthurian legends should have reached that far south one need look no further back than the late eleventh and early twelfth centuries.

In the eleventh century Italy was a battleground for many peoples. Both the Arabs and the rulers of the Byzantine Empire (which was actually the remnant of the Eastern Roman Empire) wished to claim it as their own. The feudal system was very weak in Italy, but it was the backbone of medieval armies. This meant that the peninsula had difficulty in looking after its own military needs and relied heavily on foreign mercenaries. In this case the Italians called for help from the greatest military power in Western Europe-the French duchy of Normandy. Normandy bordered Brittany to the east. John Morris believed that Brittany itself was part of Arthur's realm, which was possible. Arthur was often called "king of all the Britons" and in the sixth century that would have included the Breton. Breton tales certainly circulated in Normandy and other areas of northern France, so the Normans who travelled to Italy must have known them. From them the tales passed to the Italians and an episode from one story was carved into the Modena Archivolt.

The Normans also introduced the Arthurian legends to England. Researchers often assume that the English knew all about Arthur, but there is no evidence that this is true. Despite the fact that the two peoples were neighbours for hundreds of years the English and Welsh tried to ignore each other except when they were killing each other. The Anglo-Saxons recorded no information about their defeats in the late fifth century and denied the existence of the period of peace. The

Anglo-Saxon Chronicle records no defeats in this period and claims victories over the Britons in 501, 508, 514 and 519. Even if the timing for Badon provided by Gildas is rejected in favour of 517 as recorded in the *Welsh Annals*, clearly at least one of these battles has the wrong date. It is quite possible that they all do.

Some modern researchers deny the existence of the peace and accept the dates in the *Chronicle*. With the exception of the Romans virtually no one in Western Europe in this period recorded dates. Most of the surviving dates are guesses made by later researchers and many of those guesses are known to be wrong. For example the *Chronicle* contains two completely different dates for the founding of Wessex-495 and 519. They cannot both be right and it is possible that both are wrong.

Since the Anglo-Saxons did not even admit the existence of the two things Arthur was famous for– defeating them and maintaining the peace-they could not very well have been paying too much attention to him. Why would they? Arthur was a hero of their hated enemies; they would have had no reason to celebrate his accomplishments. Peoples in that time period did not record history as we are used to it. They boasted of their own victories, lamented the deaths of important political and religious leaders, usually only their own leaders and noted unusual natural phenomenon such as plagues, famines, and comets. They recorded no information on the heroes of their enemies, unless they were boasting of killing them. But the Anglo-Saxons did not kill Arthur, so they had no reason to mention him.

Linguistics supports this argument. Many of the names used in the English versions of the legends are in French forms. Guenevere, Lancelot, Camelot, Perceval, and Excalibur are all French. If the English had these stories they would have rendered them into English forms.

As was already mentioned in Britain itself many of the places associated with Arthur are in Cornwall. Natural rock formations in Cornwall bear such names as "Arthur's Bed" and "Arthur's Cup and Saucers," while Camelford has been suggested as the site of the king's last battle, Camlann, or even his capital, Camelot. His other main fortress, Celli Wig, was also located in the county. Two of the most interesting Cornish connections are mentioned in the *Mirabilia*. It is recorded that while hunting the great boar Twrch Trwyth, Arthur's dog, Cabal, left his footprint in a stone called Carn Cabal; if the stone were taken away at night it would magically reappear the next day. The other is the grave of Arthur's son, Anir, which had a strange property in that no matter how many times it was measured no two measurements would ever be the same. Most of these sites are of local interest only and are of little importance to the Arthurian investigator. The reference to Anir is interesting because it contradicts the more usual version of the tales that state that the king had only one child, Mordred.

The next stop is much more significant. It is Glastonbury in Somerset, more specifically the hill, called a tor, not far from the town. For many centuries the place has been associated with Avalon, the location to which Arthur's body was taken after his final battle. Avalon was said to have been located on an island, or in some versions, a hill. Although surrounded by dry land today Glastonbury Tor was not always that way. It is in the middle of a floodplain. Today it is kept drained, but for centuries heavy rains would surround the hill with water several feet deep. This made it both an impressive hill and an island. Some time around the year 1193 a writer named Giraldus Cambrensis (Gerald of Wales) wrote a book called *The Instruction of Princes*, in which he recorded a visit he had made to Glastonbury Abbey, which in those days stood at the top of the tor. While there he was shown Arthur's grave. During the reign of Henry II the abbey had burned down. When reconstruction began, a grave was uncovered and inside was found a cross that bore an inscription in Latin. There are several different versions of the inscription, but the only one based upon a depiction of the cross itself reads:

HIC IACET SEPULTUS INCLYTUS REE ARTHURUS IN INSULA
AVALLONIA CUM UXORE SUA SECUNDA WENNEVERIA.

This means: "Here lie the renowned King Arthur in the island of Avalon with his second wife Guenevere." Most researchers doubt the entire story. They point out that the abbey was in need of money to pay for it's rebuilding. The discovery of the grave of a famous person could have been used as a profitable tourist attraction. Gerald records that the excavation of the grave took place behind a curtain. It is argued that the curtain was erected so that no one could see what the monks were really up to. It has also been speculated that the cross, which has since disappeared, was a forgery. This inscription was not in the style of Latin used in Arthur's time. King Henry II, who paid a visit to the site and was shown the grave, suffered the hoax to continue because he wanted to dispel the myth that Arthur would one-day return to lead the Welsh to victory against the English.

The monks of Glastonbury had a bad habit of making similar claims. They tried to say that both St. Dunstan and St. Patrick were buried at the abbey. In fact Dunstan's grave is in Canterbury Cathedral. Ireland's three greatest saints are all buried together and a rhyme was made to commemorate this fact: Three saints do one grave fill/Patrick, Brigit and Columcille.

It is just possible that the assumption that the grave was that of Arthur was a case of mistaken identity rather than a deliberate forgery. In 1607, before the cross disappeared, a topographer named William Camden produced a detailed drawing of it. Leslie Alcock argued that the shape of the letters in Camden's picture shows that although it does not date to the sixth century, it was not made in the twelfth century either. Medieval forgers were notoriously sloppy in their use of Latin and their styles of lettering. They almost invariably used the types current at their own time. The lettering on the cross was tenth or eleventh century.[68] There is also the little known fact that the abbey went through a major building program in the tenth century. St. Dunstan was abbot of Glastonbury and later became archbishop of Canterbury. He used his position to benefit the abbey. The main building was extended so that it was actually built overtop of part of the original cemetery. The cross could have been made then. There is further evidence against the forgery idea in the fact that the cross stated that Guenevere was Arthur's second wife. In the

---

68 *Arthur's Britain*, pg.78.

twelfth century the idea that Arthur was married only once was already firmly set. The makers of the cross must have followed a different tradition that had either lapsed by the time the discovery was made or was known only locally.

According to the account the coffin was made from a tree trunk. The Britons did bury their dead in trunks of trees in prehistoric times. The tor had sacred associations for the pagan Britons and could very well have been used as a burial site long before the abbey was built there. This suggests that a war leader of the Britons was buried on the tor, apparently with his wife. The monks discovered this grave in the tenth century. At least one of them must have known about Glastonbury's association with Avalon and with Arthur. The dead man was assumed to have been a famous king, the cross was made and the grave was covered over again only to be rediscovered in the twelfth century.

A charitable view of the monks would argue for a mistake, a more skeptical approach would suggest a forgery. A third alternative is that it really was the body of Arthur. Perhaps the tenth century monks knew exactly what they were doing when they made the cross. There is not enough evidence to draw any firm conclusions on the Glastonbury burial.

If it was a hoax, some very important people were taken in by it. In 1191, Henry II's successor, Richard I, gave a sword called Escalibur to Tancred of Sicily. Richard said the sword came from Glastonbury. He would not have misrepresented the sword, which was a gift to a valuable alley and family member (Tancred had married Richard's sister, Joanna). Richard must have believed that it was genuine.

The artifacts found in the grave had a varied history. The monks themselves disposed of the coffin. They transferred the remains to two wooden chests. Edward I and his queen, Eleanor, reburied the chests with great ceremony as a propaganda ploy. Edward conquered Wales and he wished to drive home the idea that the greatest Welsh hero was not only dead, but also buried on English soil, an idea that would weaken resistance to the regime. Tancred of Sicily sent the sword to Jerusalem, where it disappeared during the confusion of the Crusades. No description of the woman's remains was recorded, the other coffin contained the shin bone of a tall man, a skull with several wounds in it, including a large one near the left ear believed to have been caused by the death blow, and a lock of blonde hair judged to have come from a woman. During the Reformation the two chests were dug up again and their contents lost. The abbey was destroyed and has never been rebuilt.

If Glastonbury was not Avalon, Arthur's final resting place in the myths, then where was it? Theories range form Ninsavallan in Cornwall to Sicily to the Far East. Avalon holds a fascination for many theorists who are convinced that it was a real place. But it cannot be pinpointed on a map because it did not really exist. Avalon is Annwn, sometimes spelled Annfwn, the Otherworld from pagan mythology. Even though the Britons converted to Christianity at an early date, many pagan characters and ideas carried on in their folk traditions and Avalon was certainly not the only pagan element to find its way into the Arthurian tales.

It was to Avalon that Arthur's body was taken after his defeat in his last battle, but the entire explanation of the scene is mythic and not realistic. As the king lay wounded he told Bedivere, his last surviving faithful knight, to take Excalibur and throw it into the water. It was not until Arthur was dying that any mention was made that the battle took place anywhere near water. Bedivere could not bring himself to throw away the royal sword. After all it did symbolize the kingship of Britain. He was to make three attempts before he was successful, and even then only after Arthur threatened to kill him if he did not carry out his orders. The number three was considered sacred to the Britano-Gaels. For example the goddess of the land could appear in three forms: a beautiful young maiden, a mature woman or an ugly old hag. When he finally did throw the sword away, a hand reached out of the water, took hold of it and pulled it under the waves. Water held mystical associations for these people. They believed that the land of the dead had to be reached by boat and it was often described as an island, they also made many offerings to water deities in their pagan days. The modern idea of making a wish and throwing a coin into water is derived from this practice. In ancient times they threw more than just coins. Wells and springs have been discovered with many different kinds of items such as statues, jewelry and swords. Such sites were usually associated with healing deities.

It should be pointed out that in Britano-Gaelic mythology there were usually two mystical realms: the Land of the Dead and the Happy Otherworld. Annwn is obviously the second of these. It was a land of healing and plenty where hundreds of years could pass in our world while only days went by in the mystic realm. An example of this idea has already been mentioned in the first chapter when discussing *Branwen Daughter of Llyr*. After the raid upon Ireland the warriors spent eighty years there with the magic severed head of Bran. This idea is an obvious connection to the legend that Arthur is still alive and will one day return. The only way that he could remain alive for centuries is if he was taken to Annwn.

When the knight returned to the place where he had left the king he found Arthur gone. The king was by that time on a ship, attended by three queens. One of the queens was said to be Morgan le Fay. Morgan was derived from the Morrigan, one of the pagan goddesses of war. In fact all three may have been she as the Morrigan had three aspects and could appear in three different guises at the same time. As a war goddess she was associated with the Otherworld. Taken as a literal narrative the sudden appearance of the ship makes no sense. How could it have arrived without Bedivere seeing it? He was just at the shore and should have had an excellent view of it as it came into land. Yet he knew nothing of the vessel until he discovered that Arthur was missing. The tale is obviously mythic. The hero was wounded, an offering was made to a goddess to ensure Arthur's safe passage to the Otherworld, the offering was accepted and the goddess came in all three of her guises to guide him on his journey.

There is other evidence to suggest that Avalon is Annwn. According to Geoffrey of Monmouth the name is derived from the Welsh word *aval* which means "apple." In Welsh tales it is often called *Ynys Avallach*, "Isle of Apples." In Irish tradition the home of the sea god Manannan is often connected with the Otherworld and said to be *ablach*, "rich in apple trees." Manannan's home was said to be the Isle of Man, which lies between Scotland and Ireland. In the *Spoils of Annwn*'s alternate version, *Branwen Daughter of Llyr*, Ireland replaces Annwn as the scene of the action. The Otherworld is a sacred island, and Glastonbury Tor was an island sacred to the pagan Britons, and after the conversions an abbey was built on it, making it sacred to the Christians. So which one is Avalon? The answer is every one of them, and none of them. Mystical geography does not follow the same rules as actual geography. In Norse mythology there was a great ash tree called *Yggdrasill*, the world tree. One of its great roots was in Asgard, the realm of the gods, another was in Jotunheim, the land of the giants, and the third was in Niflheim, the land of the dead. At the same time the trunk was in Asgard. This is physically impossible, but that did not matter, ancient mythologies were not overly concerned with physical possibilities, they dealt with religious mysteries.

There are other real locations in Britain that have legendary associations. The Romances are full of fictitious places with names like the Castle of the Four Stones and the Dolorous Tower. A charter drawn up in 1142 referred to a real place as the Castle of Maidens. That place was Edinburgh, though why the ancient capital of Manu Gododdin and the modern capital of Scotland was given that name is impossible to say. But it does suggest that some of these other colourfully named locations may have been associated with real places.

The last stop is not found on any map. Many traditions refer to the real site of Arthur's grave, but none give any easily identifiable location and several contradict each other. Any attempt to locate it immediately bogs down in a quagmire of contested translations and competing theories. Many researchers do not even mention it, except to say that it was not Glastonbury. The few who do give it any thought always come up with ingenious methods for fitting some chosen site into their own ideas. Those who believe he was mythical sometimes use this problem as evidence that he never existed. The fact is that the graves of almost all of the famous individuals from this period are long lost. Dynasties often chose one particular area to bury their dead and when that place can be identified some of the graves of specific rulers can also be identified. But since it is impossible to even find all of the kingdoms on a map, it is certainly not possible to find all of their royal burial plots. It may have been somewhere in Cornwall, but since it is not generally known that this was a kingdom (kingdom here being used in the sense that it was ruled by a king, not in the sense of an independent monarchic state), no one has even started to look for the final resting place of its kings.

Having completed a tour of Arthurian geography what remains are the stories themselves. These are rich in characters and objects that need to be examined if the figure of Arthur is to be fully understood. After all, the image most people have of him has much more to do with works of fiction written from the twelfth century onward than with a sixth century king. The history lesson is finally over. It is time to enter the realm of myth, legend and Romance.

Chapter VII

THE COURT

M OST SCHOLARS agree that there is a certain amount of myth and legend in the story of Arthur as we have it today. The previous chapters have shown that there is also a certain amount of history in it as well. This is only natural. The level of literacy among the Britons of Arthur's day was very low by modern standards. It was in fact one of the darkest periods of the Dark Ages. Written works were not read by individuals but were performed in front of audiences in order to compensate for the fact that most people could not read. Even when information was written down it was often destroyed in the wars of the period. Most books were stored in monasteries, which were isolated to keep their inmates away from the temptations of the world. Those with the best libraries were the largest and wealthiest because secular rulers granted them gifts in exchange for prayers to help the donor's souls get into heaven. This meant that the monasteries were prime targets for war bands that took advantage of their isolation to plunder their wealth.

Storytellers and bards passed on much Arthurian material orally. When a story is transmitted verbally alterations are almost always made to it in order to turn it into a livelier tale. Even when it is written down succeeding generations can make changes to it. Tales of King Arthur went through a series of convoluted developments. It should be remembered that by the time these tales were written down the Welsh had been Christian for approximately eight hundred years. Stories that had a religious significance in the pagan days were retold only for their value as entertainment. Consequently it was no longer important to make distinctions between different characters that had similar attributes. Sometimes the same character that was treated differently in various stories was split into two or more characters in order to reconcile the variants.

The Arthurian sources can be divided into two main categories: the Welsh *Triads* and the non-Britano-Gaelic accounts. The Welsh sources are contained in the grandly named Four Ancient Books of Wales. They are not ancient in the sense of when they were written, but in the sense that they record oral traditions that date back to ancient times. They are *The White Book of Rhydderch* (*c*1300-'25), *The Black Book of Carmarthen* (12th century), *The Book of Aneirin* and *The Book of Taliesin* (possibly 14th century). There is also *The Red Book of Hergest* (c1400), which is essentially a copy of *The White Book* with a few additions. These sources contain not only poems and stories but also the *Triads of Britain*. Approximately one hundred Triads contain references to Arthur.

Of the second group, the most numerous were the Romances. The Romances were works of fiction written by English, French, German and other Western European authors in the Middle Ages. The earliest surviving examples were composed by the Frenchman Chretien de Troyes in the 1170's. However Chretien himself stated that there were earlier versions of some of the stories, but they have not survived. In the terminology of the time, a Romance was anything written in one of the languages derived from Latin, the language of the Romans. More broadly it was anything written in any Western European language other than Latin. For example, the *Romance of the Rose* was a work of philosophy, but it was called a Romance because it was written in Old French. The modern association of romances with love stories was a product of the early twentieth century. Many of the authors of the earliest Romances drew on oral traditions, especially from Brittany. These sources are now lost to us as there is virtually no documentation from early medieval Brittany at all. The authors rewrote the tales to suit their audiences and it is not always easy to distinguish the original material from elements that were added later. It should be remembered that by the twelfth century the Britano-Gaelic storytellers themselves did not understand all of the references in the tales. Aside form the Romances there were also works that claimed to be history, like the *Roman de Brute* written by Wace in 1155. There are also short poems such as the *Lais* composed by Marie de France in the late twelfth century. Sometimes these contain material that is not found elsewhere that was taken from both oral sources and written works that are now lost to us.

A researcher is faced with problems not only because of the varied and often obscure nature of the sources, but also because of the nomenclature. The names of the characters in the Romances are French versions of Breton or Welsh originals, while in the surviving material written by the Britano-Gaels themselves the names are either Irish or Welsh. This means that except in cases where the Romances follow the originals very closely, it is often difficult to identify the characters from one source to another. The easiest way to examine the myths and legends in the Arthurian Cycle is to tell the story of the king as it is generally accepted and try to discover the origins of the different details.

The story began on a windswept hill many years before the birth of the hero. Vortigern was attempting to build a castle. Every time construction got well under way the structure toppled over. Of course the king was not very pleased by this and he demanded that his wise men find a way to put a stop to it. They told him that a boy whose mother was still a virgin must be found. The boy could then be sacrificed and his blood allowed to soak into the soil. That would permit construction to continue. After a search was made of the whole country a child was finally found who had a mother but no earthly father. The woman claimed that a man came to her in a dream one night and the next morning she discovered she was pregnant. The boy was taken to the hilltop to be sacrificed. Unafraid the child told the king that killing him would not solve his problem. He could reveal the truth but only if the king promised that if everything the boy said was true he would be set free. Vortigern agreed. The child said that if the king's men were to dig a deep hole they would find an underground lake. At the bottom of the lake would be two hollow stones and inside the stones they would find two dragons. Vortigern's men did as the boy directed and everything happened just as he said it would. As soon as the stones were cracked open the two dragons burst out and began fighting one another. One of the beasts was red and the other was white. At first the white one had the upper hand, but eventually the red one was triumphant and drove off his opponent. The boy interpreted the dragons to represent the two races of Britain. The red was the British and the white was the Saxons. At first the Saxons would rule the land, but after many years a great British hero, the boar of Cornwall, would arise and defeat the invaders and drive them from the island. The boy then revealed that his name was Merlin and he proceeded to make a large number of predictions, often of an obscure nature.

The dragons in the tale were the national symbols of the Welsh and the English in the early Middle Ages. It has been suggested that the red dragon of Wales originated with this story, but this is not true. Its exact origin is obscure. The red dragon as it now appears on the Welsh flag is definitely derived from the symbol of the house of Gwynedd. On the other hand the fact that pendragon may have originated as a term or title for rulers of the fifth and sixth century suggests that it may already have been the symbol of the nation as well as that particular province. The reason the design of the dragon used by Gwynedd was so important was a product of the subsequent history of the Britons. After the Anglo-Saxons gained the upper hand the territories of the Britons became divided into three parts: Cornwall, Wales and Strathclyde. It was impossible to maintain unity between these places, but it proved difficult to do so even within Wales itself. The long history of political rivalry in Wales throughout the succeeding centuries falls outside the scope of this work. Suffice it to say that Gwynedd had the upper hand more often than any of the other regions and eventually its symbol came to represent all of Wales.

The white dragon and its origins are often forgotten since the English stopped using the symbol in the eleventh century. As with so many things in Western Europe in the period, it was copied from the Romans. In AD175 the emperor Marcus Aurelius hired 8,000 Sarmatians as mercenaries for the Roman army. These people had originated on the steppes of Asia and were great horsemen. They had invaded Eastern Europe and when the Romans encountered them they were along the Danube. The Sarmatians had a banner that the Romans called the *draconarius*. It was in the shape of an oriental dragon with its mouth open. It was fitted with a noisemaker so that when the wind passed through it, it sounded like a roaring beast. This made a great impression on the Romans who adopted the banner for other units, including the Imperial Guard. The noise of the banners was used to herald the arrival of the emperor. It was because of this connection that the Britons later used the word dragon as a synonym for prince and was the origin of the title pendragon. In the centuries following the collapse of the Empire dragons were common symbols. The personal banner of Charlemagne, for example, was in the shape of the beast. Over the centuries the symbol began to fall out of fashion. In England this happened because of the Norman Conquest in 1066. A white dragon banner was carried to the Battle of Hastings, but the Normans won the battle and the Norman symbol was two (later three) lions.[69] The Crusades began in the late eleventh century and the crusaders venerated warrior saints. Saint George became popular and the story of how he slew a dragon was adopted as a symbol of the crusaders slaying the enemies of the Church. Because of this connection dragons began to be associated with the devil and became less popular symbols in Europe, but they did still appear on some coats-of-arms.

In ancient times Europeans believed that there were two distinct types of dragons. The good had bodies like lions, but covered in scales, and had long legs. Their blood had curative powers and dragon fat mixed with honey was believed to cure blindness. Evil dragons had serpentine bodies and either short legs or no legs at all. The English often called this second variety "great worms." A great many people attribute the dragon symbolism in Britain to the Sarmatians. A contingent was stationed on the island in the third century and some of their symbolism did influence the natives, but this connection has been taken too far. The style of dragon used by the Sarmatians would have been evil by European iconography, but the Welsh dragon was clearly good. The Britons may have gotten the basic idea from the steppe nomads, but they adapted it to suit their own purposes.

As for the figure of Merlin himself, it is often argued that he was derived from a pagan god. This is a natural assumption since he is now thought of as a powerful wizard. In his earliest appearances, however, his power was limited to predicting the future. The modern discoverer of the origins of Merlin was Count Nikolai Tolstoy, a direct descendant of Leo Tolstoy. In the late sixth century there was a bard at the court of King Gwenddolau, whose capital was Carlisle This bard was known by several different names including Lailoken and Myrddin Wilt (Merlin the Wild), Merddin Caledonius and Merddin son of Madoc Morvryn. In 573 he convinced his lord to take up arms against their neighbours. This plan led to a disastrous defeat at Arfdeydd (modern Arthuret, just south of Hadrian's Wall). Not only Gwenddolau but also Lailoken's beloved nephew were both killed in the battle. The guilt for having caused this disaster was said to have driven him mad. He took to living in a forest and reciting prophecies to anyone who happened by. There is a very ancient and widespread belief in the concept of divine madness. This meant that certain insane people had been granted a blessing from heaven, which allowed them to see the future. Lailoken was considered to have had divine madness and was highly respected by the Britons. He is clearly the original Merlin with a different name. Lailoken does not seem to have been a name at all, but a term that meant "twin brother." Traditions about the

---

69　Many researchers call them leopards, however there are no leopards in English heraldry. To be precise they are lions passant guardant, which means they are walking on all fours but facing the viewer. Two lions were used until the reign of Richard I "the Lionheart" (r.1189-'99) who added a third because he thought it looked better.

figure state that he had a sister named Ganieda or Gwenddydd who was married to Rydderch Hael (the Generous) of Strathclyde. It was their son who was the bard's favorite nephew. She was sometimes identified as Lailoken's twin.

The problem is that Merlin is not a name either. The original is pronounced myrthin and it means "sea-man." It was a term for a person who predicts the future, a prophet. The Britano-Gaels had a great many mystical associations with the sea and believed it could be a powerful source of magic. There were several merlins in the traditions. The *Triads* record an entry for the "Three Baptismal Bards" whose names were Merddin Emrys, Taliesin and Merddin, son of Madoc Morvryn. Although Tolstoy's identification of Myrddin Wilt as the famous Merlin is widely accepted (at least by those who do not believe that Merlin was a god), there is good evidence that he is actually an amalgam of at least two prophets. In his book *Journey through Wales*, Gerald of Wales stated that Geoffrey of Monmouth had merged two myrddin figures. One was named Sylvester and was born in what is now southern Scotland. From Gerald's description it is clear that this was Lailoken. Since neither Merlin nor Lailoken are names, Gerald seems to be the only author to record what he was really called. Gerald said the second figure was called Ambrosius and lived in the time of Vortigern.

These comments are sometimes ignored because the author often got his facts muddled and because people want there to have been only one Merlin. But the only writer to contradict him is Geoffrey of Monmouth, who was not exactly reliable either. In this case Gerald was right. The second man he was referring to was obviously Ambrosius Aurelianus. The very story of the meeting with Vortigern proves that Ambrosius was involved. The oldest surviving version of the tale is not found in Geoffrey's book at all. It is in Nennius.[70] In that version the child is not called Merlin, he is called Ambrose and there is a note to say that his Welsh name was Emrys Wledig. The story is set at Dynus Emrys (Fort Ambrosius) a real site on Mount Snowden.[71] In fact the story is about that fort and the prophecy of a coming hero was referring to the adult Ambrosius. Geoffrey himself confirmed the true identity of the character. He twice referred to Merlin as Ambrosius and both times it was during the meeting with Vortigern.[72] Then there is the *Triad* of the baptismal bards. The first is Merddin Emrys, in other words Merlin Ambrosius.

Geoffrey cut off the original ending of the story. In fact in his version the story has no ending. He introduces the concept that Merlin can see the future and then produces a long list of predictions. When the narration picks up again it has moved away from the attempts to

---

70 *Historia Brittonum*, 39-42.

71 This is actually more evidence that Britain had a central government. Ambrosius built the original fort, which is why it was named after him. But Snowdonia was in Gwynedd. If it were really an independent kingdom the Ambrsius would not have had the right to build a fortress there. He might have had the authority to order the local king to build one, but it would not have belonged to the pendragon, it would have belonged to the king of Gwynedd.

72 *History of the Kings of Britain*, vi. 19.

build a castle without explaining what happened. Geoffrey had two heroes, Merlin and Arthur. Ambrosius made the original predictions about his own future. Geoffrey deliberately changed the predictions to refer to Arthur. This meant that he had to move the incident to late in Vortigern's reign. When his narration picked up after the prophecies it recounted the rebellion of Ambrosius and Vortigern's downfall. Even if he recognized that there were two different Merlins, he had to amalgamate them for the purposes of his narration or else he would have had a child Ambrosius confronting Vortigern and an adult Ambrosius plotting the king's overthrow at the same time.

Arthur's Merlin is based upon at least two people who really lived-one before the Arthurian period and the other after it. Even when the tales were taken from history, the information was not always contemporaneous. This is an example of the Arthurian whirlpool sucking in everything from the traditions of the Welsh.

To return to the story, after he had taken power Ambrosius wished to establish a monument to the men who had been massacred by the Saxons at Vortigern's failed peace talks. Merlin suggested that they bring the Giant's Dance (Stonehenge) from Ireland and erect it on the site of the tragedy. In the earliest versions of the tale Ambrosius sent his brother, Uther Pendragon, to take it from the Irish. Later accounts claim that Merlin used his magic to bring it across the sea. This is a piece of fancy as Stonehenge has of course always been on its present site and was ancient even before the Britano-Gaels arrived in Britain.

Ambrosius achieved victories against the Saxons for a time, but a political rival poisoned him. Uther Pendragon succeeded him as king. Vortigern and Ambrosius were real people who have already been dealt with. But who was Uther Pendragon? Geoffrey of Monmouth says that he was Ambrosius' brother. We know very little about that king's family, but if he had a brother the man in question would not have been called Uther Pendragon for the very simple reason that it is not a name. In Old Welsh *uther* means "terrible" as in spreading terror, like Ivan the Terrible, and *pendragon* was a term for the supreme ruler and it literally means "head (or chief) prince." It has been stated that Brythonic names were sometimes similar to titles. But not names like this. No Britano-Gaelic name ever incorporated a term like "terrible." They used terms that boasted of royal power such as "World Ruler" (Dumnagaul) or "Over-king" (Vortigern). Next to nothing is recorded of Uther. His only real function is to be Arthur's father. The best conclusion is that in this case it is not a name but an epithet.

There are several possibilities as to the origin of Uther. He appears in written sources in two Welsh tales, the *Dialogue of Glewlwyd Gafaelfawr* and the *Dialogue of Arthur and the Eagle*. In neither one of these is he connected to Arthur. In fact in the second it states that he was the father of someone named Madog. He may simply have been a character in the Welsh tales who was chosen to be Arthur's father because their names were similar. There is also a chance that Arthur himself was Uther.

Although the Britons did not have primogenitor in the Arthurian period they did adopt it later. Medieval audiences would have needed some sort of an explanation as to how Arthur could have inherited the throne from Ambrosius. They may have passed on the legend of the sword-in-the-stone but they had forgotten what it meant. A line that described Arthur as the terror spreading chief prince could easily have provided the name simply by adding the word *mab* Old Welsh for "son of" between the words Arthur and uther. There is a surviving list of kings in a manuscript now called "Jesus College LI" that supports this conclusion. Vortigern is split into two different men, Vortigern the Elder and Vortigern the Younger. This shows that some confusion had arisen as to the fifth and sixth century rulers. Ambrosius is referred to as wledig, which proves that titles were included on the list. Uther and Arthur follow next as separate people.

According to the legends Uther became infatuated with Igerne, wife of the duke of Cornwall, Gorlois or Hoel. These are variant forms of the same name. It was a very popular name in Brittany, Devon and Cornwall. It is possible, but only possible, that this was the real name of Arthur's father. Uther tried to take the duchess from her husband by force. While Hoel was away at the front, Merlin used magic to make Uther look like the duke so that he could sleep with Igerne. He made one stipulation: if a son were born from their union, Merlin would take him and raise him. As they lay together, the real Hoel was killed in battle.

Mystical origins for heroes were common in ancient times. This story is very similar to the story of the origins of Alexander the Great, except for the insertion of the idea that someone else raised the child. The Nennius version of the child confronting Vortigern proves that a similar tale was invented for Ambrosius Aurelianus, since his mother was a virgin and his father was a spirit. Merlin's taking of the infant Arthur is often overemphasized. To some it is evidence that the characters were mythical. There seems to be no reason for it other than to have the boy raised by the wizard. There is also the fact that infant stealing is common in folktales. To others it suggests that there was a real reason as to why the young Arthur could not be raised at home. Speculation runs rampant about political intrigue and the boy's life being in danger. In fact there is a very simple explanation for this part of the story. In Britano-Gaelic society having royal children raised by other families often strengthened political alliances. Since it was part of the culture it was also part of the legends. Having children raised by foster parents (usually a single parent) was common in their tales. Within the Arthurian stories themselves it happens with Arthur, Lancelot, Gawain, Perceval and Mordred, to name the most famous examples. In other words it might be only a convention, signifying nothing.

Igerne married Uther, but he did not tell her the trick until just before Arthur was born. She had already given birth to three daughters by Hoel: Morgawse, Elaine and Morgan le Fay. Again there is a great deal of speculation about the origin and importance of these women, but the answer is obvious. The third sister is called a fay. Fays were what Western Europeans called pagan goddesses after the conversions to Christianity when they were no longer thought of as goddesses. They did not simply edit these beings out of their stories, but they were altered to strip them of their religious roles. Certain Britano-Gaelic goddesses were believed to be able to take on three forms at once. One such deity was the Morrigan, whose name means the "Phantom Queen." Morgan was the Morrigan and it is likely that the other two sisters were her other forms, a conclusion supported by the fact that Morgawse is a corruption of Morgan. It should be noted that the other sister was sometimes called Morcades, which is another corruption of Morgan. Britano-Gaelic mythology was in no way systematic. Characters often embodied very different, and sometimes even contradictory attributes. This could lead to the same characters being treated very differently depending upon the tale and also to different characters becoming confused with one another. The Morrigan was a war goddess but she could also play a sexual or maternal role in tales. In Irish legend she attempted to seduce Cu Chulainn and she went through a ritual mating with the paternal god, the Daghda (whose name means the "Good God"), while placing one foot on each side of a river. In this case she embodied fertility while he represented protection for the people.

Morgan married Urien, the very same as the pendragon Urien of Rheged. Those who believe that Arthur was mythical often overlook the fact that almost all of the real pendragons were incorporated into the legends.[73] Other traditions state that Modron married Urien. Modron was a maternal goddess who was known in ancient times as Matrona. Her name means "Divine Mother." Some have argued that Morgan was really derived from this goddess. According to this theory her name was changed in Brittany where there were traditions of water fairies called Mari-Morgans. But if Morgan were derived from the Breton word for fairy, then calling her a fay would be rather redundant. Morgan may have absorbed some of the attributes of Modron, a phenomenon that was very common in Britano-Gaelic mythology, but Morgan is derived chiefly from the Morrigan.

After he was taken from his parents Arthur was not actually raised by Merlin himself. His foster father was Ector or Antor. Ector's origins are completely unknown as he seems to have been invented for the Arthurian legends or he may have been some real man whose name did not survive in the sources. Ector had a son, Kay. The character of Kei dates back to very early sources, but he is the son of Kynyr. The name Kei appears, sometimes with different spelling, in Old Welsh works such as Poem XXXI of the *Black Book* and the story of *Culhwch and Olwen*. He is associated with Arthur at an early date and seems to have been one of the first Welsh heroes to be drawn into the Arthurian orbit. What adventures he may have had on his own are unknown. In all of the surviving material he is merely a character in someone else's story.

---

73 Of the seven pendragons known to have existed in the fifth and sixth centuries (including Arthur himself), the only two who do not appear in the Arthurian traditions are the rulers of Gwynedd, Maelgwyn and Rhun. Even they could be there. In Book X of *Le Morte D'Arthur* by Thomas Malory there is an evil knight named Malgrin, which might be a corruption of Maelgwyn. Gwynedd is called Norgales in the Romances, which is a corruption of North Wales. One of its kings was Ryons, which might be Rhun.

Eventually Uther died and there was no king of all the Britons. A competition was arranged to determine the rightful successor. Only the true king could draw a mystic sword from a stone. A great many candidates came from all over Britain to participate, including Kay and Arthur. In modern versions of the story, Arthur was Kay's servant but in the original tales the two were essentially equals. Kay had slightly more authority but only because he was slightly older. There are two popular theories as to the origin of the sword-in-the-stone. The first links it to metallurgy. The blades of iron swords were created by pouring molten iron into a mold consisting of two sections made of stone. Once the iron had cooled, the blade was pulled from the stone. The other links it to the Sarmatians, the nomads hired by the Romans and stationed in Britain. The Sarmatians had a test of strength in which they drove a sword into the ground and took turns trying to pull it out. They also had a symbol of a sword thrust into an anvil and in the oldest surviving version of the tale, which is found in the writings of Robert de Boron in the twelfth century, the sword was in an anvil and it rested on a stone.

Both of these theories concentrate on the props and ignore the plot. The first point to be made is that the Sarmatian argument exaggerates the similarities and ignores the differences. The Sarmatians had no stone, yet it is obvious that the stone was important to the Britons because even when the anvil appeared, they made a point of saying that it rested on a stone. The Arthurian story is not about making a sword or deciding a contest of strength, it is about a man proving himself the rightful king. Stories like this were actually very common in the ancient world. In the Germanic tale called *The Sword of the Volsungs,* the king of the gods, Odin, drove a sword into a living tree called Branstock, The great hero of the people, who was Sigmund, was the only one who could draw it out. A closer parallel is found in Greek mythology. *Theseus and the Minataur* was set long before Athens became a democracy. His mother raised the hero Theseus without him knowing who his father was. He proved his identity as heir to the throne of Athens by moving a special stone that only the rightful heir could move. Underneath he found his father's sandals and sword. This story has much more in common with the Arthurian legend than the Sarmatian practices, but it could not possibly have been influenced by the nomads as the tale was written hundreds of years before they came anywhere near Europe. The Britano-Gaelic aspects of the story have already been mentioned, but the Irish version should be examined a little more closely. As was already mentioned in Irish legend the king of Tara had to pass a series of magical tests. He had to mount the royal chariot without frightening the horses, and then drive the chariot between two standing stones that would magically part to let him pass through. He would then put on a special mantel that was kept by the druids. It would fit perfectly without the need for any alterations. He would then place his hand upon the Stone of Destiny, which would cry out and confirm his legitimacy. The parallels to the sword-in-the-stone are obvious: the need to find the rightful king, the use of magical tests and the fact that stones figured in two of these tests.

A few comments need to be made about the archetype itself. Tests to establish a person's credentials were quite common in ancient tales. Men who grew up far from their natural parents and then returned were common in Britano-Gaelic and Greek legends. The most famous story of this type was *Oedipus Rex*, where the hero ended up killing his father and marrying his own mother precisely because he did not know who they were. Kings and heroes were warriors, so the presence of a sword is not out of place. Stones are more rare. The Stones of Destiny have already been mentioned and it was said that among other things they represented strength. Theseus nicely illustrated this fact since he physically lifted the stone in his story. Physical strength was often used as a symbol for strength of character. The popularity of the sword-in-the-stone is relatively recent in comparison to some of the other elements in the tales. Despite the fact that the sword-in-the-stone first appears in the writings of Robert de Boron in the twelfth century, most medieval writers make no mention of it. The Vulgate Cycle (1215-'30) was the first attempt to collect all of the Arthurian stories into one connected narrative. It originally consisted of three books: *Lancelot*, *Queste del San Graal* and *Mort Artu*. Some time after these were completed two further works were written to fill in certain gaps. These were *Estoire del Saint Graal* and *Estoire de Merlin*. The Vulgate Cycle actually uses the sword episode twice, once in *Merlin* and once in *Queste del San Graal*. In the *Queste* it is Galahad who draws the sword. It does not signify that he is to be king it identifies him as the Grail Knight.

The sword that Arthur took was called Excalibur. This is a later addition; originally Excalibur was a completely different weapon. Not everyone accepted Arthur as king and wars against foreign enemies continued. Arthur's sword was broken in combat and Merlin took him to a lake in a wild section of the country. There he saw a woman emerge from under the water. She carried a sword, which she presented to the king. It was this blade that was Excalibur. In Old French "ex" or "esc" was added to the name of something to show that it was important. Geoffrey of Monmouth called it Caliburnus. In other sources it is named Caledfwlch or Calibor. These are variant forms of Caladbolg, the sword carried by Cu Chulainn in Irish traditions. The Welsh and Irish were similar people who lived close together so it is not surprising that similar objects appear in the traditions of both peoples. Excalibur was made in Avalon, which has already been identified as the Otherworld, further evidence that the weapon is mythic. It belonged to the Lady of the Lake who gave it to Arthur who had it returned to her at his death.

The Lady of the Lake herself is one of the more important "fairies" or goddesses who populate the Arthurian landscape. She is responsible for Lancelot's upbringing; she falls in love with Merlin and uses his own magic to imprison him so that he would stay with her forever. She is not usually named in the tales but when she is her name is variously given as Nimiane, Niniane, Niviene and Viviane. A Lady of the Lake is killed by the knight Balin, but this may be a different person from Viviane. In one version of the Lancelot tale the Lady also raises a knight named Mabuz. Mabuz has been identified as the god Mabon. Mabon's mother was Modron, which means that in at least one tale the Lady of the Lake was derived from the maternal goddess.

Since there seems to have been more than one Lady of the Lake it is possible that this title was not intended to represent a single goddess but rather it was a generic term that could be applied to any goddess. In Irish stories a *sidh* (pronounced "shee") was a hill or mound that contained the dwelling of a god or goddess. A common term for a goddess was "Lady of the Sidh," or banshee. In folktales the banshee acted as a harbinger of death, warning people by means of the famous "banshee wail." Goddesses sometimes performed similar tasks in the pagan mythology. It was said that on the eve of battle one of the war goddesses could be seen on the banks of a river washing the bloody clothes of those who were to die that day. A misunderstanding of the banshees' role led to them being depicted as monsters in modern literature because of their associations with death. Two of the most sacred natural phenomenon among the Britano-Gaels was hills and bodies of water. While divine beings could be associated with either of these in both Ireland and Wales, the Irish tended to prefer the *sidh* mounds in their tales while Welsh stories usually placed the dwellings of deities on islands or even under water. It is possible that Lady of the Lake was the Welsh equivalent of Lady of the Sidh.

After being chosen king, Arthur decided to marry. His bride was the daughter of Leodegrance, king of Cameliard. The kingdom was said to be between Sherwood Forest and Norgales. Norgales is the Old French for Northern Wales, in other words Gwynedd. It is impossible to tell if such a kingdom as Cameliard ever existed as it falls in a region for which there is no information.

The marriage brings us to one of the most important, and at the same time one of the most confusing characters in the Arthurian cycle. The name Guenevere is derived from the Old Welsh *gwenhywvar*, which means "white spirit" or "white shadow." The name suggests that she may have been another goddess. A great many people argue that she was a real queen, possibly Pictish, whose exploits were edited out of the stories by male chauvinistic copyists. Such an argument does not stand up to close scrutiny. Although warrior women were rare in the Middle Ages, they were not unknown. The most famous was Joan of Arc, but she was not the only one. In the late eleventh century Matilda of Tuscany made quite a name for herself by leading Italian resistance to German invasions. She even captured the Imperial Standard at the Battle of Canossa, much to the embarrassment of the Germans. If the chroniclers recorded Matlida's battlefield exploits, why should they have hidden those of Guenevere?

The argument that Guenevere's battles were simply omitted from the stories makes even less sense when Britano-Gaelic material is considered. They were not shy about recording the exploits of women soldiers. The two greatest heroes in Irish tradition were Cu Chulainn and Finn mac Cool. Both were taught the arts of combat by women. Furthermore, a woman not only trained Cu Chulainn's son Condlae, but his mother was a famous warrior queen-his parents had met in combat school. The most famous of all Britano-Gaelic leaders of the Roman period was Boudicca. She was queen of the Iceni tribe who lived in what is now Norfolk and Suffolk. She led a great, and ultimately doomed, rebellion against the Romans in the late first century. The idea of edited texts is a convenient argument for those who cannot find support for their theories in the documentation, but such ideas do not fit the context of the material. The idea that she was a Pict is another example of putting the theory before the information. Although a popular idea, there is no support for it in the sources. The only statement we have on her family is that they were of Roman origin. Given the supposed location of Cameliard, this makes more sense than making her a Pict since it was in a region where there were Roman settlements.

Another popular suggestion is that Arthur's wife was a Saxon princess called Winifred and the Welsh altered her name to fit their language. The problem with this argument is that Winifred is actually the English pronunciation of a Welsh name. The name was completely unknown until the sixteenth century. When it first appeared it was in families that had connections to Wales. The best guess is that it has nothing to do with Guenevere at all. It seems to have been derived from Gwenfrewi, a saint who was popular at that time.

Although it is possible that Guenevere was a Roman-British princess, the most likely explanation is that the "white spirit" was a goddess. This is supported by the fact that the *Triads* say that Arthur had three ladies at court, or in one translation, three wives, all named Guenevere. The habit of Britano-Gaelic goddesses to appear in three forms has already been mentioned. Many scholars believe that Guenevere was what has been called the Goddess of Sovereignty. More accurately it should be Goddesses of Sovereignty, in the plural. Irish sources name several for all Ireland, including Eriu, Banbha, Folda, and Medb. There were others who were of only a local nature. The land was often personified as a woman in the mythology. She had great authority and even took an active part in choosing kings. Guenevere was not just the goddess of the land; she was the patroness of the rule of the land. Villains often kidnapped her. This was not simply a plot device. These abductions often coincided with challenges to Arthur's authority and attempted coups. One Triad deals with the "Three Unrestrained Ravagings of the Island of Britain." In one of them Medrawt (which is an alternate spelling of Medraut, the name of Arthur's son in Old Welsh) attacked Arthur's court at Celli Wig, sacked it and kidnapped the queen. Arthur pursued him, destroyed his court and rescued her. This aspect of Guenevere's role in the tales has often been obscured by her relationship with Lancelot. However Lancelot was a relatively late addition to the Arthurian stories. He made no appearances in any of the Welsh tales or in Geoffrey of Monmouth. In Geoffrey's version of Arthur's downfall, when Mordred usurped the throne, he also forced Guenevere to marry him.

Since she represented dominion over the land on a symbolic level any action that threatened Arthur's rule was an abduction of Guenevere. The one represented the other. Medrawt challenged Arthur by attacking Celli Wig and Arthur lost the queen. He got her back again by reasserting his dominance when he sacked Medrawt's court. Arthur lost the throne to Mordred, who married Guenevere. He was the new ruler, so he became the new consort to the goddess. Arthur had proven that he was no longer worthy to be king because he could not hold the throne. However Mordred could not force the affections of the goddess. She chose her kings and consorts. They could not compel her to accept them. For these reasons both men had to die in the final conflict.

Tales that examine her relationship to Arthur support the identification of Guenevere as Goddess of Sovereignty. In the Welsh tale *Gereint and Enid,* the king finds himself in a difficult position. He has killed a famous white deer and according to custom he must now give its head to the most beautiful woman at court. Several different knights insist that their ladies should receive the prize and if their wishes are not followed, they will fight to avenge what they insist will be an insult to honour. Arthur cannot say that all of the ladies are the most beautiful and is at a loss as to how the situation should be handled. Guenevere suggests that he delay making his decision until the next day, at which time the hero, Gereint, is expected to return to court. In his travels Gereint has met Enid, described as easily the most beautiful woman in the world. The two are journeying to Arthur's court. When they arrive everyone agrees that Enid should receive the stag's head.

This tale is important in understanding Guenevere for two reasons. First of all she seems to be in possession of information that no human being could have-that Gereint's return will have a direct bearing on Arthur's predicament. No one at court knows of the existence of Enid at this point in the story, while neither Enid nor Gereint are aware of Arthur's adventure with the deer. Secondly there is the queen's stature at court-Arthur adopts her suggestion even though he has no idea as to how it could actually solve his problem. Guenevere's position in this case is similar to that of the goddess Medb in Irish tales. Medb is often presented as a queen and her kings (there are at least nine scattered throughout the tales) follow her advice on a regular basis even when there is no obvious reason for doing so. The queen's origins can even be discerned in some Romances. In *Perceval* by Chretien de Troyes, when the evil Red Knight challenges Arthur's authority he also spills a cup of wine over the queen's head. The symbolism is obvious: an insult to the king's authority is an insult to the Goddess of Sovereignty.

Another problem in identifying the true nature of the character was created by the fact that she was not drawn from one single character but was a mixture of different figures from legend. This idea will resurface when her relationship to Lancelot is examined in detail. The real Arthur must have had a wife, and she may even have been named Guenevere, but nothing of her true character can be discerned in the surviving material.

Arthur was now married. Since he was a mighty warrior, the enemies of his people had been overcome and a period of peace begun. This was the Golden Age. The king decided to create a company of heroes such as the world had never seen before. In this group were such men as Bedivere, Gereint and Yvain. Bedivere was one of the earliest figures to be drawn into the Arthurian orbit. The first mention of him comes from Poem XXXI from *The Black Book of Caermarthen* that speaks of the hero Bodwyr commanding a legion in battle along the banks of the Tryvrwyd. This river has been suggested as being the same as the river Tribriut that is included in the Nennius battle list. The fact that this is a very early reference can be seen by the use of the Latin term legion for his command. Bodwyr, or as he was later called, Bedwyr, has no quests of his own and there is nothing to suggest that he is a truly mythic figure. Like Kay he is important at court, but he does not do anything to justify that importance. It is Bedivere who throws Excalibur into the water after Arthur's last battle. Other than that, he is simply a supporting figure in someone else's tale. Both of the characters of Kai and Bedwyr may have been based upon real people. The reason that they are important in the stories is that they were important in real life. They have no quests because they were warriors and not fictitious heroes. This is only supposition, but it is supported by what is known of Gereint (also sometimes spelled Geraint).

In the legends Geraint was Arthur's nephew. In reality Arthur was present at his death at Llongborth. The real Geraint came from Dumnonia and Arthur came from Kernow, (that is Cornwall). The Cornovii tribe lived in both provinces. It is also known that at one point Cunomorus ruled both. His name is on the Dumnonian king list and a monument in Cornwall. This suggests that different branches of the same family ruled the two places. Geraint may really have been Arthur's nephew. All of what we know of the real Geraint comes from the fact that a poem about him was fortunate enough to survive. If it had not then he would simply have been another figure in the legends. Kay and Bedivere are heroes with no such poems but in the Arthurian tales their positions are very similar to that of Geraint. There is one significant difference between Geraint and the two other characters-he is the hero of his own adventure, called *Gereint and Enid.* The story is also the earliest Romance written by the French author Chretien de Troyes. In that version the hero is called Eric. Another character that is similar to Geraint is Yvain, son of Urien. He is also called the "Knight of the Lion" because he saves a lion's life and it becomes his friend. His adventures are totally fictitious; however the character is based on Owain ap Urien of Rheged, a pendragon of the late sixth century.

To return to the narrative, there was one small problem with Arthur's plan to assemble the greatest knights in the world. With so many proud warriors in the same place at the same time they began to argue among themselves as to which of them was the greatest. The disagreement became a petty squabble over who would have the best seat at the table. Arthur solved the problem by acquiring the Round Table. In some versions it was a gift from Guenevere's father while in others it was constructed by Merlin. With the Round Table, no seat was better than any other. This aspect of the tales is ancient in origin. In the Middle Ages the seat of honour was to the right hand of the king. It would not matter if the table were round; rectangular or pear-shaped, the king would have had a right hand. The basic concept is paralleled in other Britano-Gaelic tales but the table itself is unique. It may have been some sort of real conference table or an image for something else, just as the sword-in-the-stone was an image for the process of choosing a pendragon.

Britano-Gaelic war bands used to sit in a circle in their king's halls. During feasting the one judged the greatest warrior would receive the choicest cuts of meat and other fine food. This was called the Champion's Portion. He was also entitled to the biggest share of the spoils taken from defeated enemies. From Ireland comes the tale called *The Story of Macc Da Tho's Pig.* Macc Da Tho invited two groups of warriors to his home to enjoy a feast. The main course was a huge pig, as big as forty oxen. Before the meal could begin it had to be determined which of the warriors was entitled to the best cut. The characters took it in turn to slander each other and boast of their own deeds to try and convince their host that they were the most deserving. The contest ended in a brawl. It was an echo of that kind of confrontation that was behind the concept of the Round Table.

There is another possibility about the origin of the Table. There is no direct evidence to support this idea, so it is presented here only as a suggestion not as an actual theory. The idea can best be explained by using an example. For hundreds of years France was plagued by the petty ambitions and schemes of powerful nobles. Louis XIV (r.1643-1715) finally broke the power of the aristocracy and made himself absolute monarch. One of the ways in which he did this was to force the nobles to spend most of their time at court. He even built what amounted to a royal town, the Palace of Versailles, in order to house them. They were cut off from their power bases and he could keep a close watch on the troublemakers. Perhaps Arthur did the same sort of thing. Maybe the Round Table fostered peace because the kings were required to attend its meetings. They became separated from their private armies and could not conduct their private wars.

In the Romances the Table took on a greater significance. It became a symbol that transcended the boundaries of Britain of itself. In the Middle Ages the circle was considered to be the perfect shape and had great symbolic importance. The Round Table represented completeness and the equality and brotherhood of all knights. It also represented the world (contrary to popular belief, the peoples of medieval Europe knew that the world was round). The Table was the embodiment of their hope that the ideals of Camelot would be embraced all over the planet.

The stage is now set for the next act in the Arthurian Cycle to begin. With the great knights all assembled at Camelot and seated at the Round Table there must be something noble and important for them to do. They must set out on adventures to prove themselves and to win the love of fair ladies, and so begins the next phase-the quests.

Chapter VIII

The Quests

THE ARTHURIAN Cycle is crowded with literally dozens of knights and their adventures. To keep the present study to a manageable size only the major tales and characters will be dealt with here. The examination will begin with those knights who were associated with the king at an early date, and progress from there in a more or less chronological order.

The first figure was Arthur's nephew/son and archenemy, Mordred. In the Romances he was Arthur's only son whose mother was the king's sister, the sorceress Morgan. In earlier versions he was the son of Arthur's sister Anna and her husband Lot. In a Welsh story called *The Dream of Rhonabwy* he was not only the king's nephew but also his foster-son. A corruption of this may have been what led to the idea of an incestuous relationship between Arthur and his sister. Or this may have been invented in an attempt to remove the stain of incest from the king's story. Since incest did appear in many Britano-Gaelic myths, either interpretation is possible.

Mordred was the great traitor whose attempt to seize the throne led to Arthur's death and the break up of the Company of the Round Table. He first appeared in the Welsh traditions as Medrawt or Medraut. The *Welsh Annals* mentioned his death at Camlann, along with Arthur's, but neglected to say whether he was the king's ally or an enemy. This has led to speculation that he was one of the king's loyal followers. In one Welsh manuscript Mordred was listed as one of the "Twenty Four Knights of Arthur's Court." The Mardoc of the Modena Archivolt may have been Mordred, but if so he was in his more familiar role as a villain. The character's depiction in the Triads is ambiguous. Although there are over ninety Triads that deal with Arthurian material Medrawt is mentioned in only three of them. His attack on Celli Wig has already been dealt with. In another episode he insults Guenevere. However, one of the "Three Unfortunate Councils" was Arthur dividing his army with Medrawt at Camlann. This would suggest that he was one of Arthur's lieutenants who commanded part of the king's army at the last battle. It is not impossible to reconcile this idea with the usual concept of Mordred as a traitor. It has already been pointed out that it is possible that Mordred switched sides at Camlann, in which case the fact that Arthur trusted him with an important command would have been a grave mistake.

Most researchers who believe there was an Arthur also agree that there was a Medrawt but exactly what he did is hotly disputed. He may have been Arthur's chief enemy who was killed fighting the king. Maelgwyn of Gwynedd is sometimes named as his supporter and main beneficiary at his death. On the other hand he may have been one of the leaders of Arthur's army who was killed at his king's side while the real traitor survived. That would not have made the story very satisfying; it was much better to punish the villain for his treachery. Medrawt was said to have died in the battle, so his name was given to the villain. The simple answer that he was the king's son who rebelled against his father is usually not even considered, even though it is the main point that the Welsh themselves make about him.

The next figure is altogether different. Gawain is Arthur's heroic nephew, in stark contrast to the villainy of his kinsman Mordred. He is a knight who goes on adventures, which Mordred does not, and remains loyal to the king until death. He is also the greatest of the Knights of the Round Table in the early stories and a large number of tales feature him, even when the main hero is someone else. It has been suggested that he was French in origin. At least as far back as the eleventh century there were tales of a character named Walwanus who bears a striking resemblance to Gawain. Supporters of this theory are guilty of faulty linguistics. The name Walwanus is derived from Gawain, not the other way around. The original was Welsh. He was Gwalchmei, which means: "Hawk of May." For proof one need only look at his two main adventures, the testing by the "Loathly Lady" and the beheading game, both of which are definitely Britano-Gaelic.

There are several known versions of this first tale, but the one most readily available to the modern reader is "The Wife of Bath's Tale," from *The Canterbury Tales* by Geoffrey Chaucer. Two others are a fifteenth century Romance called *The Wedding of Sir Gawain and Dame Ragnell* and a ballad called *The Marriage of Gawain*. In all three an ugly woman named Ragnell saves Gawain's life on the condition that he agrees to marry her. On their wedding night Gawain is amazed to find that his wife has suddenly turned into a beautiful young woman who announces that she is under a curse. She can be beautiful for twelve hours out of every twenty-four. Gawain has to decide if it would be the daylight hours when she would be seen by other people or at night when they would be alone together. He says that she should decide since it is her fate that is in question. A delighted Ragnell informs him that he has made exactly the right answer and the curse has been lifted. From that moment on she will be beautiful all the time.

The basic story of an ugly old woman testing a hero and then becoming young and attractive is told in a much more primitive version in Irish tradition. There the hero Niall of the Nine Hostages meets an old crone guarding a well. He is in dire need of a drink but she will give him water only if he will make love to her. When Niall agrees she instantly becomes young and beautiful. She announces that she is the goddess Medb and that he will become king of all Ireland. This is a good example about how mythic tales can become told about real people. Niall Noigiallach was high king of Ireland and founder of the O'Neil dynasty who virtually monopolized the Irish high kingship for roughly six centuries. In the Gawain story the basic idea is similar, but the hero's reward is different.

The same is true of the beheading game. The best version of this story is *Sir Gawain and the Green Knight*, written by an anonymous Yorkshire man in the late fourteenth century. The story begins at Christmas just as the feast is being served. Arthur says that he will not begin the meal until something interesting happens. This is a common device used in the Romances and is the signal for the event that starts the quest. In this case the event is the sudden entrance of a bizarre figure on horseback. Not only is he dressed all in green, but his skin is green as well. The newcomer issues a challenge to all of the knights present. The hero will have the opportunity to cut off the head of the Green Knight. In one year the two will meet again at a place called the Green Chapel when the Green Knight will get a chance to cut off the head of his opponent.

Gawain is the only one who can be found to accept the challenge. It was believed that if a sorcerer was decapitated he could re-attach his head if he got to it quickly enough. After Gawain cuts off the Green Knight's head the other members of the court try to keep it away from the body by kicking it to one another. Despite this macabre game of football, the knight easily retrieves it and does not bother putting it back on his shoulders, he just rides out with it under his arm. This is a sign that he is a being of immense magical power. Gawain sets off to keep his part of the bargain. But he cannot find the Green Chapel anywhere. Eventually he arrives at the castle of Sir Bercilak and this knight offers him the hospitality of his home. When Gawain tells his host of his errand, Bercilak replies that the Green Chapel is not far away. Since it is still several days since Gawain has to keep his appointment, the hero agrees to play a game suggested by his host. Every day Bercilak will go out hunting and Gawain will stay in the castle. Every night they will give each other what they have been able to collect. On the first day Gawain is dismayed to discover that his host's wife is trying to seduce him. He fights off her advances but she does manage to kiss him. A similar incident happens on the second day. On the third day, however, she announces that she has given up and wants to be his friend. She gives him a magic sash or girdle that will keep him safe from any blow. Breaking his word to Bercilak, Gawain keeps the girdle hidden. When he rides out to meet the Green Knight he is surprised to find that the "chapel" is actually an oddly shaped hill. He hears someone sharpening something. Sure enough it is the Green Knight preparing his axe for the coming confrontation. When the hero kneels to receive the other's blow, the attacker makes two false swings with the axe before finally giving Gawain a small cut on the side of his neck. The hero's joy at being delivered from certain death is cut short when he is told the true identity of the Green Knight. He is none other than Sir Bercilak. Bercilak knows all about what has been going on between Gawain and his wife and about the girdle, it was all about the challenges that the knight had to overcome. Bercilak tells him not to be concerned about the whole adventure because Morgan planned it as a way of terrifying Guenevere. He also tells him to keep the girdle as a memento. Gawain decides that he will use it as a reminder that he is neither as honest nor as brave as he had previously thought. It is a lesson in humility.

There are parallels to this story in Irish traditions. The theme of a hero being tempted by a woman with magical powers (or possessed of a magical item) is reminiscent of the Morrigan's attempt to seduce Cu Chulainn. The parallel is very close since the Morrigan and Morgan la Fay are the same character. When Lady Bercilak is introduced she is standing beside an old woman identified as Morgan, strongly suggesting that Lady Bercilak is the goddess in one of her other forms. The beheading game itself is used in *Bricriu's Feast*. This tale consists of three heroes being set different tests by different characters to determine which of them will receive the Champion's Portion. Two of them, Loegure Buadach and Conall Cearnach fail all of the tests, but Cu Chulainn passes them. The three play the beheading game not once but twice. The first time is with a strange man named Uath son of Imoman who lives inside a lake. Uath has magical powers and can change his shape. Like the Green Knight, he takes three swings at the hero. The second challenge is from an ugly brown churl who turns out to be the magical being Cu Rui in disguise. It seems that two versions of the story have become tangled. A character named Muinremur, who is not mentioned anywhere else in the tale, plays the beheading game with the others the second time, after the second time Cu Chulainn is named chief hero of Ulster.

An obvious point is that in the Irish versions of both stories the hero becomes a leader, in *Bricriu's Feast* he is chosen the champion and with the Loathly Lady he becomes king. For some reason this fact is sometimes ignored when Gawain is examined. If only one story about Gawain were of the type where he is chosen as a leader, or if there were only two of a great many more, then perhaps this approach would be acceptable. But Gawain has only two main adventures and they are both concerned with his becoming a leader, at least they are in their Irish equivalents. There are two possibilities as to the development of the tales. The beheading game is usually believed to have originated as a tale of kingship that lost this aspect in both Ireland and Wales. If this is true then the Green Knight would represent kingship and his beheading was the passing of the king. That is why it did not harm him. Individual kings might die but the monarchy endured. The fact that in the Gawain story the beheading games are close to New Year, one year apart, supports this conclusion. In the Britano-Gaelic calendar the celebration of New Years was called Samhain ("summer's end") and it fell on what is the first of November in our time, but the festivities began the night before. It was a time full of magic when the barriers between our world and the Otherworld broke down, souls of the dead and demons could walk the land. This idea lingers on in Halloween. At Samhain the king was ritually sacrificed in three ways: burning, wounding and drowning. The other possibility is that the beheading game was always a test of courage to choose the champion. The test is repeated because the champion had to continually prove himself in order to maintain his post. In Ireland the two tales remained separate with different heroes, while in Wales they became combined. Since Gawain was drawn into the Arthurian orbit the test of kingship was altered because Arthur was the king. The emphasis shifted to tests in general and so both tales could have the same hero. Either conclusion is possible.

Gawain is a solar hero. Even as late as Sir Thomas Malory's time in the fifteenth century this showed through. According to Malory, Gawain hated Lancelot because the latter had killed his brothers. The two met in a combat that lasted all day. Gawain's strength varied with the position of the sun-the higher it was in the sky, the stronger the hero became. Another indication of Gawain's connection to the sun is the fact that in some Welsh tales his father's name was Llew. This is alternate spelling of Lleu, the Welsh version of the sun god, Lugh. This is borne out by the fact that Gawain seems to be the Welsh equivalent of the Irish hero Cu Chulainn. Both resist seduction by a goddess, and both play the beheading game. Cu Chulainn was the greatest hero in Irish tales and, until the arrival of Lencelot, Gawain was the greatest of Arthur's knights. Cu Chulainn's head radiated light, which was certainly a solar symbol, and Lugh was his father. It has been suggested that the two characters were derived from a real person. Until he was seven years old Cu Chulainn was called Setanta, while in ancient times a tribe called the Setantii lived in what is now eastern England.

This identification is highly speculative. A similarity of names does not necessarily indicate a connection. Even if there was a connection between the two, it does not necessarily follow that the hero was named after the tribe. The tribe could have taken its name from the character. Some Britano-Gaelic tribes did name themselves after important figures from their mythology. For example, the Brigante, a large tribe in northern Britain took their name from the goddess Brigit. Another argument that the idea that the character was derived from a member of the Setantii tribe is the problem of geography-the Setantii were said to have lived in "north-eastern" Britain. This is a vague term that gives only a general indication of the area under discussion. To be more precise they occupied the coastal region between the rivers Ribble and Merrsey. Neither of the two heroes is associated with that district or with the Setantii. Cu Chulainn was the champion of Ulster, which was named after its inhabitants, the Ulaid. Gawain was the son of King Lot. Lot was a real man who ruled Lothian, the district around Edinburgh. This was the land of the Gododdin. In some tales he was said to have come from Galloway, which is now in southwestern Scotland. Galloway was divided between the Novantae and the Selgovae. Neither area even bordered Setantii land. It is quite possible that the character was simply associated with the north in general. In Irish terms this meant Ulster while in Britain it referred to either Lothian or Galloway, the districts along the Pictish border.

There is evidence which points to the character being widespread throughout Western Europe and known to the true Celts. There is a ceremonial vessel that is the most famous and one of the most beautiful of all Celtic artifacts. It is 96 percent pure silver and was forged in either Thrace or Romania in the fourth or third century BC. At some unknown point in its history the cauldron was dismantled in twelve pieces and buried in a bog near Gundestrup, Denmark, probably by Germanic raiders. It has since been reassembled. The Gundestrup Cauldron depicts scenes from Celtic mythology. A hero wearing a horned helmet is shown several times. Divine beings are represented as much larger than this character and the other mortals that are shown.

The supernatural figures pictured not only include gods and goddesses but bulls as well. On the base of the artifact one of these bulls is shown dying. From this and other imagery, it has been concluded that the cauldron depicts an early version of *The Cattle Raid of Cooley*, the great epic of Irish poetry. If this identification is correct then the helmeted hero would be the prototype of Cu Chulainn and Gawain. However, this evidence is not conclusive. Many scholars believe that Cu Chulainn was not the original hero of the tale; he may not have been added to it until as late as the seventh century AD.

The problem is that although they are similar, Cu Chulainn and Gawain are not exactly the same. It is obvious that the two traditions have diverged since the Irish character has definite associations with the storm god Taranus ("Thunderer"). He has a ferocious temper, a common attribute with storm gods, and his weapons are named after lightning. Aside from Caladbolg ("Hard Lightning") which was mentioned as the origin for Excalibur, he also carried Gea Bulga ("Lightning Spear"). There is no trace of Taranus in Gawain. Gawain is rather rash, but he does not have the same temper as Cu Chulainn or the storm god. Any explanation for the origin of the character must fit both Cu Chulainn and Gawain, but the different courses of the legends makes it difficult to find the origin. The best guess is that the original hero was the embodiment of the ultimate warrior who was tested and made king or champion. In Ireland his war-like attributes were emphasized and he incorporated aspects of Taranus while in Wales it was his royal nature that came to the fore, until it was obscured by associating the hero with King Arthur's knights.

The emphasis upon testing in the Gawain stories was ultimately based upon reality, even if it was given a mystic setting. A council of chieftains selected the king from candidates chosen from the royal family and could depose him if they found his rule less than adequate. Since deposing caused problems they liked to make sure that they made the right choice, hence the need for testing in the tales. It was also believed that on a mystic level the king married the land. Gerald of Wales recorded the ceremony whereby the high kings of Tara in Ireland married the land, a rite that was still used as late as the twelfth century. In Irish legend no king of Tara could take up his duties until he had slept with the goddess Medb. That was why women played such important roles in the testing. In *Sir Gawain and the Green Knight*, Lady Bercilak standing beside Morgan has already been suggested as the goddess in both of her aspects as young beauty and old crone. Ragnell played the same role in Gawain's other tale. Medb was both young beauty and old crone in her encounter with Neil and she set several of the tests for the heroes in *Bricriu's Feast*.

Given these facts it is reasonable to assume that the woman Gawain encounters is the Goddess of Sovereignty. This is borne out by another story often associated with the hero. Arthur's nephew was prominent in a type of tale called the "Flower Bride." As late as the nineteenth century a mock combat was held in many parts of Wales every first of May. The Champion of Winter and his army captured the Flower Bride, who had to be rescued by the Champion of Summer. The climax came with a confrontation between the two leaders, which always ended in a victory for

Summer. The first of May was Gawain's birthday. It was also Beltaine, the beginning of summer and the second most holy day to the pagan Britano-Gaels.

There is a definite connection between the Flower Bride and the character of Gawain. In *The Knight of the Cart* by Chretien de Troyes a knight named Meleagrant appears at court and announces that he has captured several of Arthur's knights. Meleagrant issues a challenge that any knight may face him in combat. If Arthur's man wins, the prisoners will be released but if he looses Guenevere will join the others as a captive. The king's reaction is to ignore the challenge rather than risk the safety of the queen. However Kay tricks Arthur into allowing him to accept. When Kay is overcome, both Lancelot and Gawain set out to rescue Guenevere. The name of the story is derived from the fact that, lacking any other means of transportation, Lancelot agrees to ride in a farmer's cart. Several characters remark that it is unseemly for a knight to have to travel in such a conveyance. They express the opinion that he should feel ashamed of himself. Since Lancelot is the hero of the tale he is the one who succeeds in the quest. However the fact that Gawain is included indicates that the story is attempting to reconcile two different versions of the story. This contention is supported by the fact that after the abductor is overcome Guenevere refuses to leave until Gawain arrives.

The inclusion of Kay is significant. He is the previous Summer Champion whose defeat leads to the abduction of the Flower Bride. This incident introduces the theme of the old hero failing and being replaced by a new one, a theme implicit in the beheading game. The sudden appearance of Meleagant at court and his challenge to the assembled knights is reminiscent of the actions of the Green Knight in the Gawain tale. Furthermore Lancelot battles Meleagant twice, with the two combats taking place one year apart, the same period of time that separated Gawain's encounters with the Green Knight. The Flower Bride represents the fertility of the land, but such goddesses were also associated with the rule of the land. The Goddess of Sovereignty merged both the aspects of fertility and royalty.

In Irish legend Cu Chulainn fell in love with Blathnat, daughter of the god Midir. But Midir locked her away in a fort on the Isle of Falga. In order to rescue her, the hero enlisted the help of the magical being Cu Rui. In exchange for his help Cu Rui demanded the pick of the spoils. Much to the hero's anger the other chooses Blathnat. Cu Chulainn attempted to prevent Cu Rui from taking her, only to be overcome by his opponent. The villain buried the hero up to his neck, cut off his victim's hair and dumped manure over his head. Cu Rui abducted the woman and took her to his home. But Blathnat was no trophy bride. She took an active part in her own rescue. When the hero came to her she tied Cu Rui to the bed with his own hair and gave Cu Chulainn the villain's sword, the only weapon that could kill him.

This appears to be an Irish version of the Flower Bride motif, in both stories the hero is humiliated and must fight the abductor twice before rescuing the woman. The identification is strengthened by the presence of Cu Rui who plays the beheading game with Cu Chulainn in *Bricriu's Feast*. Another indication is the fact that a magic cauldron was taken from Midir in the raid. As will be seen on the section on the Holy Grail, the Goddess of Sovereignty was sometimes associated with a magic cauldron. The fact that the two characters were lovers shows that Cu Chulainn was the consort of the goddess.

Originally Gawain must have been the hero of his own set of legends that had nothing to do with the Arthurian Cycle. These tales dealt with being tested, found worthy and named a king or champion. When he entered the Arthurian world this had to change. Arthur was already king and there was no need to choose another. The stories stayed but their endings were altered. The "Loathly Lady" became a sort of "Beauty and the Beast" while the beheading game was turned into a lesson in pride and honesty. The Flower Bride ceased to be a Gawain story altogether and became connected to Lancelot.

The next important knight to enter the Arthurian Cycle was Tristan. Although it is a very old story *Tristan and Iseult* was a relatively late addition to the Arthurian world. This can been seen by the fact that it is quite possible to tell the tale without any mention of Arthur, Camelot or the Round Table. The adventure concerns King Mark of Cornwall who sends his nephew Tristan to Ireland to ensure the safe journey of his new wife Iseult, to Mark's court. However the hero and the lady fall in love after accidentally drinking a love potion and they begin to have an affair. Their relationship becomes known at court and several people try to make it public. Seeing that the situation is hopeless, Tristan flees to Brittany. There he marries another woman named Iseult but makes no attempt to hide the fact that he does not love her. One of his enemies poisons him. Iseult of Ireland comes to Brittany to care for her lover, but he dies before she arrives. The Irish queen dies of grief.

Where did the tale come from originally? Many scholars believe it was a true story. Near Castle Dore in Cornwall there is a memorial stone that reads: DURSTANUS FILIUS CUNOMORI. This means "Durstan son of Cunomorus." The stone dates to the mid-sixth century. Durstanus is a form of the name Tristan and the stone is in Cornwall, not far from the castle reported to have been the palace of King Mark in the tale. Many take this as proof of the basic truth of the tale. They sometimes support this conclusion by pointing out that Wrmonoc of Landevennc, writing in 884, said that Cunomorus was also called Mark. The storytellers altered Tristan's relationship to Mark to that of king's nephew so that he would not be seen to carry on a love affair with his own stepmother.

Unfortunately this conclusion does not really make much sense. Cunomorus was one of the most famous British rulers of the second half of the sixth century. He reigned in the 550's through to the 570's. He was king of Brittany, Devon and Cornwall. This means that he united all of the territory ruled by the different branches of his family. He was also greatly active in the politics of Gaul. Of all the stories that are told of him, none bear any resemblance to the legend of Tristan. As for the story itself, why would the storytellers alter the tale so that Tristan was not having an affair with his stepmother, when they freely said that Arthur slept with his own sister? And how does altering the relationship from stepson to nephew make Tristan a more noble character? The changed relationship does not remove the idea of incest, especially in a Britano-Gaelic context, since they placed great emphasis upon the extended family.

The name Tristan, or Durstan as it appears on the stone, is the Irish pronunciation of the Pictish name Durst. The Irish conquered Cornwall and occupied it until the 450's. The Pictish high king Durst I, who lived in the early fifth century, was highly respected by the Irish and passed into their legends. The story itself may be Irish in origin. There are three Irish versions, each with different characters and different details, but all telling the same basic story. Grainne, the fiancé of Finn, elopes with the hero Diarmaid. There is also the tale of Deirdre who flees to Scotland with her lover Naoise to escape her fiancé, King Conchobar. Probably the oldest version is *The Wooing of Etain* where the same story is actually told twice-with Etain fleeing from Midir to the arms of Eochaid, only to return to Midir again. Both men play the part of lover and abandoned husband. In this version the characters are divine. This is the same god Midir who tried to prevent Cu Chulainn from marrying his daughter Blathnat who was mentioned on the section on Gawain.

If the story were true then why did the Irish tell it several different times, never once setting it in Cornwall or including the "real" characters? Just because a sixth century prince had the same name as a fictional hero does not mean they were the same person. The idea of connecting the tale with Cornwall in general and Castle Dore in particular was probably the sole result of the coincidence of names. It was not until 884 that anyone made the claim that Cunomorus and Mark were the same person. Although that was a relatively early date when compared to most of the sources that have been examined, it was still over three hundred years after the erection of the monument. That was more than enough time for the Pictish hero of Irish legend to have become confused with the real prince of Cornwall.

The Irish were not the only people to tell versions of this story. Chretien de Troyes was the greatest of the early French Romancers. The sources he used originated in Wales and Brittany, and he knew the story as *Cliges*. He had no sympathy for adultery so the lovers remained chaste until after the death of the lady's husband. Aside from this alteration the story is essentially the same. There is one more version and oddly many people do not recognize it as the same tale. Although details are different, *Tristan and Iseult* is essentially the same story as Guenevere's affair with Lancelot.

Lancelot is another late arrival to the Arthurian Cycle. He does not appear in any of the Welsh sources or in Geoffrey of Monmouth. The earliest mention of him is in the Romances written by Chretien de Troyes in the 1170's. His true origins are more difficult to discern than any other major character in the Arthurian Cycle, even more difficult than Arthur himself. The name is French, or least it is in a French form that has no obvious Welsh equivalent. Chretien did not invent the characters he used they were all taken from Britano-Gaelic sources or French works derived from those sources. It has been suggested that the name was derived from Llwch Lleminawc (Llwch the Irishman), one of Arthur's followers in *The Spoils of Annwn*, who may or may not be the same as Llenlleawc who appears in *Culhwch and Olwen*. The linguistics may be similar but the characters are not. The Welsh figures were minor heroes who bore little resemblance to the great champion of Arthurian legend.

There have been several attempts to claim that he was real, but none of them are very convincing. They consist of making forceful statements backed up by questionable interpretations of episodes of various Romances. Lancelot is the archetypical hero. He is the bravest, the strongest and the most handsome of all the knights and women routinely fall in love with him at first sight. Since he is an archetype it is highly unlikely that he was derived from a real person. He is literally too good to be true.

Lancelot combines aspects of Gawain and Tristan. He is the Summer Champion who rescues the Flower Bride in *The Knight of the Cart* and similar tales. He is the young warrior of the Love Triangle. He incorporates specific details of the lives of the other characters. Like Tristan he went temporarily insane from the torments of love, a common medieval motif. According to some stories he was born in Lothian, one of the regions associated with Gawain. In order to accommodate this change Gawain's father, Lot, was transformed into king of the Orkney Isles. But this change could not disguise the truth since the name Lothian is derived from Lot. Lancelot became the greatest warrior in Arthur's court. This is the rightful position for both the Summer Champion and the hero of the Love Triangle. But Gawain held that post, so Gawain had to be pushed aside to make room. Chretien de Troyes followed contradictory traditions about the hero. In *Erec and Enide* Lancelot is listed as the third most important knight at Arthur's court, while he loses a joust to the hero of *Cliges*. But in *The Knight of the Cart* Lancelot is presented as the greatest warrior in the world and unbeatable in combat. Clearly Lancelot was from a different set of traditions that was forced, not too smoothly, into the Arthurian Cycle. His presence also caused changes to the character of Guenevere. As she became more closely linked to him, she was moved farther from her role as Goddess of Sovereignty. This is why this aspect of her personality can best be discerned in tales like *Gereint and Enid*, in which Lancelot does not appear.

Where did he come from? It is known that stories about Arthur were passed down in Brittany. It is also known that French Romancers used both Welsh and Breton sources for their works. Since he was not Welsh, then Lancelot was almost certainly Breton. At first the French simply recorded the parallel traditions, which is why Lancelot is not always the greatest knight in the stories written in the twelfth century. Soon they made attempts to reconcile the discrepancies. They combined the two traditions and in the process they confused Guenevere's function, stripped Gawain of his premier position and told the same story twice.

The only major tale left to discuss is the quest for the Holy Grail. It has had a greater impact on the minds of people than all of the beheading games and love triangles combined. The image of the elusive Grail has fascinated people as different as T.S. Elliot and Adolf Hitler. Is it real or a symbol of unattainable perfection? Is it a pagan myth or a Christian mystery? Because of the Grail's significance, it has been assigned a chapter of its own.

Chapter IX

THE GRAIL

THE HOLY Grail is the single most controversial story of the Arthurian Cycle. In recent years books about it have sprung up like weeds each one "proving" the truth of the story. They trace intricate webs of international conspiracies, secret histories, holy bloodlines and a whole range of romantic, if farfetched, ideas. An older tradition makes it the miraculous cup used by Jesus at the Last Supper. At least five different churches around the world are claimed to house it. During the Second World War Nazi agents scoured Europe for any trace of the sacred relic, while T.S. Eliot took images from the legend and used them in his great work *The Wasteland*. The idea of the quest, the eternal search, has always appealed to the human mind. Add to that the fact that the Grail is a mysterious and mystical object, and it is no wonder that succeeding generations have found the story so fascinating. There is also the fact that it is so mysterious because it is unattainable. In the film *Indiana Jones and the Last Crusade* the heroes find the Grail, only to lose it again. This allows others to take up the quest if they wish. The never-completed quest can be used as an allegory for the search for the meaning of life itself.

This may give an idea as to where the legend is now, but it does not begin to explain where it came from. Many people believe that it originated in the Holy Land, either as part of an early Christian sect or an Arabic myth that was brought to Europe by knights returning from the Crusades. But these are guesses backed up only by possibilities and suppositions, not hard evidence. The story is not Arabic. The greatest collection of legends by that people, *The 1001 Arabian Knights*, has been available in various English translations ever since 1885. Not only does it contain no story remotely like the Grail, there are no stories that contain its central theme either. The Grail legend is about the intimate relationship between the king and the land. When the king became wounded nature became a wasteland. This concept is very ancient and widespread in Europe especially in Britano-Gaelic Europe. Shakespeare's *King Lear* is ultimately derived from a myth about the god Lud. Lud (also called Nudd) was the king of the gods. London was named after him. Over the centuries the tale became confused with another god, Llyr of the Sea. In the play the title character is driven to madness just as a great storm breaks. This is no dramatic convention-the storm begins because the king is mad. With the monarch out of balance, nature is also out of balance. This connection between ruler and nature is totally alien to the Arab world. The Arabs live in a land that is mainly desert; it is always a wasteland. The idea of connecting the state of nature to the well being of the ruler simply would not occur to them.

To reject a Britano-Gaelic origin for the story is one thing, but why choose Arabia as an alternative? The answer comes from what may be the best-written version of the Grail legend, *Parzival*, by Wolfram von Eschenbach. The author, writing in the early thirteenth century, claimed that he heard the story from a famous traveling poet named Kyot. We are told that this man came from Provence in southern France. On his travels he visited Toledo in Spain, and there he learned how to read "heathen," by which he meant Arabic. The Arabs conquered most of Spain in the early eighth century and were not completely driven out again until the late fifteenth century. In one of the "heathen" books Kyot found the Grail legend. He then told it to von Eschenbach, although Kyot supposedly wrote a version of it in French before he did so.

It is amazing that anyone today would accept such a story at face value. First of all *Parzival* may be the best version of the tale, but it was certainly not the first. There are three surviving renderings of the story before *Parzival* and not one of them claims Arabic origins for it. Chretien de Troyes wrote the oldest surviving Grail Romance, an author known to have used Britano-Gaelic sources for his inspiration. Furthermore no trace of Kyot or his version of the story can be found anywhere else.

The Kyot story is very appealing for many reasons. He is a romantic figure, a traveling poet who also seems to have been a talented linguist. Not only did he teach himself to read Arabic, we are also told that he was fluent in Latin. He must have learned French too, because a native of Provence would have spoken Provencal, a language that was related to French but was not the same, much the same way that modern Spanish and Portuguese are related to each other. Kyot's Grail Romance was written in French, not his native tongue. There is an air of mystery about the whole thing. Von Eschenbach tells us that Kyot made him promise not to answer any questions concerning the Grail, as the true story must be kept secret. But if he wanted to keep it a secret, why write the story at all? That would automatically draw attention to something that he was supposedly trying to hide. All of this mystery and romance sounds much better than for von Eschenbach to say simply that he copied the whole thing from French Romances.

One further argument against the Kyot story is the fact that von Eschenbach did not know what the Grail really was. In this book the hero was seeking a stone that had fallen from heaven. Von Eschenbach was not alone in his confusion. Chretien de Troyes died before he could finish his version of the legend. He never explained what it was. It was Robert de Boron who said it was a chalice or a cup. He also introduced many Christian elements. It was de Boron who first said that it had been used at the Last Supper and was brought to Britain by Joseph of Arimathea, the man who provided the tomb in which Jesus was buried.

The oldest surviving written form of the legend is *Li Conte de Graal*, also known as *Perceval*, by Chretien de Troyes. Aside for one reference to the Eucharist, there are no Christian elements in this version at all. It is not even called *san graal*, "Holy Grail" but simply *un graal*, "a grail" as if it were a common item. Many researchers claim that there was no such word as *graal* in Old French. These people completely ignore the fact that all medieval languages, including Old French, had a variety of dialects. Roger Sherman Loomis discovered a book written by Helinand, abbot of Freidmont monastery in 1215, which defined a *graal* as "a wide and slightly deep dish."[74]

The Grail legend is Britano-Gaelic in origin. In fact it would be impossible to find a more Britano-Gaelic story, at least in its early versions. That is the problem in attempting to explain the Grail; the story began as a pagan myth and ended as a Christian allegory. The two interpretations are very different and will be dealt with one at a time.

There were a great many different versions of the story. No two are exactly alike, but there are certain ideas and details that appear over and over again. The following synopsis is not based upon any one manuscript. Instead it has been pieced together from different accounts, based chiefly on the oldest by Chretien de Troyes, but supplemented by later versions. The story begins with Joseph of Arimathea arriving in Britain with Anna, who was described as a cousin of the Virgin Mary. Anna married a local prince and gave birth to a son who grew up to become the mighty king Beli the Great. Meanwhile Joseph earned his keep as a tutor to the prince, Bran the Blessed. This episode undercuts the believability of the entire story. According to the earliest material Beli the Great was said to have been the father of Caswallon. Caswallon was the greatest chieftain in Britain at the time of Julius Caesar and he died in *c*48 BC. Obviously Beli could not have been born after Jesus had died if his son died decades before Jesus was born. It cannot be argued that it was a different man with the same name because of his epithet. Just as there was only one Alexander the Great there was only one Beli the Great.

It is highly unlikely that Beli ever really existed. His name is the same as one of the Britano-Gaelic sun gods and his eldest son was Lud, the same Lud who was the king of the gods. The whole connection hinges upon Anna. It is generally argued that the name is derived from the Hebrew name Hanna, but coincidentally it is also a Welsh name. It is the Welsh pronunciation of the name that appears in Ireland as Dana. It was also the name of the great maternal goddess in their pagan mythology. In Ireland the term for all of the deities was Tuatha De Danann, the "Tribe of Dana." As for Bran the Blessed, this is the same god of the sea and patron of the cult of the severed head who was already introduced when examining *Branwen Daughter of Llyr*. Of the five characters in the story so far, only two of them, Caswallon and Joseph, can be shown to be real people and they lived about one hundred years apart. As will become clear it was absolutely essential to bring Joseph into contact with Bran in order to make the story work.

According to the story Bran was the founder of a special family. One of his descendants was a valiant knight who was killed shortly after his young wife gave birth to a son. Fearing the same fate for her boy, the Widowed Lady (as she was called) took her child into the wild to raise him far away from any warlike pursuits. This of course was the very common motif of the hero being

---

74   *The Grail From Celtic Myth to Christian Symbol*, pg. 58.

raised in isolation. This designation, the Widowed Lady, is reminiscent of Lady of the Lake and Lady of the Sidh, already discussed as terms for goddesses. The child was Perceval. As will become clear he was not the original character. This raises the question as to where he came from. In southern Wales the name was Pryderi and he was associated with Dyfed. The tales told of him are the closest to the Grail legend as they contain the wasteland motif. In northern Wales his name was given as Peredur, son of Evrawg. The only known Peredur was son of Elifer, a late sixth century ruler of York. He and his brother Gwrgi were famous heroes who had the rare distinction of being mentioned in the *Welsh Annals* not once but twice. In 573 they defeated Gwenddolau at Arfdererydd and they were killed in battle in 580. There is definitely an Arthurian connection to these events. Arfdererydd is the same battle connected to Merlin. This suggests that Peredur was the origin of Perceval but there is no way to be absolutely certain, especially since the name of the father was different in the traditions than in history and the fact that the traditional character was connected to Dyfed, not York.

The fictional Perceval was a child of nature. He spent all of his time in the woods. One day he met some knights. Dazzled by their shining armour he mistook them for angels. When they told him who they really were he decided to become a knight and set out to find the king. On the way he came across a richly decorated tent with a beautiful woman asleep inside of it. He climbed into bed beside her, and when she awoke he attempted to seduce her. The woman resisted the hero's advances, telling him she was married. Perceval stole one kiss. He then took a ring because he misunderstood a piece of advice his mother had given him regarding taking tokens of affection from ladies. Perceval's position here is similar to Gawain's meeting with Lady Bercilak in *Sir Gawain and the Green Knight*. Both involved a beautiful woman, an attempted seduction and the hero receiving a token from the woman. The difference is that the roles have become reversed. In the Gawain story it is the woman who steals a kiss after failing to seduce the hero. As has already been stated the Gawain episode is similar to an Irish tale involving the Morrigan and Cu Chulainn.

Up until now this narration has referred to the main character as Perceval. But this has been for convenience. In several versions of the tale he had no name at this point. When asked he stated that he was called "dear son," "dear brother" or "dear master." After his meeting with the married woman he met his cousin, who told him that his name was Perceval. The episode seems to be a mingling of different ideas of nomenclature from different cultures. Several Britano-Gaelic heroes went through a process of renaming. In Irish tales Cu Chulainn was original called Setanta and Finn mac Cool grew up with the name Demne. On the other hand the dominant idea in Western Europe in the Middle Ages was that people were defined by their names. For this reason the character could not change his name without changing who he was. To get around this problem the hero grew up with no name at all. Perceval's cousin was mourning the death of her lover, who had just been slain by the Red Knight. The hero set out after the murderer to avenge the crime. This underlined the importance of his naming. At first he had merely wanted to become a knight to gain glory. Deciding to right the wrong of the murder marked him as a noble figure. It is because his true nature has been revealed that he can be named.

The Red Knight broke his way into Arthur's court and proceeded to insult the king and queen in a way reminiscent of the Green Knight and the villain in *The Knight of the Cart*. Perceval arrived a short time after the knight fled and gained the king's permission to confiscate the Red Knight's armour if he could defeat the villain. Perceval caught up with him, defeated him and took the armour. In an Irish adventure featuring Finn mac Cool the hero came across a woman whose son had just been killed. Finn tracked down and slew the perpetrator of that crime. The fact that Perceval's opponent is associated with the colour red is significant. Although they do not appear in that particular story, Finn's archenemies were the sons of Deira the Red.

Arthur was impressed with the hero's prowess, as was everyone at court. This was a common occurrence in Britano-Gaelic tales. Since the hero had grown up in obscurity he had to do something in public in order to prove himself to others. The most famous example of this type of event was the sword-in-the-stone, which showed that Arthur was the rightful king. Another example came from Ireland: while still only a teenager, Finn mac Cool defeated all of the other contestants in a hurly match, a game similar to field hockey. The losing players became angered over their embarrassing defeat and attacked Finn, who quickly overcame them by using his hurly stick as a club. It was after this incident that his name was changed from Demne to Finn.

After defeating the Red Knight, Perceval became the student of a man named Gornemant who was to teach him what he needed to know about being a knight. One of Gornemant's teachings was a warning not to be impolite by asking too many questions. This may be an example of a *geis* (pronounced "gesh"). A *geis* was an injunction placed upon a character forbidding the person from doing something or to refrain from doing something. If a *geis* were broken dire consequences would ensue. It was a two edged sword. Even if the character did follow the *geis*, he or she could still end up in trouble. A good example appears in the tale *The Pursuit of Diarmaid and Grainne*, one of the Irish versions of *Tristan and Iseult*. In the story Grainne is promised in marriage to Finn mac Cool. However at the feast celebrating the marriage she meets and falls in love with one of Finn's followers, Diarmaid. Contriving to see him in private, Grainne first attempts to seduce him, and when this fails she lays a *geis* upon him that he must run off with her that very night. Uncertain about what he should do, Diarmaid consults several of his friends, one of whom is a druid who is highly respected for his wisdom. The druid states that although it is dishonourable to elope with his chieftain's fiancé, he dare not break the *geis*. Finn seeks revenge; Diarmaid is magically transformed into a boar, which is then killed by Finn and his followers. Poor Diarmaid was in a no win situation. Breaking the *geis* would have been fatal, but following it was also fatal.

Unfortunately the only examples of the *geis* come from Ireland, not from Wales where the Grail legend is thought to have originated. However this may be the result of the timing involved in the recording of legends. The advent of Christianity brought an end to the pagan practice of laying a *geis*. The Irish conversions took place at a later date from that of the Welsh. On the other hand the Irish recorded their myths and legends hundreds of years before the Welsh did the same. As a result the Irish material contains many pagan elements while the Welsh stories went through centuries of editing by Christian bards and storytellers. The use of a love potion in *Tristan and Iseult* may have come about as the result of the search for a suitable substitute for a *geis* in the original.

To return to the story, when his training was over Perceval set out on his first quest. He reached a river in which there was a man fishing in a boat. Fish, especially salmon, were considered mystical creatures. The Salmon of Wisdom that was eaten by the Irish hero Finn has already been mentioned in Chapter One. As if to emphasize the mystic nature of the situation Perceval is informed that there is no bridge or ferry across the river for twenty leagues in either direction. A league is three miles. Twenty leagues in both directions means that the river was impassible for one hundred and twenty miles. There is no such river anywhere in Britain. Water was a common boundary between reality and the Otherworld in Britano-Gaelic mythology. Perceval had reached that boundary and was about to cross it. The man, who was a king, invited the knight to his castle. In order to reach it the hero had to climb to the other side of a mountain and descend into a valley below. When Perceval ascended to the mountaintop he saw no castle. Just as he came to believe that he had been tricked, he came upon it unexpectedly. The sudden appearance of this castle marks it as being part of the Otherworld. In Britano-Gaelic tales heroes often found the homes of the gods in abrupt ways. Simply going to sleep on a hillside or crossing a stream could have been enough to introduce a character to the land of the gods. Upon reaching the castle Perceval found his host already there, seated on a throne and waiting for him. The hero then discovered that his host had been wounded; a lance had been thrust through both of his thighs. Celtchair son of Uthechar, one of the characters in the Irish story *The Tale of Macc Da Tho's Pig*, had received exactly the same wound and a Welsh poem records that the god Bran was the victim of a similar wound.

While inside the castle Perceval was witness to a strange little parade usually called the Grail Procession. Different authors gave different versions of this Procession, but four elements were usually the same. A youth entered carrying a sword; three maidens followed him. The first bore a spear that was dripping with blood, which was caught on a platter that was carried by the second maiden. The third maiden followed behind carrying the Grail. The sun god Lugh had a spear that was covered in blood, or in some versions it rested against a cauldron that was full of blood. After the Grail Procession everyone sat down to eat and the Grail was passed among the feasters. It magically produced everyone's favorite food. Although very curious, Perceval remembered the advice of his teacher and asked no questions.

The hero spent the night in the castle. When he awoke the next morning he found the castle gone and he was shocked to discover that the Fisher King's country had become a barren wasteland. The usual way for a hero to leave the dwelling of a divine being was to find it gone. In the Irish story *Phantom's Frenzy*, Conn paid a visit to the home of the god Lugh, and his wife, the Sovereignty of Ireland. After serving Conn a feast of ribs and giving him drinks from a golden cup, Lugh spoke a prophecy in which he named all of Conn's descendents who would become king. After this the palace and the divine hosts vanished, leaving Conn alone with the cup.

The wasteland is closely connected to the belief in the king marrying the land, which has already been mentioned. Since the king had been wounded through the thighs he had been rendered sexually impotent. In the Grail legends this was only implied but in *Macc Da Tho's Pig* it is specifically stated. As the king was impotent the land, his wife, could not be fruitful. The idea of an impotent king is found in the Welsh tale of *Math, Son of Mathonwy*. In that story, King Math must spend every day resting his feet in the lap of a beautiful virgin or else he will die. The fact that the king comes into daily physical contact with a desirable woman-with her lap no less-yet she remains a virgin is an obvious indication that he is impotent. The wasteland also appears in Welsh tradition in association with the southern Welsh region of Dyfed. In the tale Dyfed's queen is Rhiannon, the mother of Pryderi. As has already been mentioned, Pryderi is an alternate form of Peredur, the Welsh original of Perceval.

To return to the Grail story, not knowing what else to do, Perceval went back to King Arthur's court. While he was there an ugly old woman appeared and began to insult the hero. This woman was the one who had carried the Grail in the procession the night before, but she was young and beautiful then. The motif is similar to the Irish story of Nail, dying of thirst, agreeing to sleep with the old hag in order to gain a drink of water. As was mentioned, as soon as she obtains his promise she becomes young and beautiful, announces that she is the goddess Medb and promises that Nail will become high king of Ireland. This story not only illustrates the idea of a goddess who can change her appearance but also reinforces the sexual connection between the king and the goddess of the land. The woman told Perceval that if he had asked the proper question the king would have been healed and the land restored. Since he did not do that, the Grail had disappeared. The hero must then go on a quest and find it again, bring it back and ask the question.

The Grail will heal the king. In *Branwen Daughter of Llyr* King Matholwch of Ireland had a magic cauldron of such great healing power it could bring the dead back to life. In this story Bran stole the cauldron. In other tales Bran had a magic dish that had healing powers. It should also be remembered that the Grail provided the food for the feasters, instantly providing whatever dishes the people most wanted. The cauldron stolen by Arthur and his men in *The Spoils of Annwn* had exactly the same power. A cauldron belonging to the Irish god the Daghda could perform the same feat. Obviously the cauldron and the dish are different versions of the same object. Equally obviously it is the origin of the Grail, since *graal* was a kind of dish. The Welsh recognized the Fisher King as Bran and if they wanted to pass the Grail off as a cup used at the Last Supper they had to find a way to make a connection between them. That is why they invented the story of Joseph of Arimathea coming to Britain and becoming Bran's tutor.

According to Chretien de Troyes, after setting out to find the Grail Perceval encountered the lady whose ring he had stolen. She was dressed in rags and rode on a decrepit old mule. She had informed the hero that because of their earlier encounter her husband believed that she had taken a lover and given him the ring as a token of her affection. Her husband decided to publicly humiliate her as punishment. She also warned Perceval that her husband was nearby and would attack him without warning if he saw them speaking together. This situation mirrors the plot of the Welsh story of *Gereint and Enid*, and told by Chretien de Troyes as *Erec and Enide*. In the tale Gereint believes that Enid has been unfaithful to him. As a punishment he forces her to ride ahead of him on a mule. Gereint then attacks any knight who dares to speak to her. This continues until the hero discovers that Enid is innocent, and the fault is not her infidelity but his jealousy. Perceval defeated the lady's husband in combat and then verified her innocence. He then ordered that his vanquished opponent should go straight to the nearest house, see that his wife was bathed and properly clothed in garments suitable for her station. The two were then to travel to the court of King Arthur, publicly recount their story and ensure that the woman was made one of the ladies-in-waiting to the queen.

Perceval eventually arrived at the Grail castle. The castle was called Corbenic. There are several ideas about the linguistic origin of this name, but the best idea points out that it is reminiscent of the Latin *corvanus*, which means raven. Bran is Welsh for raven. In his adventures along the way he discovered that he was related not only to the Fisher King but to the woman who insulted him as well. The characters in other tales were often related. Tristan was Mark's nephew, Arthur's sister was Morgan and his son was Mordred. However this aspect was not exclusively Britano-Gaelic, family connections were also very important in medieval society and were often emphasized in the stories. The castle was on an island and could only be reached by boat. The cauldron in *The Spoils of Annwn* was on an island. The one in *Branwen* came from Ireland, which is also an island. One other Welsh tale made use of a magic cauldron. It was one of the objects that the hero Culwch had to obtain before he could marry the lady Olwen. In that story the mystic article was again located in Ireland. It should also be borne in mind that Midir's island fortress contained a magic cauldron in the story of Cu Chulainn and Blathnat. The connection between the Otherworld and islands has already been explained in the section on Avalon and need not be repeated here.

Perceval eventually secured the Grail and returned with it. He then asked the question, "whom does the Grail serve?" Since the answer was the king, the question was a reaffirmation of his position as king. This re-established his connection to the land. The monarch was restored to health and the land supported growing things again. The tale was about the mystical union that the Britano-Gaels believed to exist between the ruler and the land. He had to be healed by a mystical object, the sacred cauldron of Britano-Gaelic mythology, which was associated with both healing and the fruitfulness of nature.

Much of the forgoing is not new. Many scholars are familiar with the material and have been ever since the 1960's and the first in-depth investigation of the story by Roger Sherman Loomis. Loomis concluded that the tale concerned the changing of the seasons. The Wasteland represented the winter, the Fisher King was the sun god, Lugh, and his wounded state symbolized the sun's weakness in winter. The divine woman was the Goddess of Sovereignty, who personified the land. She was beautiful in summer and ugly in winter. Loomis supported this by pointing out that in Irish tradition the most important of the goddesses of sovereignty, Eriu, was married to a deity called Mac Grene. His name meant "Son of the Sun" and Loomis asserted that it was another name for Lugh but concluded that the story was Irish in origin, with the sea god Bran being connected to the tale by the Welsh.

Although he did an excellent job of researching the tale, some of the conclusions that Loomis drew cannot be supported. The four objects in the Grail Procession (the sword, lance, platter and Grail) argue against Irish origins for the legend. Jessie L. Weston has shown that in a slightly different form they were part of the cult of Adonis from the Mediterranean world. In the Adonis cult the lance was a wand, and the Grail (or dish) was a cup. If Robert de Boron knew this it would explain why he called the Grail a cup. The four Adonis objects are still seen today as the suits in a deck of Tarot cards. Adonis was a figure from Greco-Roman mythology that was associated with the death and rebirth of plants. It would be logical to associate him with a tale concerned with the changing of the seasons. However the Romans never conquered Ireland and Irish mythology shows very little influence from Latin beliefs. The Adonis objects must have been added in Britain some time during the Imperial period. The legend must have been known to the Britons before the late fourth century, for by that time they were thoroughly Christianized and would not have been interested in adopting a pagan Irish myth and infusing it with pagan Greco-Roman elements. The changing of the seasons is such a basic part of life that the original story would have been common to all Britano-Gaelic peoples, not just the Irish. The Welsh may have known of, and even been influenced by, Irish versions of the tale but they did not adopt it from the Irish.

The evidence that Loomis himself used to claim Irish origins for the story contradicts the idea that the sea god became associated with the legend in Wales. Loomis found three Irish *echtras* (adventure tales) with parallels to the Grail legend. In all three the hero arrives at an Otherworldly palace where he is served a delicious feast. One of these tales includes a question similar to the one found in the Grail legend and another is concerned with restoring fertility to the land. In *Phantom's Frenzy*, the hero does indeed encounter the sun god and the Goddess of Sovereignty. However, in *The Adventures of Cormac in the Land of Promise*, the goddess is not present and the god is Manannan mac Lir. The Welsh version of Manannan was Manawydan, who was the chief sea god and Bran's brother. In *The Adventures of Art, Son of Conn*, the divine couple is Manannan's niece and her husband, Daire. The presence of the sea god or his relative in these *echtras* means that the practice of associating him with the Grail legend was common on both sides of the Irish Sea.

This may have been because two different stories with similar elements became confused with one another. There is other evidence to indicate the presence of another story within the tale.

Jessie Weston argued, and Loomis agreed, that Gawain was the original hero of the Grail legend. Given the emphasis placed upon the king's relationship to the land, such a suggestion corresponds to Gawain's royal associations that were examined in the last chapter. This idea would also explain why Perceval's attempt to seduce the married woman resembles Gawain's encounter with Lady Bercilak. Chretien de Troyes devoted approximately half of his version of the story to Gawain's adventures, even though Perceval was the main character. Gawain was the hero of the so-called First Continuation of Chretien's tale and the Grail Romance called *Diu Crone* ("The Crown") by Heinrich von dem Turlin. The First Continuation was a Grail related story that was added to Chretien's manuscript shortly after the author's death. The person who wrote it is unknown. It concerned Gawain's visit to the Fisher King's castle, which was on an island at the end of a causeway that extended for miles out to sea. While there the hero saw a corpse lying on a bier and a broken sword. The king, who was not wounded in this version, gave the broken sword to Gawain and asked him to attempt to repair it by putting the pieces together. When he failed to mend the blade, Gawain was told that he was unworthy to complete the quest. He then found himself on the seashore, which had been a wasteland, but now life had returned to it. Since Gawain's actions somehow restored fertility to the land that could not have been the quest he was unworthy to perform. The dead body provided a clue as to the mysterious second quest. Loomis pointed out that Perceval bore a resemblance to the Irish hero Finn mac Cool. The upbringing of the two characters was similar and they shared a tale of avenging the death of an innocent man. In the Finn tale the murderer was one of two men responsible for killing the hero's father. Finn never encountered his father's other killer in the written sources. However Loomis discovered that as late as the nineteenth century oral traditions in Ireland and Scotland told a tale of Finn avenging his father's death, but no one ever wrote it down.

The revenge motif took centre stage in the tale *Peredur Son of Evrawg*, the only surviving Welsh version of the Grail legend. Many of the familiar elements are present-the hero being raised in obscurity by his mother, his mistaking of knights for angels, a man, in this case his uncle, who undertakes to teach the hero, the injunction against asking questions, the avenging of the death of the husband of a female relative (in this instance she is the hero's foster-sister) the blood soaked lance, the maimed king and his connection to the land and the rebuke for the unasked question. The important element that is missing is the Grail itself. Instead of that mystical object the hero is shown a severed head on a platter. It is the head of Peredur's cousin and the plot concerns the hero's quest to avenge the death of his relative.

Originally the sea god may have played a part in an extended version of the revenge tale. The Irish sources used by Loomis hint as much. As mentioned Finn's enemies were the sons of Daire the Red. The name is suggestive. The colour red was used by Britano-Gaels to signify divine or supernatural beings. In the Irish tale *The Cattle Raid of Regamon*, the goddess Medb appears with red skin and dressed in red clothes. A giant who also wears red accompanies her. The text suggests that he is a god but does not reveal which one. The association of the colour with the divine can be seen even in the Romances. For example, Mabon, the son of the goddess Modron, appears in *Erec and Enide* under the name Mabonagrain. He is described as being a foot taller than the tallest knight and clad in scarlet armour.

The name Daire occurs with suspicious frequency in Irish tales, and always in connection with the supernatural. Aside from Daire the Red, men who bare the name include: 1) the father of Cu Rui, the shape-shifting Irish equivalent of the Green Knight, 2) the owner of the fateful Brown Bull, an enormous animal with human reason and the target of *The Cattle Raid of Cooley*, and 3) the husband of the niece of the sea god in *The Adventures of Art, Son of Conn*. Could it be that all of Daires were the same character? Was the original opponent of Finn/Perceval a supernatural being who was associated with the sea god? If this were so it would help explain how the sea god became entangled in the Grail legend. Unfortunately this hypothesis rests entirely on a coincidence of names and such evidence is too weak to support a firm conclusion. One argument against it is that Finn's son was also called Daire and he was certainly not the same person as Daire the Red.

To summarize what has been suggested: the Grail legend was derived from two different stories. One recounted Gawain's adventures with the sun god and Goddess of Sovereignty, his search for a mystic cauldron and concerned the passing of the seasons and the king's connection to the land. The other featured Gwynn (the Welsh version of Finn) who was later replaced by Perceval. The other important characters were the sea god and Daire the Red. It involved a blood feud and the hero's attempt to avenge the death of a family member. Both stories included a visit by the hero to an Otherworldly palace. While there the hero failed a test (failing to ask the Grail question or an inability to repair the sword). Because of this failure he was sent on a quest. The hero also participated in a feast before leaving. As time went on the two accounts became confused with one another because of their similarities. The fact that the Lugh story was concerned with fertility may have added to the confusion. Bran was also associated with fertility in that he not only owned a magic platter of plenty but also a magic drinking horn, which could provide any kind of drink. The conversions to Christianity would have added to this process. Once the supernatural characters lost their religious significance it would no longer have been necessary to keep them distinct from one another. Confused versions of both stories continued to be passed down in the oral traditions. However once the tales came to be written down it was inevitable that one account would be preferred over the other. Perceval became recognized as the Grail hero, probably because he was the main character in Chretien de Troyes' version of the story and Chretien was the most respected of all early Romancers. However, several of the Gawain variants were preserved before Perceval eclipsed Gawain altogether.

Chretien de Troyes, Robert de Boron, the anonymous author of the *Perlesvaus* and Wolfram von Eschenbach, to name the most important authors, followed the first version of the Grail legend, with differences in detail and emphasis. But there was another, very different rendering of the tale, introduced in the *Quest for the Holy Grail* of the *Vulgate Cycle* and used again by Thomas Malory in *Le Morte D'Arthur*.

The medieval world was very religious. Its people also believed in magic. There were only two places magic could come from: heaven or hell. Since the Grail was a magical item and it performed good works it had to be connected to God. Even as early as Chretien's work this is evident. His Fisher King had an invalid father who survived by eating the Eucharist served from the Grail. Later versions added more Christian elements. The lance became the Spear of Longinus that had pierced Jesus' side while he was on the cross. The Grail was turned into the cup used at the Last Supper that was put into the hands of Joseph of Arimathea for safekeeping. Joseph used it to catch some of Christ's blood as he suffered on the cross. The hero became a descendant of Joseph and part of a family line whose duty it was to protect the Grail.

These changes evolved over time. However they were sparked by a real event. In 1099 the warriors of the First Crusade captured Jerusalem and established the so-called Crusader States in order to defend it. In 1187 the Crusaders in the Holy Land were badly beaten at the Battle of Hattin and Jerusalem fell back into Muslim hands. From a European point of view this was not only a military disaster but a spiritual one as well. Ever since the first century, with the concept of the New Jerusalem in the Book of Revelations, Christian Europeans had associated the place with salvation. This image was reinforced in the fifth century when St. Augustine used Jerusalem as a metaphor for heaven in his book *The City of God*. To the peoples of medieval Europe there were two Jerusalems, the actual location and the spiritual haven, and they did not necessarily understand the distinction between them. Crusading opened the gates of heaven not merely because unbelievers were killed and the faith spread to new lands but also because the Crusaders were defending God's holy city.

With Jerusalem in the hands of the Muslims a new Crusade was organized to get it back. In the meantime a new spiritual quest was needed to fill the void. The Grail was one of several substitutes. From a psychological standpoint the Grail's importance became even greater when it was realized that Jerusalem could not be recaptured. In order to make the story work as a Christian tale it was necessary to alter it to eliminate all pagan elements. The rewriting of the work found its greatest expression in *The Quest of the Holy Grail* of the *Vulgate Cycle*. The *Quest* has been called an "un-Romance" and this is an apt description. It is not concerned with heroic deeds but rather with a journey of spiritual enlightenment. In many ways it has more in common with other medieval works of spiritual journeys like the *Divine Comedy* than it has with Arthurian Romances like *Parzival*. The man who takes this journey is a new character, Lancelot's son, Galahad.

There is some argument as to where his name comes from. Those who wish a Britano-Gaelic origin claim it is traceable to a Welsh hero named Gwalcheved. This means "Hawk (or Falcon) of Summer." It is a variation of Gwalchmai, the "Hawk of May," who appears in the Romances as Gawain, who was probably the original Grail hero. On the other hand it is quite possible that the anonymous author of the *Quest* invented Galahad. This explanation is more likely. Unlike other Romance writers the author of the *Quest* was a monk. His was a religious theme, which maintained that the other Knights of the Round Table were not worthy of attaining the Grail. Since this was the case it makes more sense for him to have created a completely new character rather than look back in Welsh sources for an obscure rendering of Gawain's name. In fact there is no evidence that he used any Welsh material at all. Everything that he needed to know about Arthur's court and the Grail itself he could have learned from reading other Romances without going to the original sources. What is more he certainly invented other characters like Sir Bors, who played an important role in the *Quest*. A non-Britano-Gaelic origin is also indicated be the fact that in the *Quest* Galahad is Lancelot's son. No close connection existed between Lancelot and Gawain in any of the older material.

Galahad's character is very different from that of any of the other heroes. He has been accused of being two-dimensional: a cardboard saint who is too much of an allegory himself to be taken seriously. This is unfair, as it ignores the fact that he is capable of strong relationships with those around him, including both Perceval and that knight's sister. Galahad's dealings with this lady are significant. Because of the nature of his character and the main thrust of the story she is not merely the hero's love interest, as so many women are in the tales. She acts as a spiritual guide for the young knight. This means that their friendship is more complex than those that exist between the heroes and the heroines of most of the Romances. Galahad is the embodiment of the ideal Christian knight whereas his father Lancelot is the embodiment of the ideal valiant knight. It is his Christian piety that makes him difficult to understand in this secular age, but is essential in understanding the medieval view of the legend. It is significant that Galahad was Lancelot's son. Lancelot was the greatest of the Arthurian knights and until the *Quest* he was also the hero of the *Vulgate Cycle*. In fact the *Cycle* itself is often give the title of the *Prose Lancelot*. According to the story Lancelot was originally called Galahad. However only the knight who completed the Grail quest could hold that name. When Lancelot was found to be too worldly his name was changed.[75] Both he and Gawain went on the Grail quest, but because it had become a spiritual journey and they were worldly knights, they found that not only could they not complete it but also nothing at all happened to them. The two complained bitterly at how tiresome the whole business was. In a way they were like the modern critics who have attacked Galahad's character. They wanted adventure and had no interest in a spiritual allegory.

Lancelot and Gawain were unfavorably compared to Galahad on several occasions in the story. The sword-in-the-stone was repeated, but this time it was used to find the greatest knight in the world. Lancelot refused to attempt it. Gawain tried, but only after being ordered to by Arthur. He failed. Galahad also attempted it at the king's request, and he succeeded. The knight also passed the test of the Perilous Seat (a.k.a. the Siege Perilous). This was a chair at the Round Table, which no one but the greatest knight could occupy. In this story the son supplanted the

---

75 This is a rare exception to the medieval belief that people could not change their names.

father as the greatest knight because of his virtuous nature. As Tennyson said of Galahad "his strength was as the strength of ten, because his heart was pure." Having established the hero's credentials, the story progressed with the introduction of the Grail. The room was suddenly filled with a great light. The doors opened by themselves and the Grail floated in, circled the company and left. Everyone present was instantly presented with his or her favorite foods. Gawain was so affected by the scene that he vowed to find where the Grail came from and to sit again at the table blessed with its presence. Since his motives were selfish (getting a good meal) he was doomed to failure before he even began. Lancelot was tainted by his adulterous affair with the queen, so he also could not complete the quest. The Grail hero was of course Galahad, but he was not alone in his success. Three knights reached the Grail Castle. The more usual Grail hero, Perceval, and a new character named Bors accompanied Galahad. He seems to have been created specifically so that the companions would number three. Three is just as important to Christian numerology as it was to the pagan Britano-Gaels. Only Galahad proved worthy of actually completing the quest, although both of the others were good enough to be allowed to see the sacred relic.

The completion of the quest did not heal a king or return fertility to the land. The story ended with Galahad meeting Josephus, the son of Joseph of Arimathea, who then accompanied the knight's soul into heaven. The Grail had become the means to salvation, the true goal of the *Quest*. The Grail legend is a good example of what happened to the Arthurian stories once they began to be written down by the Romancers. Elements that would appeal to a medieval French or English or German audience were added or emphasized, removing the tales from their Britano-Gaelic roots. But the influences were not all in one direction. Arthurian aspects had an affect on the world around them. Sometimes this influence outlasted the world were it was first felt. This is the Arthurian legacy, which must now be examined.

Chapter X

The Arthurian Legacy

A T THE risk of stating the obvious, Arthur was one of the most popular and respected figures of the medieval world. As far back as the early fourteenth century Europeans adopted the concept of the Nine Worthies. The oldest reference to them is a work called *Vows of the Peacock* (*Voeux du paon*) written in 1312 by Jacques de Longuyon. It is uncertain if he invented the idea or was merely the first person to write it down. Whatever the origin, the idea became quite popular and was used in literature, plays, tapestries and other art forms. The Nine Worthies were considered the greatest heroes who ever lived. There were three pagan: Alexander the Great, Hector and Julius Caesar; three Jewish: Joshua, David and Judas Maccabaeus; and three Christian: Arthur, Charlemagne and the crusader Godfrey de Bullion. This places Arthur in very illustrious company.

It is common today to speak of King Arthur and the Knights of the Round Table. In the fifth and sixth centuries there were knights, but not as we think of them today. Originally a knight was any warrior wealthy enough to afford a warhorse. The full title the Romans used for one was *in ordenum equestrem recipere*, "member of the equestrian order." They were called *eques* for short, a word linked to *equus*, the Latin word for horse. In all Western European languages except English, the term for knight means a horseman. For example, in German it is *ritter*. English is a Germanic language and it is not a coincidence that *ritter* looks similar to rider; they are essentially the same word. Even at the height of their power most English knights fought on foot. Because of this the English word is derived from an Old English word meaning "one who serves." Since all knights were vassals to superior lords or the king himself, they all served in a feudal sense.[76]

Knighthood as it is now understood grew out of a series of military and social reforms enacted by the Franks in the eighth and ninth centuries. The process was started by Charles Martel ("the Hammer"), and reached its peak under his grandson, Charlemagne. This change in the idea of knighthood led to an alteration in the way in which they were depicted in the tales.

---

76 By an interesting coincidence, the Japanese word *samurai* also denotes one who serves. This is because, like the English knights, many fought on foot.

The time period influenced the stories, but the stories influenced the society. By the thirteenth century knights at tournaments began organizing Round Tables where they pretended to be characters from the Romances. In the following century such ideas were taken a step further with the formation of the Knightly Orders. Religious orders such as that of the Benedictine monks had existed for centuries. The Crusades begat a new phenomenon by establishing orders of warrior monks like the Knight Templars and the Teutonic Order. In 1330 King Alphonso XI of the Spanish kingdom of Castile added a new aspect when he created the Order of the Band. It was the first such organization without an overtly religious purpose. Edward III of England followed Alphonso's lead with the Order of the Garter. Edward's stated purpose was to remake Arthur's Order of the Knights of the Round Table. The Order of the Garter still exists in Britain today. It is very exclusive and membership is an honour that can be bestowed only by the monarch. Recent scholarship has revealed that Edward originally intended to have an Order of the Round Table, complete with a new castle built as its headquarters, but when this proved too expensive (he was waging a war against France at the same time) he abandoned the idea and replaced it with the Garter instead.

Every age has interpreted the Arthurian material to suit its own viewpoint. Edward III and his contemporaries saw Arthur and his knights as being much like them, or at least idealized versions of how they saw themselves. Men tried to emulate the exploits of the heroes. Knights were trained as warriors, fighting was their profession. But they had an unrealistic view of how they should do it. They hungered for personal glory in a world where warfare was relying more and more on trained armies that emphasized teamwork instead of individual effort. Nothing exemplifies the differences between the real and the ideal more than the Tournament of the Thirty.

The Hundred Years War was the longest conflict ever fought. Despite its name it actually lasted one hundred and sixteen years. It was a contest in which England and France battled each other for control of the French throne. The war was conducted with a few years of campaigning punctuated with long lulls of little or no activity besides raiding. In 1351 thirty French knights issued a challenge to the English to send thirty of their knights to do battle. This was war the way they liked it, with no archers or pikemen or any other non-noble rabble who were beginning to dominate the battlefields of Europe.[77] The conflict lasted several days; four French and eight English knights were killed. The Tournament had a profound effect on the people of the time, at least among the knightly classes. Even when they were old men the veterans of that confrontation were treated with great honour and respect because of their achievement. The Romances were

---

77 The Tournament was not unique. In 1396 King Robert III of Scotland ordered a similar meeting between Clan Chattan and Clan Ha in order to prevent their ongoing feud from blowing up into a full civil war. The confrontation took place at Perth and ended in a victory for Chattan. There is no other historical reference to Clan Ha, but Cameron is the best guess. They were Chattan's chief rivals and it is known that they changed their name during the late Middle Ages.

popular with the nobility for the same reason the Tournament of the Thirty had been. The stories emphasized individual prowess and achievement. Lancelot and Gawain and all the others did the kind of things that these knights wanted to do but could not.

The cause of the knight's frustrations can be seen by a study of the course of the war. English longbowmen massacred the greatest flower of French chivalry on three separate occasions: Crecy (1346), Poitiers (1356) and Agincourt (1415). This was an especially bitter pill for them to swallow, as the bowmen were not only commoners, but commoners from the lowest of classes- the peasants. Peasants were viewed as little better than animals by most knights. In fact they were often seen as less important than a good horse. One point should be made about the longbow itself, although the weapon is generally associated with the English, it was actually Welsh.

The longbow had been widespread throughout Europe in ancient times. The collapse of the Empire caused the collapse of the economy of Western Europe. Roman armour was passed down for generations because it was too expensive for all but the wealthiest to have new armour made. By the mid-seventh century this armour began to wear out. The longbow was replaced by the short-bow, which was easier to make and to master. It did not have the same penetrating power, but with little good armour that did not matter. There is no mention in the sources of the longbow again until the twelfth century when an English army invading Wales got a rude shock when Welsh archers penetrated their armour at great distances. It is not known if the Welsh abandoned the longbow and then reinvented it, or if they never got rid of it. In wars in which different Welsh kingdoms battled each other ambushing enemies was a common tactic and the longbow would have been ideal for that purpose, especially since Wales is mountainous. Topography dictated weaponry. The English had bitter experience of just how effective the longbow could be. For this reason they enlisted Welsh archers into English armies and later they adopted the weapon itself for use by their own men. At both Crecy and Poitiers the majority of the "English" bowmen were actually Welsh.

The English received another rude shock, or rather two, when their enemies managed to gain the upper hand in the Hundred Years War. The first was the person who rallied the French and sent them back on the offensive. Joan of Arc was all wrong by medieval standards. Not only was she a girl (she was only nineteen when she was executed) in a male dominated world, but she was also a commoner. No wonder the French thought she had been sent by God and the English accused her of witchcraft. The second major setback for the English came when the French adopted a powerful weapon of their own.

The weapon that allowed the French to recover was the cannon. By the end of the war, France had the best artillery in Europe and their experts knew how to use it to devastating effect. Like the longbow it was a weapon of the lower classes, although not as low as the peasantry. For consolation the knights liked to retreat into a fantasy world where members of their class were supreme and those of the non-knightly classes were almost never allowed to intrude.

Another aspect that appealed to the audiences of the time was Courtly Love. In the Middle Ages Courtly Love was a code of behavior governing the proper conduct of a knight with a lady, which today is usually and inaccurately called chivalry. Chivalry was actually the warrior's code that knights followed in war. The word itself is directly related to cavalry and the French word for knight, *chivalier*, both of which are terms for mounted warriors. Courtly Love is often misunderstood today. There are those who believe that it championed adultery. Actually it was nothing more than a pattern of courtesy. As a way of being polite a knight was supposed to pretend that he was in love with any lady he met, especially if the lady were married. It was taken not only as a compliment to the woman herself but also her husband to show him how lucky he was to have a wife other men adored. Far from having a love affair, the lady in question and the man paying court to her usually did not so much as touch hands.

A man was supposed to suffer in love by *not* sleeping with his beloved. Suffering was thought to build character. The greatest achievement was to love without being allowed a physical relationship. Far from condoning adultery, married women were preferred precisely because their lovers could not consummate a union with them. This is evident in the Romances themselves. Adultery played a role in the tales of Lancelot and Tristan, but these stories are ancient Britano-Gaelic in origin. Furthermore neither of these knights was noted for their manners. Gawain was the one character said to best exemplify the ideals of Courtly Love. An important aspect of Courtly Love was that most of the time the man was not really attracted to the woman-he merely pretended to be because that was the polite thing to do. The anonymous author of *Sir Gawain and the Green Knight* used this to good affect. He turned the entire temptation scene into a parody of Courtly Love. Gawain had followed convention by telling Bercilak's wife how beautiful she was and how he loved her dearly. When she actually came to his bedroom to make their relationship more intimate, he was horrified. He had to backtrack and find a way to tell her that he was not serious without hurting her feelings.

The Britano-Gaelic tales and the concerns of medieval society often complemented one another. This was true not only in matters of chivalry and love but also in regard to the fate of Arthur as well. In the bardic sources the king's grave was listed as a mystery, while traditions in Brittany, Cornwall and Wales all said that Arthur did not die, but fell asleep. At the time of his country's greatest need he would awaken and lead his people to victory over their enemies. The Arthurian aspect of Welsh nationalism led to an English response. The long series of wars between the English and the Welsh came to an end in 1283 when Edward I (r.1272-1307) conquered Wales. Edward used a variety of methods to impose his rule. He weakened the conquered people politically by naming his own son as Prince of Wales, and militarily by building castles (many of which still stand) at strategic locations. He also made a great show of reburying the remains at Glastonbury to emphasize that Arthur was not only dead but also buried on what was then English soil. The Welsh countered by claiming that not only was the grave not that of Arthur but not even that of a human being. Llewellyn Fawr (the Great), a hero of Welsh independence, was shown the bones in 1277. He was said to have identified the skull as that of an ox, which he supposedly proved by showing that the space between the eyes was the span of a man's hand, too wide a gap for a human. This is an example of using propaganda to fight propaganda. As has already been pointed out the Glastonbury burial cannot be shown to be that of Arthur. On the other hand the idea that the English could not tell the difference between the skull of a human and the skull of a bovine is utterly ridiculous. It must have been a human skull; the question is whose skull? Unfortunately there is no way of knowing.

Arthur's popularity was assured for another reason. As time went on the Anglo-Saxons drew closer together and began to see themselves as one people. They were not Saxons or Jutes or the inhabitants of specific little kingdoms; they were the English. The idea of one people necessitated the idea of a common history, which was provided by both Bede and the anonymous compilers of *The Anglo-Saxon Chronicle*. But the situation became more complex in 1066 when William of Normandy conquered the English. The Normans were a foreign elite who saw themselves as distinct from the natives and had little interest in the Anglo-Saxon nation so they began to create a new one. The changing political situations brought about a change in attitudes. The conquest of Wales and the wars with France created the concept of a new people, the British. Not the Britons, the British. A common people need common heroes. Beowulf, the greatest Anglo-Saxon hero, would not fit the bill. He was not even an Anglo-Saxon. His popularity dated back to the days when these people had strong connections to the Scandinavian world. This held no attraction to the Welsh or the Normans and little even for the English anymore. The French hero Charlemagne would not work for similar reasons. The Normans were no longer French and neither the English nor the Welsh could identify with the Frankish emperor. But Arthur was different.

Although the Welsh had preserved the stories they were popular with the Normans because of their similarities to the Carolingian tales. Most of the adventures took place in what had become England and therefore had a frame of reference that transcended the border between England and Wales. The process of assimilation was helped by the fact that the Britons called their enemies the Saxons. Although educated English people would have recognized that the Saxons and the English were the same people, the difference in the term would actually have created a psychological barrier. The Saxons could be accepted as the enemy because although they were the English, in a way they were not the English.

Once England and Scotland became politically linked the idea could be expanded to include them as well. After all the ancient realm of the Britons did include southern Scotland. Many characters including Arthur himself, Merlin, Gawain and Lot were associated with places in Scotland, so that Arthur could be used as a hero for them too. Although the Scots may have fond memories of Robert the Bruce and the English had Richard the Lionhearted and the Welsh themselves had Owen Glendower, they could all share Arthur. The king of all the Britons became a king for all the British. Just as the difference in the terms Saxon and English helped to create a psychological barrier that made it appear as if they were two different peoples, the similarities between the words Briton and British created a psychological connection linking peoples who had been separate.

The medieval period came to an end in England in the late fifteenth century. This was a chaotic time in English history with a series of conflicts called the Wars of the Roses in which different branches of the royal family battled each other for the throne. It is not surprising that this was also when Sir Thomas Malory wrote the greatest medieval collection of the Arthurian stories, *Le Morte D'Arthur*. The story of a king who brought peace and maintained the right had obvious appeal in a time of lawlessness and civil war. The parallels were not lost on the eventual victor, Henry Tudor, who became King Henry VII. The Tudors were Welsh and Henry deliberately played on parallels to the legends by calling his eldest son Arthur. But this prince died before his father, so his second son succeeded their father as Henry VIII. The new king continued this style of propaganda. Proudly displayed in the great hall of Winchester Castle today there is a Round Table. Its legs are missing so it hangs from the wall like a work of art. It is decorated with a portrait of the king and labeled with the names of Arthur's knights. It was made during the reign of Edward III, the man who created the Order of the Garter but it was probably painted by the order of Henry VIII. In fact the portrait of Arthur bears a striking resemblance to Henry.

Over the course of the following centuries the figure of Arthur was reinterpreted over and over again to suit the needs of succeeding generations. An examination of all the incarnations would take a book in itself. This work will concentrate on a brief overview of the way in which the tales are treated today. Much of the modern image began to take shape in the nineteenth century. All things medieval became popular at that time. There were the novels of Sir Walter Scott, like *Ivanhoe*, a copy of medieval architecture called Victorian Gothic and Pre-Raphaelite painters used images from the Romances as inspiration for their works. Alfred Lord Tennyson wrote a collection of poems called *Idylls of the King*, in which Arthur was patterned after the image of Queen Victoria's husband and consort, Prince Albert. On the other side of the Atlantic Mark Twain gave the story a humorous twist in his book *A Connecticut Yankee in King Arthur's Court*. The tragedy tinged with comedy continued in twentieth century versions such as the novel *The Once and Future King* and the Broadway play *Camelot*. The tales gained a completely new perspective in the *Mists of Avalon*, which was told from the standpoint of the female characters. This opened the tales up to a much wider audience. Up until that point they had tended to be male dominated in both content and appeal.

Because there are so many different tales most modern versions tend to concentrate on certain aspects. These are usually the love triangle between the king, the queen and Lancelot, the central idea of failure to maintain the "Golden Age" of Camelot and the Holy Grail. As the position of women has changed in society, so have the female characters in the legends. In the medieval stories they were depicted in one of two ways. Some were like Morgan, conniving seductresses always hatching plots to kill the hero or overthrow the king. Others were shy beauties whose job it was to fall in love with the heroes and be a sort of reward for them once the quest was completed. Modern writers have created more three-dimensional characters that can think for themselves. Ironically that takes them closer to the depiction of women in Britano-Gaelic mythology.

Merlin has changed as well. He became the archetype of the wizard, with a long robe and flowing beard, despite the fact that originally he was a prophet, not a wizard. Many followers of the New Age of spirituality have turned him into the last arch druid of Britain despite the fact that the sources themselves insist he was a bard. Many view him with great respect despite the fact that ultimately he was a failure. In the original historical traditions he went insane after his actions led to the deaths of both his king and his nephew while in the medieval legends he could not even detect the treachery of his own pupil, Viviane, who imprisoned him forever.

Such reinterpretations are harmless, even beneficial. Unfortunately some attempts at reworking elements from the Arthurian stories have been neither harmless nor beneficial. The legends were given a sinister twist during the Second World War. Contrary to popular belief Adolf Hitler and most of the Nazi leaders were not Christians. They invented their own religion, which boasted nearly 200,000 members. It was an odd combination of superstition and racism. They believed in the literal truth of the legend of Atlantis and that its inhabitants had magical powers. When their island sank beneath the waves they fled taking the Holy Grail with them. This was supposedly some sort of magic object. The survivors of Atlantis intermarried with lesser races and lost their powers, but their most direct descendants were of course the Germans. Hitler believed that if he could find the Grail he could use its power, combined with careful breeding of pure Germans, to restore the miraculous powers of their ancestors. He scoured occupied Europe for any sign of the mystic object, he even sent agents as far away as Tibet to track down any clue as to its whereabouts.

He was not the last person to believe that the Grail was real. Since the early 1980's a cottage industry has sprung up producing books that purport to reveal a secret history buried in the legend. It has been linked to several Christian sects, the Free Masons, the Crusades, even the discovery of the New World. The basic theory is that Jesus fathered children and that families that claim descent from him still exist. They and their followers have been locked in a secret power struggle for dominance of the western world against the forces of traditional Christianity. The Grail is supposed to have had two main protectors: the Order of the Knight Templars and the Christian sect called the Albigensians. According to this conspiracy theory Wolfram von Eschenbach stated that the Templars were the guardians of the sacred relic. But the order he described was different from the real organization and works of fiction are not the best source from which to gain historical information.

This idea would not be a major problem if it did not carry with it the idea of the Templars and Albigensians being the "good guys" and their enemies being the "bad guys." The theory maintains that the Catholic Church and the governments of Western Europe, especially that of France, have been deliberately lying to millions of people for hundreds of years.

The truth is that the Order of the Knight Templars may have been suppressed as heretical but it was obviously framed by a group of secular rulers led by the king of France, Philip IV (r.1285-1314). The Orders were not popular because they maintained large armies that were answerable to their own Grand Masters, not the kings. The Templars were the largest and wealthiest of the Orders. The Church conducted investigations throughout Western Europe. The Inquisition found no evidence of heresy, except in France. The leader of the French Inquisition just happened to be a close personal friend of the king. The Inquisitions were answerable to the papacy but were financed by the secular governments. All of the rulers sent messages to the pope which said, in effect, that although there was no evidence of heresy, the Templars should be suppressed "just in case" and the monarchs should be compensated for paying for the investigation by being allowed to confiscate Templar assets.[78] It has been argued that their treasure has never been found, so it must have been hidden. But they did not have a treasure as such. This was real life, not the Arabian Nights. The Order did not have a vast pile of gold and jewels. Their assets were mainly in the form of land and livestock.

The Albigensians were a Christian sect who lived in southern France. They supposedly hid the Grail itself, or at least information about it, in their main stronghold. The attempt to include this group into a conspiracy to hide information on the descendants of Jesus is a strange thing to do. The Albigensians did not believe that Jesus had children; they did not even believe that he had a physical body. His physical form and crucifixion were illusions created to fool demonic powers. Their theology held that all created matter, including human flesh, was evil. Since Jesus was pure and good they believed that he could not have had a body and so could not have fathered any children. The conspiracy theorists explain this by saying that the Albigensians hid their true beliefs from fear of the Catholic Church. Which does not make any sense. The worst the Church could do was launch a crusade and unleash the Inquisition against them. But heresy is heresy. By supposedly pretending to believe in one heresy instead of another the Albigensians became the victims of crusade and Inquisition. So the supposed masquerade would have achieved absolutely nothing.

The idea that the Templars and the Albigensians were in league does not make any sense either. They were not allies they were enemies. They fought on opposite sides in the Albigensian Crusade, which lasted from 1203-'26. All of the elaborate theories that these books construct can be shattered in the same way. They all ignore vast amounts of information and force dubious interpretations on the evidence they do use.

---

78 Technically Templar property was supposed to be Church property. A compromise was reached in which the monarchs could confiscate the assets, but then had sell them to the Knight Hospitalers, the Templar's arch rivals. Not only did the monarchs inflate the prices, in many cases they simply refused to sell.

A more benign interpretation links the administration of John F. Kennedy with Camelot. The parallels are obvious. In both cases there was a highly respected leader who died tragically. There is also the idea that after his death things began to go down hill. After Kennedy the Vietnam War became more vicious, social unrest increased, American prestige around the world began to slip and more and more scandals eroded confidence in the government. This is an over-simplification. After all Kennedy's administration was not perfect, but then again Arthur's would not have been either. An idea's popularity is about perception, not reality.

These examples have shown that the stories have survived, but they do not explain why that should be so. One reason for the popularity of the tales is the subject matter of the stories themselves. The Arthurian Cycle is replete with adventure, love, betrayal and tragedy-four of the most basic story elements. They are universal, appearing in tales from every land and every time. The general public does not know other old stories nearly as well. Stories like *The Epic of Gilgamesh* or *The Song of Roland*, as well-written as they may be, are more limited in their scope. Also to be considered is the fact that each of the others is its own story, while the Arthurian material is a group of tales. Arthur is not really the hero of most of the Romances, but he is the linchpin that holds them together. This allows for a much wider audience. A person who does not like one particular story can probably find another that is more to his or her taste. It also permits a greater number of themes to be explored.

Another factor that has contributed to the preservation of the Arthurian material is its Utopian nature. The tales present a vision of an ideal society. The concept of such a place is a powerful archetype that has taken many forms and existed for many years. Camelot has taken its place along side the Golden Age, Shangri-la, Atlantis and of course Utopia itself as important examples of human yearning-a life without care. The Knights of the Round Table are not just adventurers; they are heroes-gentlemen and restorers of order in a chaotic world. They battle evil and do it with polished manners and proper consideration for the rights of the downtrodden. The Arthurian tales are a model of a state that can never be achieved, but in an unjust world that can be cold, cruel, and lonely such ideals are necessary to remind us of how life is supposed to be.

The most important theme in the tales is loyalty. There are many different aspects to this concept. There is loyalty to a set of ideals. It is the duty of the rulers of Britain to uphold the right, a duty that Arthur accepts by establishing the Order of the Round Table. They act as a sort of noble police force, protecting the weak from the robber barons and other titled bullies who seek to prey on the people. This is a common theme that has appeared in tales for thousands of years. Characters such as Gawain and Lancelot have much in common with Hercules and Thor from ancient mythology and superheroes from modern fantasy.

There is also the aspect of personal loyalty. Guenevere begins as Arthur's devoted wife, but then she finds herself falling love with his best friend. Lancelot is the king's loyal vassal. His ties of friendship and feudalism make his affair with the queen a double betrayal. The concept of feudal loyalty has limited appeal, but the ideas of love between a man and a woman and friendship can be appreciated in any age and any culture. The three characters become caught in a tangled web of events as they try to remain true to the ties of friendship and civic duty. At least the queen and her lover know that their actions are wrong and atone for them: she by joining a nunnery and he by praying at the tombs of the king and queen every day for the rest of his life.

Arthur was not only betrayed by his wife and his greatest friend but also by his son. Mordred is the most villainous figure. He cares nothing for duty of any kind; his only loyalty is to himself. Camelot was maintained through a precarious balance of power. If that balance were upset society would slide back into perpetual warfare and chaos. Mordred could not see this. In his selfish desire to acquire what his father had created he destroyed it. Violence is not the road to paradise. Arthur used war for a purpose. Battles were a means to an end. That end was a defeat of the enemies of his people and the establishment of peace. Mordred exemplified the phrase Gildas used of fighting wars that were civil and unjust.

In centuries past men and women who achieved great feats were believed to have a special connection to the supernatural world. The legend that Alexander the Great was the son of Zeus has already been mentioned. If a person was considered to have such a connection it was a short step to the idea that they could even conquer death. This is known as the "sleeping king" motif. Arthur is the most famous of the sleeping kings, but he is not the only one. For example the German Emperor Frederick II was also said to be sleeping and would one day awaken and lead his people to glory. The medieval attitude towards Frederick was often expressed with the phrase: "he is dead, yet not dead."

There is another kind of immortality. It is based not upon actual life, but undying fame. Arthur has found this form of immortality. So have many other characters in his tales. It is possible to find numerous people today who are called Arthur or Vivian or Morgan. The name Guenevere has evolved into Genevieve and Jennifer. These names have passed into our popular culture and are used by people who often have no idea of their origins or significance. An everlasting name is the kind of immortality longed for by the ancient warriors such as Achilles and Beowulf. In ancient heroic societies like Homeric Greece or Anglo-Saxon England or Arthurian Britain the greatest wish of the warriors was to be remembered. A reputation so famous that succeeding generations would still speak of the hero's deeds long after he was dead was considered the most significant achievement that could be attained. In Greek legend Achilles deliberately chose a short life with assured fame while the Irish hero Cu Chulainn asked his king for arms, despite the fact that it had been prophesized to him that any man who received arms on that day would die young but would be remembered forever. He said he would gladly die young to achieve that kind of reputation.

An illuminating story was told about the Irishman Dunlang O'Hartigan, who may have really existed. Just before the Battle of Clontarf a beautiful woman was said to have visited O'Hartigan. She offered to allow him to live for two hundred years in a land without sorrow, where no one died, if he would agree to stay out of the battle. O'Hartigan refused the offer and was killed while fighting in the front lines. Had he accepted, if he were remembered at all, it would have been as a coward. Arthur has achieved what Cu Chulainn and O'Hartigan wished for. However in Arthur's case what is remembered is mostly fantasy. Whether or not this would have upset the real pendragon of the Dark Ages is impossible to say. The important thing may not be who he really was but what succeeding generations have made and will make of him.

It is difficult to foresee a time when the exploits of Arthur and his knights will not be remembered. Every age needs heroes. A hero who has proven to be adaptable and can survive for centuries in many different cultures is exceptionally hard to get rid of. As long as there is a need for him and as long as each new generation can continue to rework the tales the quests will never really end. Sir Thomas Malory most aptly summed up Arthur's legacy in the fifteenth century. In Chapters 6 and 7 of Book XXI of *Le Morte D'Arthur* Malory recounts how Bedivere leaves the place where the three queens have born Arthur away in the boat. He then enters a chapel and finds a newly created tomb. On it are carved the most famous words associated with the king: HIC IACET ARTHURUS, REX QUONDAM REXQUE FUTURUS-here lies Arthur, the Once and Future King."

Bibliography

Alcock, Leslie, *Arthur's Britain*, Penguin Books Canada Ltd, Markham, Ontario, Canada, 1983.

Ashe, Geoffrey, *The Discovery of King Arthur*, Henry Holt and Company, Inc., New York, New York, 1985.

Ashe, Geoffrey, *King Arthur's Avalon: The Story of Glastonbury*, William Collins Sons & Company Ltd. Glasgow, 1987.

Ashe, Geoffrey (ed.), *The Quest for Arthur's Britain*, Paladin Books, a division of the Collins Publishing Group, London, 1987.

Ashley, Mike, *The Mammoth Book of British Kings & Queens*, Robinson Publishing Ltd. 1998.

Attwater, Donald, *The Penguin Dictionary of Saints*, Penguin Books Ltd, Harmondsworth, Middlesex, England, 1965.

Baigent, Michael, Leigh, Richard, Lincoln, Henry, *The Holy Blood and the Holy Grail*, Corgi, London, 1983.

Barber, Richard, *King Arthur in Legend and History*, Cox & Wyman Ltd, London, 1973.

Bede, Sherley-Price, Leo, (trans.), *A History of the English Church and People*, Penguin Books Ltd, Harmondsworth, Middlesex, 1964.

Burton, Sir Richard, (trans.), *Tales from the Arabian Nights*, Selected from the book *A Thousand Nights and a Night*, Braken Books, London, 1985.

Branston, Brian, *The Lost Gods of England*, Oxford University Press, New York, 1974.

Bulfinch, Thomas, *Bulfinch's Mythology*, Random House of Canada Limited, Toronto, 2004.

Castleden, Rodney, *King Arthur: The Truth Behind the Legend*, Routledge, 29 West 35 Street, New York, N.Y., 2000.

Chadwick, Nora K., *Celtic Britain*, Newcastle Publishing Co., Inc., North Hollywood, California, 1989.

Chadwick, Nora K., *The Celts*, Penguin Books Canada Limited, Markham, Ontario, Canada, 1987.

Christie-Murray, David, *A History of Heresy*, Oxford University Press, Oxford, 1989.

Coghlan, Ronan, *The Encyclopaedia of Arthurian Legends*, Element, Inc., Rockport, Ma., 1993.

Cormac mac Art, Cleary, Thomas (trans.) *The Councils of Cormac*, Doubleday, 2004.

Cummings, W.A., *King Arthur's Place in prehistory: The Great Age of Stonehenge*, Alan Sutton Publishing Inc., Wolfeboro Falls, N.H., 1993.

Day, David, *The Search For King Arthur*, De Agostini Editions, Griffin House, London, 1995.

Dixon, Philip, *Barbarian Europe*, Elsevier-Phaidon, an imprint of Phaidon Press Ltd., Oxford, 1976.

Dumville, David N., *Briton and Anglo-Saxons in the Early Middle Ages*, Ashgate Publishing Company, Brookfield, Vermont, 1993.

Editors of Time Life Books *What Life Was Like Among Druids and High Kings*.

Ellis, Peter Berresford, *The Celtic Empire: The First Millennium of Celtic History, 1000 BC - 51 AD*, Constable and Company Limited, London, 1990.

Ellis, Peter Berresford, *Celt and Saxon: the Struggle for Britain AD 410 - 937*, Constable and Company Limited, London, 1993.

Eschenbach, Wolfram von, Mustard, Helen M. and Passage, Charles E. (trans.), *Parzival*, Random House of Canada Limited, Toronto, 1961.

Evens, H. Meurig, *Welsh-English, English-Welsh Dictionary*, Mippocrene Books, New York, 1993.

Fife, Graeme, *Arthur the King*, Sterling Publishing Company, Inc., New York, N.Y., 1991.

France, Marie de, Burgess, Glyn S. and Busby, Kieth (trans.), *The Lais of Marie de France*, Penguin Books Canada Ltd, Markham, Ontario, Canada, 1986.

Gantz, Jeffrey (trans.), *Early Irish Myths and Sagas*, Penguin Books Ltd, Markham, Ontario, Canada, 1984.

Gantz, Jeffrey (trans.), *The Mabinogion*, Penguin Books Canada Ltd, Markham, Ontario, Canada, 1985.

Garmonsway, G.N. (trans.), *The Anglo-Saxon Chronicle*, J.M. Dent & Sons Ltd, London, 1986.

Gilbert, Adrian, Wilson, Alan, and Blackett, Baram, *The Holy Kingdom*, Bantam Press, London, 1998.

Gildas, St., Morris, John (gen. ed.), Winterbottom, Michael (ed. and trans.), *The Ruin of Britain and Other Documents*, Phillimore and Co. Ltd. London and Chichester, 1978.

Giles, J.A., (ed.) *Six Old English Chronicles*, George Bell and Sons, London, 1900.

Gimbutas, Marija, *The Language of the Goddess*, Harper and Row, Publisher, Inc. New York, N.Y., 1989.

Goodrich, Norma Lorre, *King Arthur*, Franklin Watts, Toronto, 1986.

Grant, Michael & Hazel, John, *Who's Who in Classical Mythology*, Michael Grant Publications Limited & John Hazel, 1973.

Green, Miranda J., *Dictionary of Celtic Myth and Legend* Thames and Hudson Ltd, London, 1992.

Grimal, Pierre, *The Dictionary of Classical Mythology*, Basil Blackwell Publisher Limited, Oxford, England, 1985.

Heaney, Marie, *Over Nine Waves, A Book of Irish Legends*, Faber and Faber, London, 1994.

Hill, David, *An Atlas of Anglo-Saxon England*, University of Toronto Press, Toronto, 1981.

Hutchings, R.J., *The King Arthur Illustrated Guide*, Dyllansow Truran, Cornwall, 1983.

Ingram, James, (trans.) *The Annales Cambriae*, Everyman Press, London, 1912.

Jackson, Kennith Hurlstone (trans.) *A Celtic Miscellany*, Penguin Books Canada Ltd, Markham, Ontario, Canada, 1977.

James, Peter and Thorpe, Nick, *Ancient Mysteries*. Ballantine Publishing Group, 1999.

Katz, Brian P., *Deities and Demons of the Far East*, Michael Friedman Publishing Group, Inc., 1995

Lass, Abraham H., Kiremidjian, David, and Goldstien, Ruth M., *The Dictionary of Classical, Biblical, & Literary Allusions*, Ballantine Books, 1987.

Laing, Lloyd, *Celtic Britain*, Charles Scribners & Sons, 1979.

Lehmann, Johannes, *The Hittites, People of a Thousand Gods*, William Collins Sons & Co. Ltd. Toronto, 1977.

Loomis, Roger Sherman, *The Development of Arthurian Romance*, Harper & Row, Publishers, Incorporated, New York, N.Y., 1964.

Loomis, Roger Sherman, *The Grail: From Celtic Myth to Christian Symbol*, Roger Sherman Loomis, 1964.

Malory, Sir Thomas, Cowen, Janet (ed.), *Le Morte D'Arthur in Two Volumes*, Penguin Books Limited, Markham, Ontario, Canada, 1986.

Markale, Jean, Hauch, Christine (trans.), *King Arthur, King Of Kings,* Prayot, Paris, 1976.

Mason, Eugene (trans.), *Wace and Laymon: Arthurian Chronicles*, J.M. Dent & Sons Ltd., London, 1986.

Matarasso, P.M., (trans.), *The Quest for the Holy Grail*, Penguin Books Canada Ltd, Markham, Ontario, Canada, 1988.

Matthews, John, *Gawain, Knight of the Goddess: Restoring an Archetype*, The Aquarian Press, Thorsons Publishing Group, Wellingborough, Northamptonshire, England, 1990.

Minary, Ruth & Moorman, Charles, *An Arthurian Dictionary*, Academy Chicago Publishers, Chicago, Illinois, 1990.

Monmouth, Geoffrey of, Thorpe, Lewis (trans.), *The History of the Kings of Britain*, Penguin Books Limited, Markham, Ontario, Canada, 1987.

Morris, John, *The Age of Arthur: A History of the British Isles from 350 - 650*, Redwood Press Limited, Trowbridge, Wiltshire, 1973.

Nicolle, David, *Arthur and the Anglo-Saxon Wars*, Osprey Men-At-Arms Series #154, Osprey Publishing, London, 1986.

Pearce, Susan, *The Kingdom of Dumnonia: Studies in History and Tradition in South- Western Britain A.D. 350-1150*, Lodenek Press, Padstow, Cornwall, 1978.

Phillips, Graham & Keatman, Martin, *King Arthur: the True Story*, Century Random House, London, 1992.

Ritchie, Anna, *Picts* HMSO, Edinburgh, 1993.

Savage, Anna (trans.) *The Anglo-Saxon Chronicles*, William Heineman Ltd, London, 1984.

Shirer, William L., *The Rise and Fall of the Third Reich A History of Nazi Germany*, Fawcett Crest, New York, 1992.

Squire, Charles, *Celtic Myth and Legend*, Newcastle Publishing Co. Inc., 1975.

Stewart, R.J. & Mathews, John (eds.), *Merlin Through the Ages*, Blandford, London, 1995.

Stone, Brian (trans.) *Sir Gawain and the Green Knight*, Penguin Books Canada Limited, Markham, Ontario, Canada, 1987.

Tapsell, R.F., *Monarchs, Rulers, Dynasties and Kingdoms of the World*, Thames and Hudson Ltd, London, 1983.

Troyes, Chretien de, Owen, D.D.R. (trans.), *Arthurian Romances*, J.M. Dent & Sons Ltd, London, 1987.

Vaughn-Thomas, Wynford, *Wales, A History*, Michael Joseph Ltd., London, 1985.

Wilkins, W.J., *Hindu Mythology: Vedic and Puranic*, Lewis Reprints Ltd., Tonbridge, Kent, 1974.

Withycombe, E.G., *The Oxford Dictionary of English Christian Names*, Oxford University Press, 1977.

Yonge, Charlotte M., *History of Christian Names*, Macmillan and Co., London, 1884.

Printed in the United States
By Bookmasters